China Sweet & Sour

2004

Did you eat?
Book 1

Virginia Heslinga

3clocks
publications

China Sweet & Sour

This book is dedicated to the hardworking teachers, students, administrators, superintendents, community leaders, and individuals it has been my honor and privilege to work with in China. I am thankful for the gifts of those communities where I experienced generosity, hospitality, help, friendship, as well as shared hopes and goals for young people who are the future. I also dedicate this book to the Amity leaders, staff, and volunteers, who strive to meet a wide variety of needs every day and every season.

publications

Published by 3clocks Publications, LLC

China Sweet and Sour: 2004

Book 1 in the Series **Did You Eat?**

Copyright © 2025 by Virginia Heslinga

eBook ISBN: 978-1-964590-00-4

Paperback ISBN: ISBN: 978-1-964590-99-8

Audiobook ISBN: ISBN: 978-1-964590-01-1

Cover and Interior Design by Gordon Saunders

Publisher's Note: This is a work of creative non-fiction. The author has presented the events accurately and fairly to the best of her abilities. Although all the incidents in the book are based on fact, names and some identifying details have been changed to protect privacy.

China Sweet and Sour: 2004 is the first book in the series, 'Did You Eat?' The title for the series is based on asking about a person's well-being. As with, 'How are you?' asked quickly and casually in the USA, a specific answer is not expected. Actually, 你吃了吗 (Nǐ chī le ma), literally translated, 'Have you eaten yet?' is a sign of courtesy. In the mid-twentieth century China experienced years of famine. Millions of people starved. Food symbolizes nourishment, hospitality, and happiness.

In addition to telling a story, the book aims to provide insight for reflections, cross-cultural communication, respect, service, and appreciation of other cultures. The author and publisher make no claims to provide any type of professional advice expressed or implied.

Foreword

"Nations, like individuals, can only learn by their own individual experience." **Pearl S. Buck, 1963**

"China is now the storm center of the world...whoever took time to understand this mighty empire would have a key to politics for the next five centuries." **John Hay, United States Secretary of State, 1899**

"What most distinguishes Confucius from other founders is that he inculcated a strict code of ethics, which has been respected ever since, but associated with very little religious dogma, which gave place to complete theological skepticism in the countless generations of Chinese literati who revered his memory and administered the Empire." **Bertrand Russell, The Problem of China, 1922**

"Hope is like a path in the countryside. Originally, there is nothing - but as people walk this way again and again, a path appears." **Lu Xun, 1921**

Contents

Characters

Note: Names of people have been changed for privacy.

The Summer English Program (SEP) is sponsored through Amity, a Chinese Non-governmental organization (NGO).

An NGO functions independently of any government with the objective of improving social conditions. In China, the government reviews NGO plans and gives final approval or suggests changes. NGOs are typically non-profit institutions. They are sometimes called civil society organizations and are established on community, national, and international levels to serve a humanitarian cause.

Jessie: an administrator from Amity who takes teams to new locations and checks on living and teaching conditions for the works of the Summer English Program (SEP).

Pastor Isaiah: assistant pastor at the church near our host school.

The 2004 Amity Team in Wuhai

Kathryn: Nurse, MSN, lifelong Massachusetts resident

Jaye: physical education teacher and lifelong Illinois resident

Doug: Business professor in Boston, Massachusetts

Tia: Elementary school teacher's aide and lifelong Massachusetts resident

Virginia: BA, MA, English and Language Arts, from Holden, Massachusetts

Wuhai Teachers and Students

NOTE- a senior middle school is the equivalent of a senior high school in the US. A junior middle school equates to a junior high school environment in the US.

Emily: Mandarin Chinese and head of the English department at our host school.

Erdeen: Indigenous Mongolian and Virginia's classroom assistant. Her name means precious gem, jewel.

Kent: A leading female teacher at a senior middle school and Kathryn's classroom assistant

Jenna: A young highly skilled teacher of English and Tia's classroom assistant

June: A middle school teacher, whose husband, Yuze, plays the guitar and knows many songs in English.

Ye: A senior middle school student, proficient in understanding and speaking English

Walt: A senior middle school teacher in Wuhai who asked about Abu Ghraib

Cassie: An outgoing young teacher of English

Delia: A talented teacher in calligraphy who also taught English, Doug's classroom assistant

Thomas: Once had been a science teacher but was told to switch to English for his school

Penny: Wife of Thomas and an English teacher at a vocational technical college.

Peter: Taught at a junior middle school not far from our host school.

Jeff: A teacher in a vocational technical junior middle school

Koshing: (ko shing) A middle school student in Jeff's class

Xiong: (shong) A middle school students in Jeff's class

Terry: A young woman and member of the Wuhai church near our host school and a teacher at a vocational technical middle school

Larry: A young teacher who asked about President Bush declaring war in Afghanistan

Principal Chen: The leader of our host school

Vice-Principal Zhu: The assistant principal at our host school

Tongzhi Wang: The Communist Party Representative (CPR) for our host school

MeiLi: A young Amity staff member from Nanjing

Naomi: A college student and translator in Beijing who attended a house church

Joel: A Wuhai church member who had a friend who drives for a company in Beijing

Timothy: A friend of Joel and a driver in Beijing

Chapter 1

First Day, First Class, Beyond a Nightmare

Vomiting in front of a group of four dozen professional teachers never appeared in any plan or even in my imagination of worst first-day teaching scenarios. People have fears before the first day of a new school year. Even as an experienced teacher with twenty-six years working with students from pre-school through high school, I still felt nervous. Before me sat teachers of English in western Inner Mongolia. Their wooden desks and bench seats, arranged in rows, crowded them into a room for high school students in the top-ranked high school in the city. These teachers had given up their vacation to take a special summer course. Now, I would start our class by getting sick in front of them.

Faces of the class members began to show concern in lifted eyebrows and puzzled frowns at my frozen stance. Something I had eaten at breakfast had been spoiled or whatever the Chinese would say for rotten. I couldn't explain how I felt to my assistant because I didn't dare open my mouth. I stood as still as a manikin. The ninety-degree temperature in the unairconditioned room gripped me like a heating pad squeezed around my body, yet I had chills. How could both feelings happen at once?

The teachers in front of me made up one of the five classes that would run for three and a half weeks in a portion of a city that bordered the deserts called Wulanbuhe desert and Gobi. This class provided students with their first in-depth experience with a native speaker of English. The opportunity came through Amity, a Non-Governmental Organization (NGO). The Amity organization called this training time the Summer English Program (SEP). All the participants were teachers of English. They knew grammar and punctuation at an expert level but had low comprehension of spoken English and a lack of skill or confidence in speaking English.

The SEP participants needed practice comprehending and speaking English plus strategies for teaching English. Some English teachers had asked their principals if they could join the SEP. Willingly, they gave up their summer vacations to participate in the SEP with the hope of improving their teaching of English. Others in this SEP had principals who told them to attend this unusual training. Teachers in China did not say no to a principal. Honor given to authority figures still followed the ancient traditions of this country with almost five thousand years of history.

And here I stood in front of the class about to start the experience of this class by throwing up. Not one of these SEP participants had ever met a Westerner in Wuhai. Only a few had ever met a native speaker of English.

I took a slow deep breath and swallowed back the sour churning sickness. Then I took one step forward to the edge of the large wooden desk. Fifty-five pairs of eyes studied me intently. Why was this happening?

Praying in silent desperation, I begged, "Please God, please help me not to throw up." In my life I had seen answers to specific prayers, but God and I had not been on the best terms for almost two years.

In just seconds, I knew my prayer was not going to be answered, not in the way I had hoped. Vomiting in front of a full new class of adults was disgusting. Dizziness and nausea caused me to reach out and put my right hand on the smoothly finished surface of the large wooden teacher's desk. Our class was on the school's top floor, the fourth floor. The wide windows were open on both sides of the classroom letting rare breezes offer some relief while the temperature rose. I looked toward the door that stood wide open.

Could I make it there and throw up outside the class-room? A balcony path ran along each of the upper floors of this building. I did not want to be sick all over the balcony. Everyone taking classes on the upper floors used the balcony walkway like we used hallways in our schools in the US.

I saw my bottle of water but did not dare to try to pick it up, not even moving slowly. Perspiration covered my fore-head. Shivers swept over me from the pain in my churning stomach. I had to move!

I took steps as fast as I could out the door, rushed across the balcony walkway, grabbed the railing, and leaned forward. Below, the flat hard packed ground appeared empty. I let the sour misery erupt, gagging, coughing, and completely embarrassed because everyone in the class could hear me vomiting.

My white-knuckled hands gripped the railing while I felt the sickening after-heaving sweat. I felt it all over my body and kept a survival grip on the railing. The disgusting mess far below would be cleared by a groundskeeper.

I leaned on the railing. My energy was gone. The dizziness faded, but I still did not move. I blinked tears away before they could spill and add to my mortification. Why did this have to happen to me now? I'd never gotten sick like this in any school.

What had caused this awful start? At breakfast, we had choices of tea or coffee, porridge, hardboiled eggs, watermelon, and something called *jiaozi*. I had chosen the smallest *jiaozi* that looked like crescent moon-shaped versions of ravioli. Only a few of these small *jiaozi* appeared on the platter of many. I had no food allergies, and if I had a fear of unusual foods, I would not have signed on to teach in a remote area of China.

The head teacher of the English department of this host school came up behind me and put a gentle hand on my back. Emily had the responsibility of being the main coordinator to the Amity teaching team. I had not heard her approach, but the feeling of her gentle touch caused tears to come to my eyes again.

"Are you all right, Ms. Virginia?"

I stepped away from her, knowing that I smelled like the sick mess I'd spewed. "I think I am now. Something from breakfast soured my stomach. Will the class wait if I go back to the dormitory, take a quick shower, and change my clothes?" I blinked away my tears. "I will hurry back. It might take me twenty minutes."

"Do you not need more rest?"

"I will nap this afternoon when we have the long break." Because this area of Inner Mongolia was so hot, classes would stop at noon and not resume until three. If I skipped lunch, I could have more than two hours of sleep.

"Go then, Ms. Virginia. Your assistant, Erdeen, and I will have the class spend time talking with one another. They are from many different towns and schools. They can try to learn about one another."

"Thank you, Emily." She had a couple of decades of experience teaching large classes, and she had top fluency in English of all the teachers in our host school. The younger teachers showed respect for her in all their interactions.

I hurried along the cement walkway to the stairs. My lightweight blouse and skirt clung to me. For the first day, I had tried to dress casually in a feminine outfit. All the Chinese and Mongolian female teachers I had met seemed to have that combination of clothing.

How would they feel about me after this awful start? Amity had arranged this summer English training opportunity for teachers in remote regions where people rarely met Westerners. In this city, only a handful of leaders in the entire city had spoken with people from the West. Some Germans and Australians came in 2000 to study desertification. Those speakers of English did not have British or American accents. Once everyone in China learned British English, but now the American pronunciation and idioms had become more popular.

I could hear some of the talking from the classrooms where my team members had their classes of forty-five to sixty students. I even heard some laughter as I hurried down the stairs. Two staircases per floor, eight flights of stairs to the ground level, out onto the packed dirt and past the mess I had made.

By the time I opened the door to my room, a sheen of

sweat from being sick and hurrying through the grounds to the dorm caused me to rush to shower. The shower's lack of a curtain or any kind of curb like threshold created a foreign configuration for me. Inches of pipe sticking straight out of the wall in the small room caused everything to get wet.

It didn't bother me now. I wanted to feel clean before returning to the classroom. The old saying, 'You never get a second chance to make a first impression,' came to mind. Could I have a good restart?

Chapter 2

Smiles from the Heart

I walked as quickly as I could back to the classroom building. My teammates were working hard to connect and encourage the adult students in their classrooms. Kathryn, a nurse, seemed friendly but had expressed the need to check her blood pressure at least four times a day and insisted she must keep to a set schedule. Kathryn had trained nurses and had a take charge attitude.

Tia, a petite brunette, looked pretty, seemed sweet and meek. I wondered how far her soft voice would carry. Would her thick Massachusetts accent inhibit student understanding? She had been a kindergarten assistant teacher for two decades.

Jaye was the most athletic looking member of our team. I thought she fit the stereotype of an American heartland girl. She kept her long blonde hair pulled back in a ponytail, and her blue eyes drew attention as much as her hair. Jaye, a physical education teacher in a Chicago suburb, could project her voice well.

And then there was Doug, the only male member of our

team. He had a few decades of experience teaching accounting and business courses in a small college in Boston. Doug had worked with Amity in 2002, in the northeastern section of Inner Mongolia. He'd told us that the climate there had cool temperatures, frequent rain, thick grassy plains, and forests, but some of the foods were appalling. He didn't want to talk about it in case it made us nervous about this experience.

Doug, at six foot two and with his solid build, fit the saying, 'large and in charge.' I wondered if his mannerisms suited a lifelong bachelor approaching retirement age or if rumors of him working for the CIA might be true. I'd heard that from two people who had also worked with Amity in 2002. Where did they get that idea about Doug and the CIA? I guessed it was gossip from someone on his previous team. He did not share personal information but had wide traveling and teaching experiences plus broad knowledge about places.

I saw a figure in the doorway of my classroom and waved. Someone had been looking out for my return; it was Erdeen. Each member of our team had a classroom assistant, someone fluent in Mandarin, Mongolian, and better than most in English. Erdeen had told me her Mongolian ancestors had lived in this area long before the Chinese government decided to establish Wuhai in the mid-1970s. When she saw me from the balcony, she rushed to the staircase.

I paused and glanced toward the place where my breakfast had hit the ground. No trace of it appeared. When we had our first team meeting in our dorm accommodations, Doug talked about the variety of jobs and pay in this region. He said groundskeepers knew they had a good job for this locale. They put effort into maintaining the best possible appearance.

"Ms. Virginia! You are back so quickly. You are feeling better?"

"Yes. Much better, Erdeen." She took my arm like I was a ninety-year-old and walked beside me to our classroom.

The students in my homeroom also were my first period class. I could see and hear them talking with one another until Erdeen and I entered the classroom. As soon as a few students recognized I was back, they turned to sit facing forward on the miserable wooden benches at their small wooden desks. Because of the heat the women did not wear stockings. Good thing, as the wooden benches had so many rough spots that stockings would have been ruined.

Erdeen left me at the large teacher's desk and moved to stand to my left as I faced the class. She obviously planned to run to my assistance at the first sight of need or word from me. With the sunlight streaming in the big window near her, Erdeen had a glowing background that suited her smile.

Anyone who wanted to see a true Mongolian beauty could find one in Erdeen. She had long dark auburn hair, deeply tanned skin, narrow slant to stunning green eyes, a nose longer than the Chinese, high cheekbones, a heavier upper lip than lower lip, and slim body. She had the beauty of a top model, but not the height. Erdeen was the only fully Mongolian woman in my homeroom.

I turned from looking at Erdeen's smiling face to focus on my class. Each member of our team would see all the classes each day. We had a schedule. Homeroom from 7:50 a.m. to 8:10 a.m., first class, from 8:10 to 8:50, a break until 9, second class from 9 to 9:45, a break until 9:55, third class 9:55 to 10:30, a break until 10:40, fourth class 10:40 to

11:20, and the fifth class, from 11:20 a.m. to noon. We had the most time each day with our homeroom class.

After returning my students' smiles, I noticed that they each had a name card on their desks. That was an activity we had planned for all the homeroom classes. Students would carry these cards with them to each class and put them on their desk to help our team to use names. At the end of the day, the cards would be collected. The name cards also had the homeroom class name in small print below the student's name. Our classroom assistants would collect the name cards and put them out on the desks each morning.

The movement of students from class to class did not usually occur in China. Both junior and senior schools in Wuhai had class sizes between forty-five and ninety. Students in these large classes stayed in their classroom and teachers moved from class to class. Because we had decorated our classrooms and brought supplies for what we would teach, we chose to stay put and have the classes move. The breaks gave them a chance to change positions, walk a bit, and socialize.

The school did not have any cardstock paper for the name cards, so we had purchased it from a stationery store in town. Each student folded a piece of the paper in half long ways, hot dog length as my elementary students would say. Our SEP students wrote the name they desired for use in the classes on the side that would face the teacher. On the back they put seven adjectives and five verbs to describe themselves.

Broad smiles and the name cards showed me that they had worked with vocabulary while I had prepared to return to the class. Erdeen had obviously given out the markers we had also bought for each class. The name cards showed the style of each individual student. Calligraphy held high value in Wuhai, and some name cards had the beauty of a highly skilled calligrapher.

"Your name cards look wonderful. Would you please each say your name and read the words you have put on the back of your cards?" I asked and stood with my left hip against the desk. I knew better than to sit on the desk.

The previous day, I sat on a teacher's desk in one of our team meetings. Emily, the head teacher had gasped. Then she told us, "No one sits on a desk. People put their hands, books, snacks, and sometimes rest their heads on their desk. We do not sit our bottoms on desks."

The teachers, giving their names and the descriptive words, spoke slowly and clearly. Anyone who has taken a foreign language class likely can remember the stress of speaking the language out loud, to the teacher, in front of everyone in the class. This class involved teachers who had all asked their students to speak a foreign language aloud. I wondered if they thought of that as they took a turn speaking. Did they grow in sympathy for their students?

In China, it seemed that any glimmer of failure disturbs and worries individuals. Everyone realizes children make mistakes while learning. The same is true for teens and adults learning a new language. We mimic sounds and may say them incorrectly for a while before we master the words.

At home, and here, I knew too many students felt self-conscious or fearful of making a mistake. In our training time in Nanjing, we'd learned that in China, the pressure of being the only child allowed to a Han family caused students to feel they must reach high levels of achievement. They did not want to fail their parents and grandparents. More than ninety percent of the population of China was Han Chinese.

Since 1980 the government allowed Han Chinese only one child.

When each class member had a turn speaking, with a short time left, we took out the Amity textbook, *Learning English,* by Don Snow. Amity gave each student this textbook. We would use it, and the students would keep it. They could find ideas and strategies to use with their own students after this summer training time.

What they found in the text's Unit I was a lesson on why language teachers should be language learners. We ran out of time before we ventured far into the first unit. I gave the class an assignment based on a question Amity said teachers in remote areas heard often from their students. Why should I learn English? For their homework they had to think of at least three reasons and bring them to class in the morning.

As they left class for their first break, I stood by the door. I said alternately repeated phrases as they departed: "Goodbye. See you later. Have a good morning. See you this afternoon."

The next group arrived with smiles. I used a set of welcome words and greeted each student. "Good morning. Good to see you. Welcome. Hello." The morning passed quickly, but I felt like a crushed warm marshmallow when the last group left at noon.

Erdeen appeared alongside me when the last person was out of sight. She handed me a bottle of red tea. Our whole team had found these common bottled teas refreshing. I'd heard Emily speak formally in English to the class assistants, so I kept that tone.

"Erdeen, thank you. You are an excellent coworker and help to me."

"I could do better," she responded automatically. In

China compliments are not given often and are rarely received with a simple thank you. "Now you will have lunch and rest, Ms. Virginia?"

"I am going to skip lunch today. This drink and maybe another will be all I need, plus rest. I am looking forward to a nap. I was surprised to learn that you had a rest time here in the afternoon, like they do in Mexico and in many other countries where the days are so hot. It makes sense."

Erdeen seemed about to say something when Emily came to the door. My teammates were beside her.

"We are going to lunch now." Emily said.

"Are you all right?" Tia asked. "We heard you got sick and left class."

"I'm okay now. I just need a little extra rest."

"You should sleep during the long break," Kathryn told me. "I need to do that every day or my blood pressure goes up."

"See you over there," Jaye said. She took her pony-tailed all American girl gym teacher self energetically toward the stairs.

Doug studied me with some concern, then nodded. He and the rest of my team went to the stairs. Emily had not moved from the doorway.

"I think I will use the time to rest, Emily. I do not need lunch."

I saw Emily exchange a glance with Erdeen as if to say,' Now what do we tell her.' Emily stepped into the room and said, "I have to ask you not to do that."

Chapter 3

Frozen Anger

"Please come to the teachers' dining room for lunch, Ms. Virginia. It is important that our cook apologize."

"Apologize? To me?"

"He has been a good cook for some years here, but he made a mistake today. If he does not apologize to you, I fear he will lose his job." I looked from Emily to Erdeen and she nodded in agreement. No way did I want the cook to lose his job because I got sick. No one else had, so how could he be responsible?

I went to lunch walking alongside Emily. Erdeen followed us. When we entered the teacher's dining room, we went to a table where Doug was talking with two of our other classroom assistants. Before we sat down, a large Mongolian man with a white bib apron over his clothes and a white cap-style hat on his almost bald head approached the table. He bowed slightly in my direction, then spoke in a subdued tone to Emily.

"This is our cook." Emily said to me. "He wants to apologize to you."

Everyone in the dining room fell silent. I felt my face grow warm and knew I must be blushing. I felt bad for this man's embarrassment. He looked like he might be about fifty, and here he was apologizing to a female foreigner in front of other people.

Although I felt weak and tired, I stood straight and regarded him with respect. He spoke in Chinese, then waited for Emily to translate.

"I take responsibility for the poor food that made you sick this morning. I am sorry and will prepare all meals with more care."

"Thank you. I am fine now." Emily translated to him in Chinese. He didn't smile, but nodded, bowed to us, said thank you, and goodbye, then left the room.

When I sat down, Tia's assistant, Jenna, leaned toward me and said, "The cook is lucky he did not lose his job for getting a foreign guest teacher sick."

Emily heard our conversation. She explained. "He should take responsibility. He did not make enough *jiaozi* this morning. He went out and bought a few from a street vendor. They were smaller than the *jiaozi* he makes. They were not fresh. You probably ate those. He could lose his job because he did that. The school expects him to cook fresh food for guests each day. He apologized. You have accepted his apology. Principal Chen will allow him to stay on as cook. Our meals in this dining room should be healthy and delicious, but they do not always have the required flavors for excellence.

"The required flavors for excellence?" Kathryn asked.

Jenna supplied more information, "In our country, we

are taught that an excellent meal has sweet to help us appreciate the sweetness of the earth, bitter to remind us of the element of fire, sour that connects to the preciousness of wood, salty to make us appreciate having water, and spicy to remind us of wind and the warmth we need when it is cold."

"Wow! Did you memorize that?" Jaye asked Jenna.

Jenna blushed, and before she could say anything else Emily gave more information on the sweet, bitter, sour, salty, and spicy elements. "What Jenna said is well known, but there are health connections too."

"I'd love to hear those," Kathryn and Doug said almost in unison. When we spoke with the Chinese people, Amity advised us not to use contractions, to say the whole words distinctly, but we often forgot this rule. I would try to remember to remind people at our team meeting. For now, I stayed quiet and listened to Emily.

"Sweet because it can improve the mood, but it is best if it comes from something natural like grapes or berries. Bitter foods strengthen the stomach and improve saliva. Sour counteracts greasy foods. Salt improves awareness of flavors and can help preserve food too. Spicy warms the body and relieves unhealthy heat in the body."

"Unhealthy heat?" Tia asked.

"Do you mean, inflammation?" I asked Emily.

"Yes, that is the word. Thank you. Every cook, chef, and family know that in traditional Chinese medicine, the flavors affect the health of the body. If we had formal dinners or banquets here, our cook would need to ensure that there were dishes with at least the important five flavors."

From Emily's explanation, I understood why the cook felt responsible. So much that happened in any day could be set at the feet of someone else's role or responsibility. Ultimately, I believed that God could prevent misery, but many days he didn't. I often longed to see interventions for others or myself. Why had I chosen the street food *jiaozi*? I might never know. Could God have had a lesson for me in it? Have more humility?

I ate only small portions of two of the lunch choices, soup, and a piece of bread similar to a yeast roll. I wondered about the leader of this school who made the rules for everything on this campus.

Principal Chen had power in this community beyond leading the Number 1 Senior Middle School. As a leader and achiever in this community, Principal Chen held long-term membership in the People's Republic of China (PRC) Communist Party. He had given us a polite and slight smile at the welcome reception, but any other times we had seen him, he presented an inscrutable face to everyone, not just us foreigners.

I left the lunch gathering as early as I could and told people I was going to take a nap. After the rest time, classes would resume, and each afternoon the students would change classes only twice. They would start in their homeroom for thirty minutes, and then have almost an hour with two other teachers.

In my room, I sat down immediately where I slept on a single bed nearest the window. The room had no closet. There were two single beds with a night table between them. Since there was no larger table or desk, I set out teaching materials, supplies, and my suitcase on the second bed.

I rested on a firm mattress atop a solid platform made of wood instead of box springs. I knew I could rest but did not know if I could sleep. Images and questions filled my mind. I thought about my decision to apply to work with Amity's SEP.

When I struggle with something or someone, I feel best if I work. If I can do a necessary project or something good for someone else, at least it's positive action when I'm upset or angry. I had done that for years growing up in New Jersey. My home life had disruptions because of a sibling's death that changed my father's mental and emotional balance. After leaving home for college, I found some stability. I also met the man who would become my husband, and we had enjoyed thirty-two years of marriage before I made this trip to China.

We had also recently moved to a new home in Massachusetts, and I felt dissatisfied with the unplanned changes I had encountered. Most of the time I felt a grinding wheel of anger. An ungrateful spirit that replaced my previously positive outlook. It had started to affect my relationship with my husband.

Jerry and I had investigated Worcester County and the church that wanted my husband to be their pastor. We had not spent much time in Holden. In fall and winter before Jerry made his decision, we took trips north to check the area. The winter seemed milder than we expected, far milder than winters we had experienced in Williamstown, Massachusetts, in the early years of our marriage. I did not like snow, cold, or ice. Even as a child I had not enjoyed sledding, playing outside in the snow, or ice skating.

We thought the move would work well for my husband and for me, but in a year and a half, that had not proved true. In our first winter in Central Massachusetts, so different from twenty mild winters in Cape May County, New Jersey, where I'd had a full-time and longtime teaching career, all I could get in Worcester County were substitute teaching jobs. In the dark days of winter on below freezing mornings, I left early, often right behind the snowplows because I needed to arrive at the schools before the buses. Jerry only had to walk twenty feet to the church building and his office.

After one deep snowstorm, I came home from teaching in Barre, a half hour drive in good weather, but an hour in heavy falling snow, and went right to bed.

Jerry came upstairs and found me. "What are you doing?"

"I'm hibernating."

"You can't sleep through the winter."

"Watch me," I responded and pulled the covers over my head.

Jerry prayed that something would break me out of the frustration and depression I let only him see.

"You know, Ginny, depression is frozen anger. Are you angry with me for accepting the job here?"

"No. We both thought this looked like a good change. It was a joint decision for you to take this pastoral position. You wouldn't have accepted this job if I had said, no. I know I could have refused to move, and we would have stayed in New Jersey."

"Are you angry about our life changes in general?"

"I like variety."

"I know you like to choose the variety. You like change but with control. Will you tell me more about your anger?"

"It's hard to say."

"You mean to say to me or to put into words?"

"I don't want to talk about it. Talk can't change our situation now."

"Talking could help you and me."

"I'll be repetitious if I put it into words. I love teaching in public schools, and I can't get hired full time here because of teachers' union pay requirements. It's cheaper for schools to hire new teachers than someone with experience. I don't like subbing. We were told several times by people on your search committee that Massachusetts needed teachers. They should have said jobs were available for low-paid beginning teachers."

"The people who told us were right. The state does need teachers. The people who invited us to move here didn't know what the teachers' union pay scale required or how it would affect you finding a job. So, you're angry with those people?"

"No. They didn't intentionally deceive us. I'm angry at myself for believing them. I should have done additional research."

"There's more isn't there? I can tell you know what makes you most angry."

"Yes. I do know. I feel tricked. You know, when I first walked into the house, through the side door and saw the kitchen with that full wall brick fireplace, like my grandparents had in Maine, I thought, 'This is great.' That nineteenth century wall connected to some of the best times of my life. Old houses have character. This 1896 house is as historic as the church. Holden Baptist Church has a fascinating history. I read it right after we moved here."

"I knew you did that, and I knew you liked this house. You said the third floor had a perfect area for an office for you."

"But then we found that even with the electric heater, it was too cold up there. It is too cold all over this house. When we deliberately visited here in November and in March, there was no snow, not even in the woods. There were no below-zero temperatures. Only after we moved here did we find out it was the mildest winter they've had in a decade."

"So, you feel tricked by the weather?"

"I believed what I saw and experienced. There wasn't any sign of winter, no snow, no ice, not in November or in March."

"You said you were tricked."

I knew Jerry was prodding me to name the real focus of my anger. I glared at him.

"God is in charge of everything, right? We prayed about the move. It seemed what we should do. Everything progressed smoothly so that we could come here."

Jerry came close and put his arms around me. I pulled away from him.

"I'm angry at God. I really am. He could intervene. He could provide a career where I could teach, a place to teach full-time with coworkers I could have as friends. Subbing is miserable. I had a wonderful career and coworkers. And here? Nothing but subbing."

"We saw God leading us to this place. We both did. You agreed."

"We thought we did, and for you it has worked out well. I just don't want to sub from now until retirement age. And winters like this past one will make me wish my life away until you can retire, and we can move south.

"I haven't felt warm in this house for over a year. This winter we had record snow, with icicles as long as swords hanging from the house, and just as deadly.

"I wear sheepskin boots in this parsonage because the insulation is nil. I know the trustees are discussing blowing insulation into all the walls, but when? Yes, I feel tricked into being here. I don't blame the people here. I don't blame you. We thought God led us here, and it would be good for both of us. I feel stupid and tricked."

"Ginny, I still believe that God wants the best for both of us here. Can't you trust that maybe your best just hasn't shown up yet?"

"How long oh Lord?" I heard my sarcastic tone. "Jerry, I know you do believe and trust that there will be something good for me. I don't see or feel that because I'm angry with God. There. I said it. I feel tricked by God, and I am angry at God.

"This spot will be good for you and for the people in the church and community because you always get involved in helping a town wherever we live. Here, you have to walk a whole twenty feet to get to your office in the church while I'm driving on ice and in snow for jobs as a substitute teacher all over this county. I should have looked into this move for my career as much as for yours."

Jerry sighed and left the room. I didn't call him back. He knew the source of my anger now, and he still trusted this spot would be good for both of us. I didn't see it.

I needed something constructive to break me out of the seething inner turmoil. When I heard about Amity's SEP, it seemed to offer a change that would make me see everything from a different perspective. Jerry told me he felt nervous about me going so far to a country like China where the government kept surveillance and heavy-handed control over daily life and definitely preferred atheism over faith in God.

Jerry knew I felt unhappy in our new home, the old

parsonage in the center of Holden. I tried not to show my frustration, anger, and sadness to others. I'd learned early in life that hiding feelings preserved peace. Jerry preferred talking out feelings. As different as we were, we'd made it thirty-two years together, and I wanted to continue with him.

Chapter 4

Worth a Try

To try to get to know people, I listened to conversations during the church's coffee social time. One Sunday morning, soon after telling Jerry I was angry at God, I heard some people talking enthusiastically about working with Amity in China. They had done a Summer English Program with Amity and loved the experience, but then they sounded sad. "Great though it was, we could never do it again."

"Why not?" their friends asked.

The answer, "Because China's summers are so hot! We felt like we were in Miami in the summer."

That very day, I searched online and filled out an Amity application. If God didn't allow me to get a job I wanted in Worcester County, I'd take a different route to a rewarding teaching experience. I'd get out of the Worcester Hills. If God had dropped me into a place that had snow measured in feet and below-zero temperatures for weeks, I'd go someplace guaranteed to be warm and work teaching English.

Ah, but would God let me do this? I stepped toward the

experience. If God wanted to stop me, my application would be rejected.

Volunteering, helping other teachers, getting out of Central Massachusetts, having an inside view of a totally different culture, and being warm every night and day sounded ideal to me. I knew I had avoided talking to God in these unhappy months. Perhaps some time in China would show me, as time teaching English in Mexico once had, that God waited for me to talk to Him, and to trust Him again.

When my birth family went through their worst years, I looked for constructive ways to be away from home. Our pastor found projects that I, as a teenager, could do with families he knew in the Rio Grande Valley and in Mexico. Tutoring other teens, working picking fruit with migrant families, and teaching English to groups of children where the school was a lean-to helped me gain a wider perspective on life. I also learned that talking with God built hope and resilience in me. My mother, father, and brother never showed interest in my time away from them, and I chose not to talk to them about working out spiritual struggles or hopes for the future.

Now, family and friends disagreed with my idea of going to China. My choice to work with Amity upset my parents. They had fears and prejudices toward China.

When I visited my parents, my father, a Korean War veteran, told me if I needed to do volunteer work in another country to choose a place other than China.

I explained that I had just received the formal invitation from the school where I would work. It was a region more like Mongolia than what he knew about China.

"It's in a northern province, Dad. It's called Inner Mongolia Autonomous Region."

My father laughed, a harsh negative rasp of a laugh. "China has an area called Autonomous? I hope you don't believe that."

"There are a few Autonomous provinces in China."

"Don't believe it. You can't be that gullible about autonomy in a Communist controlled country."

"Why is there an Inner Mongolia? Is there an outer one?" Mom asked.

"Outer Mongolia would be what we call Mongolia." I began to explain. "Early in the twentieth century, Mongolia tried to have independence."

"But China didn't accept that idea, did it?" My father interrupted with an angry 'I told you so' tone of voice.

"Yes, Dad. China tried to stop Mongolia from separating, but Russia sent troops and pushed Chinese troops south. China kept the area that is now called Inner Mongolia."

"And what is the name of the city where you will be?"

"Wuhai. W-u-h-a-i. Pronounce it like Woo high."

And the region? Do you have to say Inner Mongolia Autonomous Region every time you talk about it?

N-e-i M-e-n-g-gu. In China it is called, Nei Menggu. It sounds like Nay Mungo as far as I can tell, but probably will sound different there.

"China keeps tight control on everyone. I expect they try to wipe out traces of Mongolian culture."

"Dad, Amity has sent teams to this province before this year. They have reported there are schools for families who want their children to be immersed in the Mongolian language and culture. They learn Mandarin, yes, but the minorities in China, from what I've heard, have more choices and respect than minorities have in many countries. Also, since Mongolia has been much more open to the world, their culture has changed in many ways because of the mixing with foreigners. It turns out that if someone really wants the purest experience of Mongolian language and culture, they can find that in Nei Menggu."

"Do you hear yourself? You have just admitted that China has chosen to keep that region isolated, disconnected. How can you believe you will have safety and respect while you are living and working there?"

"Dad, according to Amity which has been doing this Summer English Program for over fifteen years, any town and school finds it an honor to have a volunteer team of native English speakers helping teachers of English to improve in speaking and listening skills. They respect and value teachers."

"But I bet they don't pay well. You are going at your expense? Right? No pay?"

"We paid for our airfare and a small lump sum that supports Amity's training and housing. They have five days of cultural training before the experience and have all the volunteers gather for a couple of days at the end of the weeks of teaching. The host school provides rooms and meals for the volunteers. Some places give the visiting teachers a field trip or two so they can learn more about the region."

"Probably just feed you miserable food, and the dorm room could be like prison. What about your health?"

"I am buying a special short-term policy for any emergencies, but Amity assures us schools do their best to give us a healthy environment and safety."

"Spy on you all the time likely, bug your room and classroom."

"I am not going alone. Amity has gathered a team from Massachusetts that will include me."

"Do you know the other people?"

"No, but they are Christians."

"The Communist government persecutes Christians."

"Amity is a Christian NGO, Dad. It's been around since the late 1980s. The government appreciates the education and medical volunteers Amity brings to the country. The people on my team filled out the same application forms that I did. People list their religious outlook, something about their faith practices, and attitude toward service. This is a great opportunity.

"What's an NGO?" Mom asked.

"It's a non-governmental organization. NGOs are in countries all around the world. They help the country to meet the needs of the people. The government approves their efforts but does have a say in who the volunteers are or where the volunteers can go."

"Do we have any NGOs in our country?"

"Lots. People just don't recognize them as NGOs. We have some you have given money to, World Vision International, Samaritan's Purse, Goodwill Industries, the American Red Cross. I bet we have thousands in the US."

"And you really feel this is a good idea now?"

"Yes, Mom. I expect that I can help teachers of English, and I'll learn about the real China, not just what we have heard, read, or think is China."

"You can't learn that in weeks. You can't trust the Chinese." Dad said.

"It would not be fair to drop out now, and I really wanted to see China this way."

"Fair doesn't matter in China," Dad said with his grump-iest growl.

"Amity submits everything for approval and review by their government."

"Can't you see what you're getting yourself into?" Mom added in support of my father's prejudices and concerns.

"Mom, our government, like other governments, reviews applications for people to work short or long term in the country."

I showed them a folder with information about the Amity program. Unfortunately, they came across one of the Amity forms requiring a choice. Did I want to be cremated or have my body shipped home if I died in China?

Mom and Dad insisted, "Have your body shipped back! If you choose cremation, they could send us any ashes, and you could be in a prison there or kept in some hospital so they can take your organs for Communist leaders who need organ transplants!"

My parents, lifelong conservative Christians, were not a bit swayed when I told them more about Amity. I explained that when China decided to open more to international connections, in 1985, a Chinese Christian man from Nanjing, Reverend Ting, started Amity, a non-governmental organization (NGO). The Rev saw that western businessmen and politicians who came to China did not provide a positive example of the West. Rev Ting decided to seek volunteers from Western countries who worked in medical and education fields who would go to areas that did not have contact with foreigners.

While thinking of the actions of Rev Ting, I fell asleep. When the alarm woke me, I sat right up feeling as though the couple of hours rest had been two minutes. As I got ready to return for the afternoon classes, I thought of a book I'd read before we moved to Massachusetts, *Are You Running with Me Jesus?*

I hoped the answer was yes. After today's humbling start to my teaching in Wuhai, I didn't know what help I could expect from God. All over the world, people without belief in God coped with disappointment and physical challenges. They made it through those struggles. I could too.

People's Republic of China (PRC)

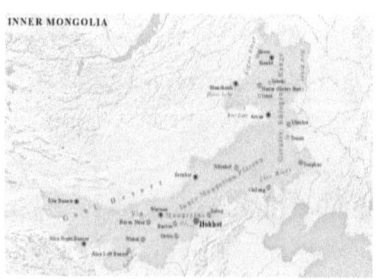

Inner Mongolia Autonomous Region, Wuhai is in the west on the curve of the Yellow River.

Wuhai Prefecture. The airport is north of this view. The Yellow River is to the west. Note the curve of the Yellow River on the left of this photo. Mountains are to the east, and layers of desert and more mountains are beyond the Yellow River behind the mountains.

Chapter 5

Plans and Overrides

Getting sick this morning wasn't the first big surprise since we arrived in Wuhai. Amity expectations counted on the commitment of volunteers to follow the Amity rules and guidelines. The set rules for teachers required that we use the Amity textbook in the mornings. For the afternoon classes, we each could have extra time to work on morning concepts or present content and activities related to each team member's special area.

Because of my degrees and experience, I would introduce famous educators from around the world and their theories and strategies. We would practice activities and discuss the educators and their ideas. Each week I would also present major American holidays and celebration customs. The students would tell me about their major holidays, the significance and their traditions for celebration.

Tia would explain and teach early childhood stories and activities and ask her classes to tell their stories. Kathryn would present health lessons related to different ages, and her class would discuss China's ancient medicine practices and modern choices. Doug would present information on businesses and corporations around the world and engage the class in talking about local businesses and entrepreneurship. They would discuss creating personal financial goals. Jaye would teach about American sports and training for health and strength. They would practice some motions, moves, and maybe learn the basics of baseball.

Then, before Jessie, our Amity escort to Wuhai, left us, she surprised us by overriding an Amity rule about who could be in the SEP. Every area that applied for an Amity English teaching team had far more applicants than the program could accept. Consequently, Amity limited applications by not taking teachers from vocational technical middle or senior middle schools.

Tuesday evening, Jessie's last evening with us, showed us surprises could even change the rules. Memories of Jessie deciding that an Amity rule had to be put aside came to mind whenever I saw Terry or Jeff. Terry was in my homeroom class, and Jeff was in Doug's homeroom. They were not eligible for the program, yet here they were.

After the day's teaching finished, we met in Doug's room to tell one another what had gone well and what had been difficult so that we could adjust the plans and problem-solve together. Dinner would be served at seven in the faculty dining room.

Doug's room was the largest because the Chinese administrators regarded the only man in our team as the team leader. He had a desk, chair, night table, and small chest of drawers besides the two single beds we women had. None of the rooms had closets.

I hoped we could discuss our feelings and observations regarding how Terry and Jeff fit into the classes. Did the other students accept them? I hadn't seen any negativity toward them today.

This first afternoon of classes, I had presented physician and educator, Maria Montessori, to all the groups. Eventually we'd look at Piaget. Plenty of educators from around the world gave me content that would easily fill afternoons for weeks: Albert Bandura, Mary McLeod Bethune, Robert Coles, Jaime Escalante, Viktor Frankl, Lev Vygotsky, and of course, Kong Qiu, known as Confucius in the West. I hoped by the time we looked at Confucius the class could consider new strategies and goals for teaching beyond their traditions. Students' needs were changing in this century.

When the last class finished at five-thirty, I stood at the door. Again, I repeated a variety of phrases to each of the students. "See you tomorrow. Farewell. Have a good evening. Goodbye. Good work today." Then I would start over.

I was not surprised when I realized Erdeen stood beside me. "Thank you for your help today, Erdeen. I watched how you worked with people all day, and yet you still kept an eye on me."

"Tonight get good rest, Ms. Virginia."

We walked out of the classroom, and instead of seeing my team, I saw Terry waiting for me.

"Ms. Virginia, may I speak with you, and walk with you toward the dorm?"

"Yes, Terry." I turned to Erdeen. "Thanks again, Erdeen. See you tomorrow."

She smiled and went to the stairs ahead of Terry and me.

At the top of the staircase, when Erdeen was no longer in sight, Terry stopped and said, "When you were sick this morning, I prayed for you. Now I see that you worked hard all day. I tried to pay attention in classes, but I prayed for you during the day too."

Then Terry, one of the youngest female teachers in my homeroom, took my hand. We walked down the flights of stairs together. Female and male friends often held hands on a walk, a sign of friendship. I had seen this in other countries too.

When we were on the pathway to the dorm, Terry asked, "Will you have dinner here tonight? "

"Yes. We had a welcome dinner Sunday night, and I think maybe another one is planned for this Friday. Tonight, we will eat here at seven, but we meet after classes to discuss the day and our plans."

"Thank you for coming here. I thanked all the teachers today. Jeff and I know it is a miracle that we were allowed to be in this course."

"You do very well, both of you."

"Now I say good night, Ms. Virginia."

I smiled, gave her hand a squeeze before I let it go and said, "See you tomorrow. Do not forget your homework, at least three reasons why anyone who lives in Wuhai or this prefecture should learn English."

We knew the ages of our students from the identification information they had supplied to enter the Amity SEP. Because of the way that Terry and Jeff had joined the program, we didn't have those details from them yet. Jessie didn't seem concerned about not having their forms when she admitted them into the program. I wondered what had made Jessie open to changing and to overriding Amity rules.

Chapter 6

Team Talk and Fears

We gathered on time in Doug's room, but discussion about our first teaching day seemed brief. We had all felt the nerves of hoping for a good start. They voted me first prize winner for having had the roughest start. I could at least smile at their joke.

For a moment we were silent with our own first day recollections. Then Kathryn asked, "Do you remember how odd it felt to be the only Westerners on the plane from Hohhot to Wuhai? It seems long ago, but it was just days."

"I remember. At least when we traveled from the other airports there was variety in passenger looks." Jaye replied. "I'm used to diverse classes where I teach in Berwyn."

"Is that a suburb of Chicago?" Tia asked Jaye.

Doug answered before Jaye. "Berwyn is about ten miles west of Chicago."

Jaye frowned at Doug and stayed silent. The rest of us stayed quiet too. Doug didn't seem to realize how much he jumped in to answer questions with facts.

Kathryn spoke next. "The men on board from Hohhot to

Wuhai did not look Chinese. Mongolian all, I guess. I never imagined there were so many tall men in China. They filled the airplane economy seats with their barrel bodies."

"They stared at us," Tia said quietly. "They were very obvious in staring."

"We were the only women on the plane, and Western women," I added.

"And you're a blonde with blue eyes, Jaye." Kathryn laughed. "They'd have a lot to talk about when they got home."

"Everything looked so brown and barren from the air for most of the flight," Jaye's comment had a tone of concern.

"This area is very different from northeast Inner Mongolia where I was last summer," Doug said. "The Gobi on one side of this city, the Ordos on the other, both cover the plateau of Inner Mongolia. It's the second largest plateau in China after the Tibetan plateau."

Kathryn rolled her eyes. Jaye frowned again. I sighed, and Tia asked,

"Have you been to Tibet, Doug?"

"No. No I haven't. Right now, foreigners can only go there as part of an approved tour group, and I'm not sure I'm up to staying any length of time at that high altitude."

Kathryn changed the topic. "Remember when Jaye looked out the window and said, 'Look at the M&Ms coming toward the plane!'"

"I knew they were umbrellas!" Tia said with a smile.

"They looked like M&Ms coming out to the tarmac." Kathryn remarked.

"Who carries umbrellas in the gorgeous sunshine?" Jaye asked. She wore flip-flops, just as she had on the day we arrived. Amity had told us to wear enclosed shoes when teaching, but all Jaye had brought were flip-flops and gym shoes. Today, on the first day of classes, she wore flip-flops, gaucho-style trousers, and a T-shirt. At least Jaye had not worn one of her brightly colored spaghetti strap tops that she had shown us during the training days in Nanjing.

Wuhai Airport, Inner Mongolia, (Nei Menggu)

Tia said, "I'm glad we had Jessie with us. Wasn't it scary knowing that we were going to be the first Westerners ever to stay here. I don't like to stand out at home, and it feels just as uncomfortable here to be the odd one everyone stares at." Tia spoke with more volume than I had ever heard from her.

"And we're not just visiting Westerners. We must be representatives for Amity." Kathryn added. This did not seem to make Tia feel better.

"We represent Amity, our country, and Christians." I added.

"No pressure," Jaye said. "Actually, one really good part about being the first Westerners to stay here, is that we can stop traffic just by stepping off the curb. It's safer crossing the street when people stop and stare at us. Didn't you notice that when they gave us a walking tour of the area yesterday? No one seems to pay regular attention to whether the streetlights show red, green, or yellow."

"Jessie was sure we'd be fine here." Tia added. "She checked the areas where we would live, the classrooms, the equipment, the dining room, and the computer lab."

"I don't think she checked the school restrooms. I can't believe that's all the students have, and the teachers too." Kathryn's words reminded us of the one long narrow building that served as the students' restrooms.

One side was for girls, one was for boys, and nothing different for teachers. In the girl's room was a trough, a long cement slanted trough. Anyone using this bathroom facility straddled the trough and watched their deposit travel down the slope. If it didn't move, there was a faucet at the highest end of the trough. Turning on the faucet made whatever was in the trough flow downhill toward the drain.

Jaye said, "It's a good thing this dorm is close to the classrooms. I jog back to the dorm for a Western style toilet. I was in a teacher's dorm room yesterday, just down the hall. Four women share it, and their bathroom is the same as ours, except they have the Asian hole in the floor for a toilet."

"They have that in many countries, not just Asia," Doug informed Jaye.

She briefly made a little girl angry face at him and continued, "As for checking, I wonder if Jessie inspected the computer lab. She should have asked for us to have more access. It's our only chance to connect with home, and I think we need more than just the break time after lunch. I feel so cut off by having only a couple of hours a day to be able to send and receive email." We agreed.

"I wonder if the people who met us at the airport felt nervous about how we would feel with these accommodations." Kathryn said.

"The principal, the vice principal, some of the top teachers, and the superintendent of all the Inner Mongolian schools made an impressive greeting line." Doug recounted as if picturing the welcome again.

"Emily' saying, 'Welcome to Wuhai,' when she stepped forward let me know she was the leader of the teachers," said Kathryn.

"The other teachers all said something too. 'Welcome.' 'Please share our parasols.' 'The sun is very hot today.'" Tia added. "I felt truly welcomed."

"I remember the warning, 'You need to be careful in our desert sun. You must take care,' Jaye added.

"I wonder if the terminal will be finished before we leave. So much of it is still under construction." Doug said.

"Do you remember that we could see construction workers along the roof and one corner of the building working in the sun's glare? They work here like that too through these dry hot days removing all the old barracks. I wonder how much they're paid. Probably below what they should get." Jaye noticed and commented on physical actions.

"The oldest buildings near us are the ones the school is removing," I mentioned.

"They look like barracks from the 1940s," Jaye added.

**Demolition of 1940s buildings in Wuhai
summer 2004**

Kathryn said, "Jessie pointed out the best features of this school, a new Olympic size track, outdoor exercise equipment, a science building and a modern new administration building with a wonderful auditorium we can use for the afternoon once a week when all the classes meet. Plus, the four-story classroom buildings are new, even if the furniture is old.

"And did you know this dormitory building has three small apartments on the first floor? Delia was with me and helped me have a conversation with the head housekeeper. The apartments are for the woman who is the head housekeeper, one for the cook, and one for the man who is the head of grounds keepers."

"The second and third floor dormitory rooms on each end of this building are for teachers. They just have bunk beds," Doug added.

"Doug, your room is nicer than any of ours," Jaye commented. We all looked at him, but he had no response.

Tia said, "Cassie told me that the students who go to this high school and who come from tiny little towns far away have rooms on the second and third floor. They have bunk beds too, four to six students in a room. Some students only go home on long holidays because they live far away. Travel expenses are high for them."

"Tough for them," Jaye said, "But I'd like to change the subject and ask, do you realize that the wall that goes around this entire campus is ten feet high? The only entrances are the front gate, which is guarded, and the little side gate at the end of the alley on this side of the dorm building, but it can only be used by people who have keys." Jaye looked annoyed. "I don't like being walled in. The street outside the gate at the end of the alley right here by the dorm would be great to explore. The gate is locked, so we have to get the housekeeper to let us out. I suppose I can point and try to get her to open it. I haven't attempted that yet. I don't want to have to ask. I don't appreciate this restrictive environment." Jaye's negative vibrations filled the room.

Tia tried to add a positive note. "Emily told me that the area where the barracks are will be a beautifully landscaped garden for students, faculty, and staff."

"Well, I'm glad we women took them up on the parasols offer at the airport. The sun is so strong here. Even the air seems super-hot," Kathryn said.

While we stood in the huge rectangle of the air-conditioned terminal, the parasols came down. Jessie talked with our hosts in Chinese. We could see their respect grow at her fluency.

The brand-new airport had not been busy. No other flights were arriving or departing. The huge side and front glass windows revealed no houses, apartments, stores, or any kind of buildings. I did see men taking our luggage out of the wide automatic front doors to three large gleaming black cars parked near signs indicating a no parking zone. I got lost for a moment in the memory of our arrival and did not hear the next couple of comments.

"You feeling all right Virginia?" Kathryn asked me.

"Hmmm?"

"You weren't with us for a few moments. We started to talk about last night, Jeff and Terry, and Jessie's abrupt decision to let them join the SEP."

"She knows herself and this country. Don't you think she has enough experience to make the choice that she did?" I asked.

"She listened carefully to Terry and Jeff speak English while they translated for us," Tia sounded tentative. "Jessie would know if her decision would offend the authorities and host school, wouldn't she?"

"Maybe not," Doug added. "Maybe it has never happened before last night. We can't know if Jessie received a warning about changing the rules on who can join the SEP at the last moment."

"I think of the Amity warnings often, like avoiding any mention of the three Ts, Tibet, Taiwan, and Tiananmen. I plan to avoid offending hosts, local people, or authorities." Kathryn nodded emphatically as she recalled the Amity cautions.

"That meeting last night seemed unreal, but Jessie took it in stride. So, shouldn't we? How did you feel?" I asked.

"I was frightened. I thought it would get us into trouble right at the start of our time here," Tia added.

Jaye surprised me by agreeing with Tia. "I wondered if our time here would be over before it started when Emily told us who had come to talk to Jessie."

Doug just looked around our group. He took a breath as if getting ready for a big announcement or a long speech.

Chapter 7

Confronting Surprises

"You do remember that Jessie said we need to make prayer time together a part of each day, personally and as a group. And Jessie encouraged us to trust that God would help us through whatever came up because so many people who support Amity would be praying for us." Doug said in his deep professorial tone.

In her usual gentle voice, Tia said, "It was easy to talk with Jessie. She made me feel more confident, especially when we prayed together, I didn't feel so nervous about teaching. I think our prayer time, before Emily's knock at the door, gave me a feeling of strength."

"I don't think anything we said or prayed about prepared me for Emily's news," Jaye responded. "My mind wanders during prayer. None of us could have guessed what was going to happen. I thought Emily must be joking."

"I can't imagine Emily joking." Tia said.

"What must Emily have thought?" Kathryn asked.

I recalled that unexpected knock on the door Tuesday evening. It had made me wonder again about the warnings of my family and friends. Everyone in my parents' generation, both relatives and friends, warned me about listening devices planted in rooms so that the authorities would know what we thought, planned, and felt. Had anyone listened to us in our personal sharing about our concerns, our teaching, and our prayers? Did they record our conversations in the rooms? How could we ever know?

Doug had opened the door. Emily stood there and had an authoritative presence even though she was petite. Emily always seemed comfortable in guiding us through school, schedules, and cultural expectations. Yet at that moment last night, Emily had an expression of confusion mixed with tension. She looked past Doug to Jessie. "Excuse me, Ms. Jessie, Some people have arrived. I think they must meet you."

"Must?" A few of us echoed.

"A request was given to Principal Chen for this meeting. Principal Chen approved the request. He called me to arrange the meeting. The person is a pastor in the church near this school. He has two young teachers with him."

"And we must meet him now?" Jessie asked gently.

Emily paused as if unsure of her next words. "Ms. Jessie, he told me..." Emily's voice trailed off. She looked at us as if she didn't feel comfortable giving the message.

"What did he tell you, Emily?" Jessie asked again.

"He told me God told him to talk with the Amity leader and teachers." Emily spoke slowly enunciating carefully. As the head English teacher in this number one school, and person over all our assistants, she sounded formal in speaking with us.

Jessie walked toward Emily. We all stood. "That's fine

Virginia Heslinga

Emily. We will be glad to meet with him. Should we meet him here?"

"I have led him and the two teachers who are with him to a conference room in our administration building. Please come with me. You and all the team."

Doug leaned toward Jessie and asked, "What do you think it is about, Jessie?"

She replied, "I cannot guess, but we should meet the pastor and the teachers with him. Wuhai has two registered churches. It is common for SEP teachers to go to the registered church nearest their host school. People know that the volunteers who work with the SEP have Christian faith. Wuhai has one registered church on each side of the city. One is less than a mile from here. Maybe that is where this pastor works."

Jessie headed down the hall following Emily. We followed them.

"Will this create a difficulty for us, a private meeting with a pastor?" Tia's voice wavered like ripples from a stone thrown into a pond.

"Every school that gets an Amity team, as well as the local, provincial, and national governments, know that our teachers go to church in the town where they live and teach unless there is no church in the town. We do have some areas where there are no registered churches, and no foreigner should go to an unregistered house church because that creates problems for the locals and for the visitor."

"Would the pastor know this?" Jaye asked as she came alongside Jessie.

"Yes." Jessie smiled at Jaye.

"But why should he think he had a right to demand to

46

talk to you?" Jaye's concern and suspicion oozed through her question.

Jessie answered, "He gave Emily the reason quite clearly."

Jaye's frown showed that she did not appreciate that response. Of all our team, Jaye had seemed least interested in any spiritual discussions or prayer time. I still had not resolved my anger toward God, but I prayed each day for other people and for our work in this SEP.

We entered the new modern administration building. Emily pointed toward the stairs and started up them. Doug would have followed next, but Jessie stopped and said to us, "Here's is a reminder, if you haven't realized it yet, learn it now. Every day will have surprises in China. Embrace them, learn through them, and remember that the Lord is always with you."

On the second floor, Emily, still ahead, opened the door to a rectangular conference room. She stepped back so that we could pass her and enter the room.

The walls were plain white. A huge picture of Chairman Mao, framed in red and black and matted in gold dominated a wall to my left at the far end of the room. Anyone would see Mao's portrait upon entering this carpeted space.

Floors throughout the school complex were cement or tiled, some plain tile, some decorative. We had not experienced springy carpet in any school room, but this room had it, a deeply cushioned ruby red medium pile carpet.

In this far western region of the People's Republic of China, Mongolian people honored Genghis Khan. The Mongol leader appeared on the wall across from me. He stood portrayed in a black and white etching, lightly tinted with a wash of clay red. His depiction was only half the size of the portrait of Chairman Mao. And Genghis Khan's image had only a simple black frame.

Also, on the long wall across from me was a huge map of Wuhai. It showed districts, the surrounding mountains and deserts, farmland and mining areas, the downtown, the train station, the airport, the cement production plant, mining sites, and the curves of the Yellow River that touched the city.

To our right on the end wall, we saw a flag of China, totally red with a large gold star and four small gold stars around the large gold star. In the wall beside the flag were two squares that looked like vents. Emily noticed that we looked around. She even picked up on our longer pause as we looked at the two squares.

"The squares are for air-conditioning, and one is an intercom system." She indicated that we should take seats at the long polished dark wood table. Eighteen armchairs surrounded the table, eight on each side and one on each end. These were the most comfortable chairs we had seen or used at the school.

Jessie, Tia, and I sat with our backs to the door. Before I sat down, I glanced at the wall behind us and saw a row of photos of the school building and architectural drawings for areas still in development. Doug, Jaye, and Kathryn walked around the end of the table and sat across from Jessie, Tia, and me.

Genghis Khan looked over their shoulders. No one sat in the end seat below the flag, and we all had a clear view to the distant wall where Mao stared above our heads. He could have been looking at the flag.

After we were seated, Emily left. We looked at one another, but we didn't speak right away. I wondered as I stared at the two vent-like openings if anything we said in this room would be heard live or recorded. Amid the tension of waiting for Emily to return with the pastor, I asked Jessie, "What is the symbolism of the stars on the flag?"

"The big star represents the Communist Party. The four smaller stars represent the workers, the peasant working class, the bourgeoisie, and the national leaders."

Emily reappeared with a dark-haired, clean-shaven, stocky Chinese man of average height. He wore a dark suit and tie, a white shirt, and black dress shoes. The two young people who followed him into the conference room wore clothes like the teachers we had interviewed. I guessed that both teachers were in their mid-twenties.

"This is one of the local pastors." Had Emily said that extra clearly for anyone who might be listening? "The young woman attends the nearby church where this pastor works. The young man does not. They are friends and teach at a vocational junior middle school here in Wuhai."

The pastor smiled, tipped his head toward each side of the table, and chose to sit in the end seat under the flag of China. I thought that must be the foot of the table. Surely the other end seat, with Mao's portrait behind it, must be the head of the table. The two young people went around to places across from us and beside Kathryn.

Emily asked Jessie, "Will you be comfortable translating, or should I stay?"

"I think we will be fine," Jessie answered. No specific introductions had been made. The young woman looked Mongolian, similar to Erdeen. She had light brown eyes with the same fold that marked Mongolian eyes, which were different from Chinese. The young man had a slight build, but was taller than the pastor, and he looked Chinese.

The administration building had air-conditioning. This room had no window. The extra-large flag of China was like a bold splash of red against the white wall.

Jessie translated as the pastor spoke. "I am Pastor Isaiah. This young woman, Terry, is a teacher in a vocational school. The city knew foreign teachers would arrive, but it is a pity, the vocational teachers cannot be in this program. Terry asked if I could help her to meet the foreign teachers because we knew Amity teachers visit churches, and the church I serve is closest to this school. I told her I would try to help her. She has loved English since she was a young child. She studies daily listening, reading, and with singing songs."

I admired the hope and trust the young woman, Terry, had shown in her pastor. When she felt disappointment that she would not meet or even see the teachers from America, she had gone to her pastor for help. He not only had brought her to the school but also had invited her to bring her non-church-going friend, Jeff.

Jessie spoke to these unexpected guests in her beautiful Mandarin, always a surprise to people. The pastor, Terry, and Jeff looked amazed by her excellent Chinese and complimented her. Terry spontaneously turned to us and translated their praise.

In her kind voice, Jessie said, "Terry, would you and Jeff like to take turns now translating what your pastor and I say for this team of teachers? They do not know more than a few basic words in Mandarin."

Terry and Jeff nodded their agreement, delighted with the task. I suspected that Jessie asked them to translate so that she could see their level of English without asking interview questions. In her two decades of living and working in

China, Jessie had gained a gracious technique of gathering information without making someone feel nervous.

"I brought these teachers to the front gate," the pastor told us. "The guard heard my request to meet the foreign teachers, and he called the principal. The principal said a teacher would come and take us to meet you.

"We heard that Amity teachers are Christians. They come as volunteers during their vacation time from work in English-speaking countries." The pastor made this a statement, but it seemed like a question. Terry translated smoothly.

"Yes," Jessie answered, this time in English. "Most of the people who work for Amity and who come as volunteers are Christians. Rev Ting started Amity because he saw that the businesspeople and politicians who came to China did not provide a positive example of the West. He sought volunteers from the medical and education fields who could work in remote areas with people who had never met a Westerner or a native speaker of English." Terry translated Jessie's words into Chinese for the pastor.

"We know that many Western teachers come for paid work teaching English in our big cities like Beijing and Shanghai, where they meet other foreigners and visit tourist sites." Pastor Isaiah added. Jeff translated this directly.

"Rev Ting knew that." Jessie continued in English. "He desired more interaction be available in the countryside for China's people. He had a hope to improve relationships with Westerners, native speakers of English, who could spend time working as volunteers. Amity volunteers and locals could learn about one another's culture.

"Teaching English is needed around this nation. Remote areas became a focus for Amity. Teachers in the provinces

distant from cities with international visitors do not have expo-
sure to people speaking English. Teachers become discouraged because it is difficult for students to stay motivated to
study a language that they think they will never use. They do
not expect ever to meet a native speaker of that language."

It seemed that Jeff conveyed this well. We saw Jessie
smile at his English translation.

"May we pray together before we talk more?" Pastor
Isaiah asked.

Jessie nodded. When the pastor prayed in Chinese,
Terry translated. I peeked at Jessie. Her eyes were closed,
but she continued to smile.

"Heavenly Father, we ask for guidance, wisdom, and
encouragement for the teachers in this room and for all those
working with Amity. We thank you for people who would
come so far to work for no pay to help our teachers improve
in teaching English. Thank you for this chance to meet with
a brother and sisters from America. Amen."

I glanced again to my right at the intercom and
wondered if there was a camera there too. The tension in my
body told me I also wondered if we would all be in trouble
because of this meeting.

Then the pastor said, "Let us sing a song we may all
know." With a smile, he launched into a song I learned as a
toddler, "Jesus Loves Me." He sang in Chinese, but we
recognized the melody. When Jessie started singing along
with him, so did the rest of us. She sang in Mandarin. Our
team sang in English. Jeff stayed silent.

"That meeting was surreal, wasn't it?" Kathryn asked
after we had shared our memories of our previous and most
unusual evening.

"Crazier than Dali's art," Jaye affirmed.

I agreed and added, "If this meeting was recorded, it would probably be the first and only time the song 'Jesus Loves Me' would be recorded from this high school conference room or any high school conference room in Inner Mongolia of the People's Republic of China."

Doug said, "As soon as we finished singing, Jessie asked Terry to talk about teaching. Could you tell that Jessie was evaluating Terry's English level?"

I answered, "Yes, I could tell. Terry's English is smooth. She's younger than many teachers in the program. It reminded me not to judge a person's ability by their age, where they work, or where they live. Terry's English is as strong as Emily's. That might not endear Terry to other teachers in our classes."

"And then Jessie smoothly asked Jeff to talk about himself and teaching." Doug added, "I thought Jeff looked uncomfortable when we were singing. It's pretty obvious he is not familiar with Terry's church life."

"Jeff's English fit in the high-level category too. How ironic. Because they teach in a vocational middle school, they couldn't even interview with the SEP. That doesn't seem right." Jaye observed.

Doug told us, "The numbers of teachers applying for SEP stays so high that the program had not expanded to include teachers from vocational or technical high schools. The only vocational technical staff who could apply had to teach at a vocational technical college. We have one student in that category."

"Who is it?" Jaye asked.

"Penny, wife of Thomas," Doug replied. "I interviewed

them. They're newlyweds. Thomas has better English skills, but Penny is close behind him."

Tia added, "Weren't you surprised when both Terry and Jeff said they listened to songs in English, mainly folk songs that told stories? John Denver and *The Captain and Tennile* they knew best. They are some of my favorites too. Oldies."

"They said they watched whatever English programs CCTV offers." Jaye said. "What is that, Doug?"

"China Central Television."

Jaye continued, "I guess they don't watch any of those gross horror movies we saw in the video store a couple of blocks from here. China probably wouldn't allow them on television stations."

"Videos in places like Wuhai are rarely the actual movie. They've been illegally copied and have made up content and ripped off portions of other movies that are all spliced into the movie people think they're buying. They're poor-quality." Doug added.

Jaye said, "I watch some pirated videos at home, not horror movies. They're actual movies, just not good quality. None of them have spliced odd parts in them."

"Did you feel uncomfortable when Jeff and Terry stopped speaking?" Kathryn asked. "I thought that their expressions showed they were embarrassed by how much they had talked or that they were wondering if they had done a good job translating."

"Jessie's response surprised them." I said, "You could see they were shocked, and even the pastor appeared surprised. She sounded definite when she said, "I cannot change the rules of the whole organization, but I can admit these two teachers as SEP students based on my evaluation of their preparation in building their English skills. I will work to help find ways Amity can admit more vocational technical teachers next year. I will talk with the Amity leaders when I return to Nanjing."

"The pastor spoke up right away," Jaye said. "I think Terry and Jeff were too shocked to say anything."

Kathryn added, "I believe the pastor was sincere when he said, 'We came here hoping only to have a chance to meet with the foreign teachers. We did not intend to ask for places in the program.' When Terry translated his words, she looked teary."

"Jessie believed they had not come to try to get into the program," I said. "Jessie did well in asking them for translation help at the church on the Sundays we are here. They accepted her idea when she told them, 'The administration knows that we expect our teachers to be able to visit a local church each Sunday. Terry and Jeff can be interpreters.'"

Doug added, "Jessie helped them to feel fully accepted when she told them, 'We want to have one interpreter for each Amity teacher. Right now, we have only Emily as an interpreter for this Sunday. The assigned translators will sit near these teachers and whisper translations to them. Each teacher has a Bible in Mandarin and English, but translators will have to help them find the correct passage since they will not understand what is announced.'"

Kathryn added, "They looked astounded when Jessie said, 'You two should plan to start in the program with everyone tomorrow. That is the first day of classes. It is best to be in from the start. These teachers have named their classrooms after cities in America. Jeff, you join Doug's class, Atlanta, and Terry, you join Virginia's class, Miami.'"

Jaye laughed, "It was funny when Jeff said, Thank you.

Yes. We will go to Atlanta and Miami tomorrow.' It sounded like they would get on planes and go to those cities."

Sighs circulated among the team. We'd been remembering rather than planning ever since we'd arrived in Doug's room. We felt like our energy was fading with the arrival of the evening. I looked at my watch and announced, "It's almost seven. We should go to the dining room. Not that I want to eat anything else, but it seems important that we show up at meals."

As my team stood, Kathryn said, "Do you think it was all right that we just did a little bow to the pastor and didn't shake hands or anything?"

"Yes, and the pastor blessed us. I loved that." Tia said. "When he said, 'I wish to bless you,' I felt relief, and was glad for a blessing. Weren't you?" We nodded in agreement.

I remembered how Pastor Isaiah had bowed his head and raised his hands up in the position of holding them over someone's bowed head. He spoke, "Lord Jesus, I ask you to strengthen and bless the efforts of Amity, these foreign volunteer teachers, this school, the city leaders, the teachers here for training, and our city. Thank you for the gracious gifts you bring into our lives."

Just after I finished recalling Pastor Isaiah's blessing, Jaye said, "Hey, do you remember that as soon as the pastor prayed and blessed us, Emily opened the door to the conference room. Do you think that was a coincidence? How did she know that was the exact moment our meeting finished?"

"Do you really believe in coincidences?" Doug asked Jaye. She stayed quiet.

"I miss having Jessie here. She could switch so easily in coping with surprises and speaking." Tia sighed.

"I heard Emily compliment, Jessie. She said, 'You were

kind, Ms. Jessie. I always thought special programs should be open to anyone interested if they had the qualifications." Kathryn said.

Doug asked, "Do you know that sometimes Amity can return to an area where they had a team the previous year. Government decisions take priority over Amity choices. No one knows why the central government in Beijing chooses to give some areas a team two or three years in a row, but it has happened."

I said, "I didn't know that, Doug, but let's go back to our first consideration. We were starting to talk about how Terry and Jeff are doing in the classes when we detoured to the events of last night. Can we say how we think Terry and Jeff did today, and whether the other students accepted them?"

"I thought everything went smoothly." Kathryn answered.

"They had a better start than you did," Jaye remarked. "What a first class you had! Hello class. Excuse me while I go barf over the balcony." And Jaye laughed.

Tia frowned at Jaye. Kathryn and Doug did not laugh. Then Tia said, "Terry and Jeff did well in my time with them. Everyone seemed friendly to them. I hope that continues. I feel nervous without Jessie. I couldn't believe how early she had to leave."

"Jessie is skilled at being the bridge between the teams and the schools, but she was almost stumped at the ceremonial welcome dinner!" Jaye laughed again and looked directly at Doug. "You threw Jessie more than a simple curve ball in that ceremony."

Doug didn't respond. Instead, he walked to the door, opened it, and indicated that we should leave. None of us spoke as we walked to the small faculty dining room.

Without Jessie we really would have had an awful start. Jaye seemed to enjoy prodding sore points, my sickness and Doug's startling choice at the welcome dinner.

Doug had shocked everyone, Chinese, Mongolian, and American. At the Amity training days, we had learned that every location had a grand ceremonial dinner. Usually it was held on the Sunday evening of the day the Amity volunteers arrived. Jaye could joke about Doug's actions now, but I wondered if we could have prevented or at least warned our hosts of the unusual problem with Doug and alcohol.

Chapter 8

Embarrassment in the Yurt

On our first evening, the same group that had welcomed us at the airport took us to the edge of the city nearest the mountains. A wide-open field lay at the base of the closest hills, and we saw a few scattered trees. A low fence and dozens of goats with wool in earth tone shades plus some white and black could be seen in the twilight. In the field, some of the largest yurts I had ever seen stood like tented mushrooms.

A long low wall with lights illuminated the space that was just wide enough for the single file of our glossy cars. We saw a path to yurts ahead of us. We exited the cars and followed the trail to a yurt twenty times the size of the traditional round dwellings for a Mongolian family. Emily had explained that these huge yurts existed for celebrations.

Hosts stood outside to welcome us as our arrival qualified was as a great event. Waiters in Mongolian costumes escorted each of us to our seats. I followed a young woman in Mongolian headdress, wearing a long dress with a sash. In her role as the main translator for the school, Emily told us that the woman wore a *deel*.

A *deel* is a long tunic with long sleeves and a high collar. Some have buttons on the right shoulder. *Deels*, like tartans, show family connection and social status.

With a smile, the young woman in costume led us to a seat at the circular table. The men and women who guided our group to our places in the yurt all wore *deels* with sashes of bold contrasting colors. Other men wore tunic tops with colorful sashes, dark trousers, and boots.

I had read about yurts as soon as I learned that our assignment would be in western Inner Mongolia. A yurt is a round tent style of Mongolian homes formed over lattices of woodwork. In family size yurts, the wood support structure is simple, but not in this one. Layers of white, blue, and gold silk adorned the doorway. Colorful flower arrangements stood on pedestals scattered around the yurt. The glowing beauty of the wood, bright white tent and colorful silks, embroidery and sashes on the servers' primary color costumes made me feel like Dorothy surrounded by beings on the Yellow Brick Road.

The huge circular table had been made of sections of curved sectional tables. Thirty people could sit around this table. An opening on one side of the arrangement allowed waiters to bring food into the center open area to serve each person. All the servers looked like the family of Genghis Khan. Carvings and pictures of Kahn appeared around the yurt. The walls were constructed in a texture similar to waffles. and the ceiling looked like sapling beams with a golden glow arching to the center of the rounded roof.

Most of the ceremonial outfits of the local Mongolian attendants, white tunics, dark sashes, and blue trim for the men showed symbolic colors of their devotion to earth, sky, water, and air. The women greeters wore long *deels* in vibrant red and gold also trimmed with blue. On their feet were summer boots that looked like embroidered felt for the women and decorative leather on the men.

The celebration yurt in Wuhai

Both men and women wore long sleeves. The male clothing looked looser than the female clothing. The teachers chosen by the school to sit as assistants next to each of us explained that the colors had significance. White is used to symbolize goodness, holiness, and positivity. Green and blue represent the natural world. Like indigenous people around the globe, the Mongolians have deeply ingrained respect for the earth. Green represents all things growing. Blue represents the sky, water, and eternity. Red represents fire, strength, bravery, and love. Yellow represents education, enlightenment, and joy.

Emily told us that the headwear was called *toortsog*. The young entertainers and musicians, and later, a singer, wore varied styles of *toortsog*. I had seen these head coverings in museums and documentaries, but not on people talking with me. The clothing varied from thirteenth century Genghis Khan outfits to modern traditional robes. Headgear included the same wide range of years and was made of leather, wood, wool, felt, and cloth.

The toortsog can be plain or colorful and have beads, trim, or both.

It seemed like we had walked into a vast version of a genie's dining room. After we took our seats, music started from the opposite side of the yurt. I wished that the music teachers I knew could see the combination of young and very ancient looking individuals playing the two stringed horse-head fiddle, a larger four stringed instrument, a lute, something that looked like a dulcimer, small drums, and miniature cymbals.

While the musicians played the dinner time music, a young couple sang, and servers came around and poured milk tea into bowls at our places. Emily explained to me that Mongolian milk tea could come from sheep, goats, camel, cow, or yak. The milk tea, called *suutei tsai*, had a strong flavor of its own.

"I rarely drink milk tea," she said, "But the school

wanted you to have a full sampling of important Mongolian beverages and foods. Chinese think clear teas are better for health than milk tea." I could see the other members of my team had assistants near them to explain about the food and drinks.

Small bowls scattered on each section of the huge round table contained optional ingredients commonly added to milk tea: salt, grated cheese, toasted millet, yogurt, and butter. People chose what they wanted to include, drop it into the bowl of beige color milk, and either wait for it to sink to the bottom or stir it with one of the *kuaizi*.

"Why do you add salt to tea?" Jaye asked quite loudly. Her seat was a few chairs away from mine. Jaye loved salt and even carried a container of salt with her. Amity had told us never to ask for salt, pepper, or spices because that would imply the food did not have a good flavor. It didn't seem to dawn on her that pulling out a huge container of salt could be insulting, but she didn't need her salt at this dinner because of small bowls of white or pink salt near each place.

Emily answered, "If people drink a lot of this tea, salt reduces the bitterness of the dark strong black tea. This helps prevent what is called, in English, acid reflux."

I didn't want to add butter to tea, but I added millet, a pinch of salt, and yogurt. I had a seat near Principal Chen and noticed that he put a bit of everything in his tea. If anyone wanted an example of an unreadable and inscrutable power person, Principal Chen would be someone to study, so I decided to watch his choices.

After we were given milk tea, Emily stood and introduced the people we had not met earlier, town administrators, and some head teachers from other schools, both Chinese and Mongolian. Each section of the round table had one foreign teacher, a translator, and local dignitaries along with the school authorities.

Emily was the translator nearest me. She named each item brought to the table starting with the appetizers: bowls of grain, fresh yogurt, pine nuts, Mongolian glazed meatballs, cabbage cups with meat, crispy beef, potstickers with ginger and chili, sesame chicken balls, spring rolls, and sweet and sour pork. I was very glad I had learned how to use chopsticks before making this trip.

Our hosts watched us. Beside our dinner plates, small dishes for appetizers disappeared as soon as they had been used. Waiters replaced them with clean plates. We also had forks, knives, and spoons. None of us used those implements for any of the appetizers or for the meal. I hoped that impressed the hosts. We all had developed competent skills with chopsticks.

As for drinking the milk tea, we had held back waiting to lift the mug size bowl until we saw our hosts and assistants drinking the milk tea. When we followed the custom of drinking milk tea by lifting the large bowl with both hands, I thought of how appalled my prim and proper New England aunts would be by the custom.

There was also one small glass handleless glass cup, rounder than a shot glass, but about that tall, at each place. Emily said that would be for ceremonial drinks made during toasts. It never crossed my mind to think there could be a problem of lifting a glass in a toast. Wouldn't everyone at such a dinner as this one do that?

A young couple circled the table as part of a Mongolian welcoming tradition. Emily explained that they would pause beside each of the visitors, not just us but also the superintendent from Hohhot, sing a song of blessing, and offer us a blue scarf. The beautiful blue silk looked like the sky and the auspicious days it represented. Different colored scarves can be offered at ceremonies, but blue shows the high respect.

Emily told us to stand when it was our turn for a greeting. The Mongolian woman sang and indicated that the honored person should lift their hands while she put the scarf, called a *khadag*, over the guest's hands. A young man beside her lifted what seemed like a rounded silver shot glass. The translation of what he said to each person acknowledged Father Sky, Mother Earth, and appreciation for all the ancestors.

They did a hand motion upwards to sky, down toward the ground, and then to head and forward as they named Father Sky, Mother Earth, and the ancestors. Then, the cup was offered. Jessie received this greeting first because she held the role of administrator from Amity. We watched her carefully as she received the silk scarf across her uplifted palms. Then the small cup had been placed in her hands.

Jessie did not choose to imitate the hand motions, but she did lift the cup to her lips. We couldn't tell if she sipped it or not. I thought Jessie made that unclear on purpose. She smiled and passed the cup back to the young man.

He moved on to the next foreigner, Doug. As the man on our team, and a tall one, Doug drew attention. With smiles, people watched him in this greeting ceremony.

The scene stopped for me.

Too late I remembered that in the Nanjing training time, when the subject of liquor and toasting came up, that Doug had told us he did not drink alcohol, not ever. He had pride in his membership in the twenty-first century temperance union. Did Jessie know? This presented a chance for mammoth social embarrassment!

With gracious fluid motions, the woman gave Doug a blue scarf. The young man beside her lifted the cup toward him. Doug did not move to take it. The ceremony froze as if someone hit a pause button.

Doug needed to take the cup and speak, but what could he say that would not be a rejection of and an insult of this gentle and lovely welcome? Studying Doug, I thought he did not care that by refusing to even make a motion as if to sip the liquor that he could offend both the Chinese banquet etiquette and the Mongolian hospitality .

With the dignity of a man sure of his choices, Doug said, "I will need some tea."

The Mongolian couple stood still. They looked to the host who had welcomed us into the yurt. He did not understand. He turned to Principal Chen. Then they both looked at Emily.

"Jessie!" I looked at her and spoke in a loud whisper of alarm.

Chapter 9

A Vow Made Him Do It

"We've lost you again?" Kathryn said softly to me as we reached the faculty dining room. I felt like a month had been packed into Wednesday, or at least into the time from Sunday evening until this moment.

"I was remembering our welcome dinner and Doug refusing to take the cup of liquor."

"Oh my gosh! That made me have a hot flash of embarrassment. Honestly, I haven't been that consumed by heat since I'd had hot flashes, years ago. Doug asking for tea, I just want to forget that."

I nodded and tried to switch gears to focus on this dinner. We had been told that when we had dinner at the school, it would be at seven o'clock. If the host school took us out to dinner, we would leave the school at seven thirty. No one mentioned whether we would ever be guests in homes in the city, but we had discussed this in Nanjing.

In our training days, each of us mentioned how special an experience it would be to have a meal in a local's home.

None of the people connected to the school or community were expected to do anything other than give us a room and a couple of meals a day. Breakfast and supper would be what host schools would definitely provide.

Above the cafeteria main hall for students, were a variety of dining rooms. Chinese prefer to dine in rooms for just their group. Our group would be at least ten people for every meal, our team and five SEP participants selected to keep us company. Emily explained that the students who had a turn to have informal conversation with the Amity team over a meal thought it an honor.

Doug had told us that when he worked with Amity in the northeast of Inner Mongolia, they had teachers at their meals too. Then he added, Chinese rarely let foreigners have time alone. Individualism and ideas of foreigners are suspect.

I noticed we were seeing the same people as mealtime companions. This caused me to remember that sometime this week the team needed to find a broader way to offer informal conversational English to all the students. Amity called these additional conversational opportunities English Corners and recommended starting them in the second week of teaching. I glanced at Doug and wondered if he would bring up an idea for English Corners before Friday after-noon. We seemed to struggle with cohesion as a team, prob-ably because we hadn't known one another at all before landing in China.

Tonight, we had Delia, Thomas, Erdeen, Kent, and Peter. They commented on the first day of class and asked questions about our homes, families, and jobs. The meal was noodles, optional sauces for the noodles, braised mutton, cherry tomatoes, and stir-fried vegetables, tea to drink, and a fruit cup for dessert. Amity had, in the training time, presented the typical earnings and meals in each of the provinces where teams would work this summer. I looked at the food served to us and knew this was more than the typical family would have for supper in Wuhai. Our hosts were still providing special generous guest fare.

I tried not to show my longing to go back to my room and to bed. My mind whirled with memories and concerns. Being on guard and a need for caution regarding each word and action with my team and with the SEP students tired me out.

When I finally returned to my room, I thought about the rest of that first ceremonial dinner, but that wasn't the worst part of our first night in Wuhai. Kathryn said she got chills from embarrassing events. I had told her I got stomachaches and headaches reviewing stressful moments.

After bringing the ceremony to a standstill with his request, Doug had to repeat his wish for tea instead of liquor. Emily stood with the poise of a diplomat, but the other English teachers looked like they had just been slapped awake. The servers who had been moving around the tables pouring the strong liquor, *baijiu*, into the small handleless cups at each place, froze holding the *baijiu* aloft.

When Emily stated Doug's request in Chinese, for a moment the principal and superintendent frowned—but they quickly erased negative expressions. If a guest seemed rude, that did not mean they would be rude in return.

Jessie stood and spoke in her fluent Chinese. Emily translated softly to me as Jessie explained that Doug had taken a vow as a young person to never drink liquor. The Chinese have a deep respect for vows. However, Chinese men would think it crazy to make a vow never to drink liquor. Chinese and Mongolian men faced judgement of strength by how much they could drink without appearing drunk.

The superintendent nodded and spoke to the nearest waiter. A cup of tea was given to Doug. I felt embarrassed that Doug's preference had come out so publicly. We should have let Emily know ahead of time. We had talked so little about our preferences and backgrounds, and we had not shared any of that information with Emily.

I knew that Doug had not attended the sessions on cultural expectations in Nanjing, but I thought that was because he'd already heard the presentations in his previous work with Amity. He told us only that he did his own exploring and reading in the days we had for cultural training in Nanjing. We hadn't questioned that either. Did Doug feel that he knew all he needed to know because of his other trip to China? Or did he have other reasons?

Doug held up his cup of tea like Jessie had held the alcohol. Now, content with tea, he tipped the cup and drank it all after saying the drink up toast, "*Gan bei.*"

"*Gan bei,*" said the principal, superintendent, and other local leaders. They all drained the small cups of *baijiu* by their plates. Immediately the servers refilled them.

I doubted that Doug realized how smoothly Emily and Jessie had rescued us from the embarrassment of his vow that seemed like rudeness. On the way to the dinner, Doug had said he did not like ceremonial dinners. They were long, and he didn't appreciate even seeing the huge quantities of food when so many people were too poor to afford one meal. He railed against the drunkenness that everyone who drank ceremonial cups would experience. He could have been a character in a grumpy old man movie.

Kathryn, Tia, Jaye, and I completed the welcome ceremony. We accepted the cup and blue silk scarf, tried sipping the liquor, and even imitated the gentle hand motions acknowledging sky, earth, and ancestors. A steady parade of food came out in trays and platters almost the entire time we were in the yurt.

The music on the haunting strings of Mongolian instruments became more festive throughout the evening. More toasts from one administrator to another, from teachers to administrators, and from teachers to our team came through the courses and the socializing. I only did *gan bei* twice, once with the principal of our host school and once with the superintendent of schools who had come from the capital, Hohhot.

Jessie gave a toast in Mandarin. As a Westerner and a woman, they did not hold her lack of draining a glass in *gan bei* against her. She knew the right phrases to compliment the principal on his hospitality, the sumptuous dinner, and the specialness of the local traditional environment, including the food, and music throughout the evening. The Mandarin and Mongolian people smiled over Jessie's gracious toast.

For the men, the toasting offered a chance to build respect. Sharing drinks promoted good *guanxi*, or relationships of mutual respect. The toasting would continue off and on throughout the dinner. Jessie had warned us that sometimes people would get up and walk around the table to toast someone. She had emphasized that whenever toasting someone of higher status, a person should hold their cup lower than the other person before clinking the glasses lightly.

Jaye did not like the first taste she had of the *baijiu*. She said it reminded her of vodka. Tia had a sensitive stomach so only sipped even the mildest wine and liquors. Kathryn said she enjoyed celebrations and liquor. She would happily toast.

Because of drinking wine and other liquors with my Italian family, I decided I would sip and toast. I didn't want to get drunk. The *baijiu* liquor that our hosts called wine and served in small cups had a potent effect. I watched the principal, our main host. How did he do so many *gan beis* and not seem a bit drunk?

I noticed that shortly before the principal toasted, he had something to eat, one of the many appetizers or a large spoonful of yogurt. In the United States, I had never liked yogurt, but this freshly made plain yogurt had a thicker texture, like heavy whipped cream but not as sweet a flavor. I tried to mimic the principal's choices before taking a drink of the *baijiu*.

Doug did not mind appearing as an oddity to the Chinese. I wondered if he might have used the temperance membership as a shield because he knew that men in this culture were expected to *gan bei* all through a celebration. In Nanjing, I'd heard of some SEP teachers claiming to be vegetarians because they feared they might be served the meat of some animal they would never knowingly eat, but no one warned us about the amount of drinking at ceremonial dinners or of the strength of the *baijiu*.

The Chinese and Mongolian female teachers rarely did a full *gan bei*. Emily told me ahead of the dinner that none of the conscientious young female teachers liked drinking alcohol. They thought only women of low character would get drunk.

Some administrators and male teachers seemed to enjoy knowing that the women did not want to drink. But the women would do so to avoid offending the leaders or someone who toasted them. These men would toast the female teachers just to see them take a drink. I heard resentment in Emily's voice when she explained this to me.

The meal's courses contained a variety of flavors suited to the Asian idea that proper meals should have sour, bitter, sweet, spicy, and salty flavors. The feast in front of us had opulence in colors, shapes, scents, textures, and tastes.

What did the Mongolian waitstaff think while serving the abundant delicious dishes? How did they feel serving people who were getting drunk through dozens of toasts? Were they and the other staff able to take the leftovers of this meal home?

Full-time workers in low level jobs might earn the equivalent of sixty dollars a month. The migrant workers seen all over construction sites in China could hope to earn thirty dollars a month. Then they would try to live on a fraction of that minimal amount and send the rest to their families. Knowing people survived on so little made me self-conscious over the extravagance of the welcome dinner.

It was dark when we left the huge yurt to go back to the school. I remembered leaning back against the comfortable car seat and feeling that my eyes were tired and sore. In fact, my eyelids felt like they had a lining of fine sandpaper.

That first night in my room, I placed a cloth soaked with cool water over my eyes to ease the pain in my lids. Getting into bed fast seemed the best choice. I was thankful to have packed a portable CD player. I needed something soothing this first night in Wuhai.

This was not the night to try to listen to the CDs of Pimsleur lessons in Chinese that I had brought along. I also had a CD of Elvis singing hymns, a CD of Evie Tornquist's most popular songs, and Sandy Patty's *Take Hold of Christ* album. I expected each of these would help me through the weeks ahead, soothing me each evening and reminding me of the qualities of God's love. I felt unhappy that I was struggling to trust in that love, but after so many instances of seeing God at work, it felt wrong to just move forward on my own power. I couldn't just ignore my spiritual dissonance. I thought of the man who said to Jesus, "Lord, I believe, help my unbelief."

The pillow was not as hard as the bed, for that I was thankful. I'd never had any problems with my eyes and didn't even need to wear glasses. That first night the sandpaper feeling in my eyes was odd. It worried me, but I closed my eyes and listened to music until I fell asleep.

The next morning, I could barely open my eyes. The sandpaper feeling had increased. My eyes had been sore last night, but now they hurt like they had been rubbed raw. I did not strain to push my eyes open more than a fraction. My eyes had no tears.

I rushed to the bathroom to stick my face in water. I heard sounds of concern coming from the hallway, along with someone crying. Jaye, Kathryn, and Jessie also had this eye problem, and Tia was crying in fear over not being able to open her eyes. Here on Monday, our first full day in Wuhai, the entire team faced near blindness.

Emily, Erdeen, Jenna, and Cassie rushed to each of us, the four of them in almost as much distress as we felt. Emily and the sweet young teaching assistants gathered around us alternately speaking Chinese at high speed and offering soothing phrases to us in English. "We will help you." "You will be fine." "We have a hospital."

We heard noises of dismay from the far end of the hall.

Doug and the superintendent of schools from Hohhot had the same eye impairment. Emily led questioning about what we had done before going to bed or during the night. The other teachers stepped back wondering if our condition was contagious.

Chapter 10

Eye-Openers

We all had slept with the window open to enjoy the cooler night air.

Our team stood together. The superintendent stood near Doug. Jessie told us that they had first wondered if we had a Western eye disease, but the superintendent from Hohhot had the same symptoms. His condition showed that it was not just a foreigners' problem.

Emily called the principal with the concern of an unknown disease and talked about taking our team to the hospital. While Emily was on the phone, Erdeen explained that Wuhai had a lovely hospital newly expanded and equipped in early 2003 because of concerns about the bird flu, but no cases of bird flu arrived in the Wuhai region.

The principal called a doctor who reached the school in fewer than fifteen minutes. The physician looked younger than most of our team. Principal Chen and VP Zhu arrived just a minute before the doctor.

"Dry eyes," the doctor stated after examining us. Jessie translated his other information. "In the desert environment, foreign guests need air conditioning and eye drops. Eye drops will not totally take care of the problem but will help to hydrate dry eyes to relieve stinging, burning, and scratchy feelings."

We had all these symptoms. Sleeping with air-conditioning would help us, the doctor proclaimed. Tears protect eyes. We should get eyedrops that would act like tears, but all of us would need air-conditioning and should use eye drops each day we were in Wuhai."

Our principal had been frowning from the moment he'd arrived. His frown did not disappear when he nodded and immediately sent out teachers to purchase eye drops and air-conditioners. He told them to return as quickly as possible.

Jessie explained that the principal would be concerned that he might be perceived as having inadequate preparation for the foreign visitors and for the superintendent from the more temperate climate of Hohhot. No school fortunate enough to be chosen by the central government to host a team of foreign visitors wanted to have anything negative on their hosting record.

We found relief with eyedrops. Jessie said we should gather in her room before going to breakfast. In our group time, we expressed thanks to the Lord. Although we were sorry to see someone else suffer, it helped that the administrator from Hohhot shared the sensitivity to the dry desert air so that we did not get taken to stay in isolation at the Wuhai hospital as diseased foreigners.

Even though Doug had worked in Nei Menggu in 2002, he had been far in the northeast thick with grasslands and streams. No dry eye problem emerged there.

Jessie had shared this miserable eye difficulty with us. She realized that in all her years in China, she had never spent time in a desert environment. The country was vast. Jessie didn't think any Amity administrator had visited all the regions.

Through our Sunday afternoon arrival, the ceremonial dinner, the misery of the dry eye problem from Sunday night to Monday, Jessie had experienced them and encouraged us. Monday and Tuesday, Jessie had planned to stay with us and help with the interviewing of the teachers who had applied to be in the SEP. Because we would group them by abilities, we needed to engage in as much conversation as we could while interviewing. With Jessie's guidance, we worked out a schedule for classes and interviewed at least 260 teachers.

Jessie reminded us again that in China, we would be wise to expect any day to have a surprise. She told us to build an attitude of flexibility and to ask the Lord each day for wisdom, grace, and strength. I knew she was right, but my anger still held me back from talking easily and often to God.

Having Jessie with us gave us a sense of security, but now she was gone. We had finished all the interviews to determine ability level. We had met a local pastor and accepted Jeff and Terry with the hope that Amity could find a way to let teachers in vocational schools apply for the SEP. We had made it through the first full day of classes after saying goodbye to Jessie at 6:00 a.m.

Now came the hard part. Amity had offered us wisdom based on experience and training for the main Mandarin culture of China in our days in the huge city of Nanjing. We'd had the opportunity to go to seminars on everything from using *kuaizi* to avoiding cultural no nos. That training time, in the international conference center with four-star hotel comfort, surrounded by lush beauty of plants, ponds, and trees seemed a world away from Wuhai.

Amity staff supported and guided us through each day in Nanjing. Unless we could cultivate a collaborative sense of service and a sensitivity to feel and see God at work in our team, we would live as remote coworkers. Without shared goals, we would be doing a job together, but reliant on other strangers from a totally different culture.

* * *

On our second day of classes, we learned that at the end of every school year in China, after the crucial exam had been completed for junior and senior middle school students, the scores were posted on the school gates for everyone to see. Pressure to avoid low scores placed a heightened pressure on students, teachers, and administrators. I could hardly imagine the anger and actions that would arise in the United States if the test scores of every student were displayed in public next to the student's name.

Teachers in China feared those test results as much as the students. Pay increases or other perks came to teachers whose students had high scores. Shame discouraged those whose classes had the lowest scores. Our students asked if the United States placed pressure like this on the students and teachers. We could only tell them that although individual names and scores were not posted, some places did put pressure on teachers. Pay raises in some cities and states came to teachers of classes with high test scores.

My afternoon classes focused on topics related to teaching techniques and strategies, but I emphasized that any questions were welcome. The teachers in China learn English in close study of grammar, punctuation, and spelling, and they tried to pass on these skills to their students. Interacting and questioning rarely occurred.

These teachers who were our students did not learn practical applications for managing students. In 2004, the old Confucian view of students listening to and obeying their teachers still reigned. Few parents or teachers wanted to admit that students were changing. I introduced examples of pedagogy from organizing grade books to attention grabbers to varied strategies for different kinds of learners. Kinds of learners? That concept opened a whirlwind of questions. In their educational system, only the traditional elements of learning appeared in schools.

Teachers needed help even considering varying lessons and classroom practices. With the pressure on Chinese students, teachers needed to learn how to give students a chance to move or talk during hours of close reading and writing. Teachers of the upper grades had full classrooms of fifty to ninety students, a tough challenge for anyone.

Our SEP participants needed strategies to prevent disinterest, discouragement, or discipline problems. I wondered how much we could help the teachers see ways to change the ingrained patterns of teacher centered, book centered learning with an emphasis on rote memory. Close reading and memorization did not lessen the stress of failing students. My classes affirmed that teachers, families, and right up the chain of command to vice-principals, principals, superintendents, and city leaders felt the strain from fear of failing scores.

Students and their parents sought to avoid any mistakes. The effort to succeed, especially in a culture where a family is allowed only one child causes that child to feel extra stress about failure. They must bring hope and success to their parents who sacrificed to make sure their child had opportunities to advance beyond the economic level of the family.

In an Amity introduction to China seminar, I learned that the population of China in 1949 was approximately 540 million people. In 1980, four years after Chairman Mao's death, stricter laws, unevenly enforced, spread across the country to try to ensure that Han Chinese families had only one child. People said this should have been named a 'one birth' policy because twins or triplets counted as one birth.

Only ethnic groups within the country could still have as many children as they wanted. It appeared that no one could imagine any of the more than fifty ethnic groups would equal the number of Han Chinese. In 2004, the Han population neared 80 percent of the 1.3 billion people in the country.

After decades of the one child policy, many students had no aunts or uncles or cousins. If grandparents lived nearby, they took an active part in raising the one child. Our SEP students told us that people with careers counted on the help of grandparents in caring for the child so the parents to go to work to earn what they could toward a better life. All over China, grandparents took care of their one grandchild.

How did they treat the child? Did they spoil and affirm them like the grandparents I knew in Western countries? No. I learned the answer to that on Thursday too, when I praised the class for bringing in so many good answers to the homework question, 'Why should I learn English?'

At my compliments for their effort, they looked embarrassed not happy. I asked why they seemed uncomfortable with a sincere compliment.

"We don't compliment simple tasks like completing homework, Ms. Virginia." Kent spoke up clearly.

"Why not? Doesn't it help to encourage students to know they have done a well?"

"Our families and teachers have emphasized modesty, restraint, and harmony."

"I recognize those as Confucian values. *Kǒngzǐ.*"

"Those values are still strong here, Ms. Virginia." Terry told me. "My parents think compliments will make a person arrogant." Many students nodded in agreement.

My face must have shown that I was uncomfortable with this information. John gave another view for the lack of praise for children. "Ms. Virginia, much praise can make a child feel that they must keep doing high-level work. I think this can cause students to feel unhappy and make them willing to cheat."

Following John's comment, we had an intriguing discussion. With the Amity goal of having SEP students listen and speak, this afternoon seemed a success. Even in our largest class, they took turns conversing as a whole group and in small groups. No one talked over one another. These teachers showed concern and respect for their peers' ideas, and they waited patiently for their own opportunity to speak.

This second day of teaching, Thursday, passed smoothly, but I was still very tired when the team gathered in Doug's room for a review of what went well and what didn't. Tia looked more tired than I felt, but the rest of the team still had energy.

We looked forward to the shorter teaching day on Friday because of no afternoon sessions on Fridays. Many teachers had come from a distance, and a shorter Friday schedule would allow them to travel home. Those who came from the farthest smallest towns had found places to stay in Wuhai, or in the host school dorm if they did not have family or friends to host them. They could have at least one or two full days at home before they returned to Wuhai Sunday evening or early Monday. I felt sorry that we had not realized how much this SEP experience required personal sacrifices for the participants.

While I thought about how difficult this SEP was for our students who lived hours away, the conversation among my team had taken a different tack. I registered a strong negative tone from Kathryn. To cover my distraction I said, "I'm sorry Kathryn. Would you repeat that?"

"I just said, for the afternoon enrichment classes, I really can't do it every afternoon. It will wear me out. Three o-clock to five thirty raises my blood pressure. I felt that today. Out of all of you, Tia's and my Boston accents make our English the most difficult for students unless we constantly speak really slowly. I usually talk fast and use contractions. I have to remember to avoid contractions. That's tough for me."

"Most of our students learned listening to British English. Boston is similar, isn't it?" Jaye asked.

"Not close enough. I feel pressure each day to speak slower and to enunciate. It's stressful."

"Kathryn, our afternoon teaching time comes right after a three-hour rest time." Doug responded.

"We don't have the enrichment classes on Friday so that the students who commute can have an early start to their weekend. If we're going to have a big group activity each Wednesday from now on, that just leaves Monday, Tuesday, and Thursday. I'd like to just do one of those afternoons, Monday. I have more energy at the start of the week."

"And what should your students do on Tuesdays and

Thursdays?" Doug's tone sounded calm. I wondered if he really felt that way. I did not think I could sound that calm if team members backed out of set responsibilities in the first week of classes.

"They could be divided among the other classes."

"Class size would be so much bigger then." I remarked.

"We have ninety desks in our classrooms. They can switch around and find a seat. Could you believe it when we got the tour and saw so many desks and benches in the classrooms?" Kathryn's response showed that she was determined to have a changed schedule.

"I was shocked," I admitted. "I told Emily that if a principal opened a door to a high school classroom in the US and the teacher saw desks for ninety students, the teacher would probably quit. The largest high school class I've had is forty-five."

"If Kathryn is going to have Monday," Tia said, "I'd like Tuesday afternoon off. Monday, we jump into work. Tuesday I could catch my breath to finish out the week. This is a lot of work even with all the Amity materials and tips. Being the main teacher instead of an assistant is difficult. I never do this at home. I am not sleeping well. I need more rest to adjust to teaching hours."

"I'll take Thursday then," Jaye smiled as she declared her preference. "Doug, you and Virginia are used to teaching full days, having one class after another. If I have four classes in a row, all I do is give some directions and oversee my physical education classes. Then they do the activities."

"So, the three of you would like to have one afternoon a week away from your classes?" Doug did not sound at all perturbed. His facial expression did not show any frustration or anger with this new challenge to successfully complete the full expectations for the SEP. I felt anger rising up at the majority of the team asking for less work. I hoped it didn't show, but inside I steamed.

"Yes," came the unified answer. Doug looked at me.

"Virginia?"

I didn't want to show my negative feelings, so I probably sounded mild, like Goody-Two-shoes with my response. "I can work with the change, Doug. The enrichment hours fly by for me. Working with a huge class of motivated adults is much easier than with high school students in the US."

"This is highly irregular, changing the plan and the schedule, unless there are health reasons." Doug's tone did not reveal whether he was making an observation or an attempt to dissuade them from asking for a free afternoon each week besides Friday.

Tia said, "I haven't got a physical condition, but I feel very tired every day."

"Even with the air-conditioning now in our rooms?" Jaye asked.

"Yes. I'm sure I should go to the doctor when I get home," Tia added.

"I just want an afternoon to explore without someone going with me. All the assistants and students will stay here for classes. The school can't be serious about us not going anywhere alone." Jaye's resentment about the host school's requirement to have someone accompany us anywhere seemed to have a corrosive effect on our discussion.

Doug didn't argue with her. He only said, "We each need to commit to being at the full class assemblies in the administration assembly hall every Wednesday for the movies, special activities, and discussions. If you have one afternoon a week, besides Friday, free, then commitment to all the other teaching times must be strong. Does anyone have a problem committing to these?" We shook our heads, no.

Doug took the role of leading through this unexpected change. The Chinese hosts might regard him as the leader because he was the only man of the group, but he was shouldering that task with a bunch of women who were not of one mind or heart on the plans he obviously thought had been settled. I would ask him how this compared to his first Amity experience.

Jaye stood up, looked at Doug and said, "So, are we done meeting for today?"

Doug stood as well. Then we all did. I admired his closing response to Jaye. "I think we've discussed all we can this evening. We need to remember that no classes or any individual in our classes should ever feel like their Amity teachers do not want to spend time with them. They work hard and want to do their best for their students and schools. Their time is precious, and they are trusting us with it."

Jaye's smile was more of a grimace. She left the room without another word to us.

Kathryn and Tia followed, saying their "Goodnights."

I waited until they seemed out of hearing distance before I said, "Does this make you think none of them will agree to the other big part of the program Amity wants the teams to do? I mean the informal English practice, English Corners. Did you avoid bringing it up tonight because of this change for afternoon plans?"

"Yes. The mood didn't seem right to remind them we're supposed to give at least an evening a week to English Corners."

"What was your team like in 2002? Did you know one

another before you came here? Did you have less trouble sticking to plans?"

"We did know one another. It was a Baptist Association-based team. Some of us had been together on short-term missions to Brazil a few years ago. We sketched out a plan before we ever got to China, refined it in the training time, and stuck with it. Plus, we gave two evenings to anyone who showed up for casual conversations in English.

Amity wants the English Corner activity launched with enthusiasm and energy. When that happens, it becomes as popular with the townspeople as with our students. Some of my 2002 group members did more. They went to parks and shopping areas and talked with anyone who approached them. People did approach them. We certainly didn't look like anyone they had encountered. We enjoyed the English Corners as much as the people who talked with us."

"Don't you think we could do the same?" I asked him.

"Only if we had all come here primarily to teach and serve."

Chapter 11

A Hazing and Limits to Power?

A t least we made good progress in our first three days by using the textbook Don Snow created for Amity. Students had practiced close reading focusing on details and grammar all their lives, so a textbook provided a familiar framework. The "Why Should I Learn English" chapter brought new ideas and our list had grown. I posted the answers in the classroom and said we would continue adding reasons during our weeks together.

The classes laughed when I said, "When your students ask you this year, why should I learn English, start giving them this list of reasons. I think they will stop asking."

On Friday we looked ahead at the chapter about what is the best way to learn English. "Is there a best way, Ms. Virginia?"

"We will investigate that more next week. I am sure you will have good ideas for the discussion. Enjoy your afternoon whether you are traveling far or staying nearby."

"What are you doing, Ms. Virginia?"

I almost said resting and planning, but Emily came into

the classroom before I could respond. "I am sorry to interrupt." Emily didn't look like she wanted to say more in front of everyone, so I joined her at the doorway, and we stepped out onto the balcony.

"I have been to the other classes. There is going to be another dinner tonight. Many school principals and some administrators will join us. Principal Chen wanted me to visit each Amity teacher and tell you we will leave for the dinner at seven-thirty. We will meet at the school's front gate."

I nodded. What else could I do? Jessie had warned us that ceremonial dinners could occur more than once a week. At least everyone would know that Doug would just drink tea. With his choice accepted, I hoped nothing else could go wrong over liquor.

"And tomorrow we are leaving for the day trip at seven. If the team wants breakfast, we will have it at six, but we will stop for a full meal on our way to the special location our principal has chosen."

"Thank you, Emily." I gave her a smile as my mind whirled with thoughts of another ceremonial dinner. The next day we were due to have a full-day field trip. Only minutes remained in the morning session. The students would probably be glad for the early ending of studies each Friday. Listening for hours to a foreign language takes more energy than people realize unless they have had that experience.

I walked back to the dorm, and I thought of Jessie's warning. Because I would teach about major holidays in the US, before week one concluded, I should make sure the school's Communist Party Representative knew what I was teaching.

Jessie said, "You are teaching about all the holidays, so

you will mention some topics and stories not commonly presented, mostly religious and faith concepts. Your students will learn the origin and practices connected to Western holidays.

"Every school has a Communist Party Representative. If you think you are going to present something that might be misunderstood because it is connected to faith beliefs, check with your assistant, or talk to the Representative. Each class will have party members. Like everyone else, they will listen carefully to anything you say and report anything concerning."

"Isn't every professional person here a member of the Communist Party?" Jaye had asked with suspicion in her voice.

"No. Some people do not join." Jessie could see our surprise, so she told us, "They see no need if they have a life that satisfies them. Only those who want to advance to higher positions or who want to be known as strong supporters of the government join the Party. The Party members have to pay dues, like what people pay to unions in the US."

"Yes. Any unions I know about have members pay dues, "Jaye added. "Usually, people complain about what they have to pay. They wonder if their dues just fund the conventions that the leaders attend."

After this conversation with Jessie, when I had a chance to speak alone with Emily, I asked her. "Do you know about unions in the US?"

"Yes. We learn about them when we study your country."

"I'm in a teachers' union, and I have heard that being a

Community Party member is like being a member of a union. Are you a party member Emily?"

"The party dues seem higher than what many people feel dues provide. I have not joined the Communist Party."

"How can you be a top teacher and not be a member?"

Looking quite serious, she answered. "My husband has been a member since he went to college. He is well respected here and in Beijing. He did not require me to join."

* * *

The important officials of the high-level schools and city administrators arrived when we did, at a sleek and ostentatious modern restaurant in the nicest hotel in the center of Wuhai. In that hotel or dining room, we could have imagined ourselves in any major city in the world. This place would be rated as a five-star hotel and restaurant.

Each of our classroom teaching assistants, plus three young male teachers from Doug's homeroom class had a seat at this dinner. Was this an honor to the male leader of our team or did the administrators want the young men to see Doug did not drink liquor?

Jeff had been invited to attend. This surprised me. He sat near the other male teachers at the far corner of the tables arranged in a rectangle. I studied Jeff's expression and thought he looked uncomfortable.

This dinner would end our first week in Wuhai. The feast appeared sumptuous, with appetizers, more than a dozen courses, and tantalizing flavors from meat pies, to baked fish, and something Emily said was a truly Mongolian dish, *buuz*. Any kind of meat, in this case mutton, flavored with salt, onion, and cumin filled a tennis ball size dough pouch. That was the *buuz* on our table.

Toasting started even earlier than we had expected on the basis of our last feast, but there was no lovely scarf ceremony. A waiter put a pot of tea next to Doug just as the toasting started. Some jokes emerged as our host principal toasted Doug.

Conversation was slow because it had to emerge with translations between eating and toasting. Anyone could toast after the formal welcomes and compliments to all the leaders and foreign guests. Doug never touched the liquor. Tia, Jaye, and I took sips when we shared toasts, and Kathryn continued to enjoy some large sips.

Baijiu could make a person drunk with just a few *gan beis*. It's a distilled liquor regarded as one of the most famous in the world. The leaders all had chauffeurs, so I suspected that they did not care if they drank too much. Nothing seemed uncomfortable until halfway through the meal when a school leader toasted Jeff.

Obviously surprised, Jeff stood as was customary. The leader, also standing, did a *gan bei*, so Jeff did a *gan bei* returning compliments and praise. They both sat down, but in a minute, one of the vice principals stood and complimented Jeff on being included in the SEP. He did a *gan bei*, so Jeff had to return a thanks and a *gan bei*. My team had worried about how the teachers would accept Jeff and Terry. We hadn't thought about how the administrators might feel.

Immediately, one of the young male teachers stood up and said a congratulations to Jeff. He did a *gan bei*, so Jeff needed to respond with another *gan bei*. Everyone knew vocational schoolteachers had not been scheduled for inclusion in the SEP. I wondered if some of the administrators and our students had suppressed resentment toward Jeff and Terry. Both had a smoothness and vocabulary few of our students could match.

Could I look at all this toasting with Jeff positively, like a super welcoming? No. It seemed like some sort of hazing test. Who would suggest or organize hazing to remind Jeff of his place as a teacher in a junior middle vocational school? Or was I wrong and this was a friendly test of Jeff's strength?

I looked at Principal Chen, the main host. He did not smile when another leader stood and said he also had not realized that Jeff was a vocational schoolteacher. Principal Chen did not show any expression when the leader saluted Jeff with compliments, did a *gan bei,* and waited for Jeff to stand and give a return toast. Jeff, now wavering with the high proof liquor and multiple *gan beis,* rose slowly. He looked red in the face, but he complimented the leader, did a *gan bei* and fell back onto his seat.

I looked at Emily. Her lovely face had no expression until her eyes met mine. Once, I commented to Terry that Emily had features that people of the West associate with Chinese beauty. Terry told me that Emily had a lucky face. Terry explained that meant auspicious features inviting good fortune, success, and well-being. Emily's brown eyes usually had a bright sparkle appropriate to her spirit.

But I saw Emily look in Jeff's direction and frown. I guessed that what I suspected--a hazing or a test was happening. For the entertainment of the initiators, whoever they might be, they were getting Jeff very drunk. Would anyone have done this without the top administrator's approval?

Jeff had dared rise above his assigned level at a vocational technical school to be a part of a program for schools that equipped students to attend a university. Someone had decided to remind him of his irregular admission into this summer's SEP. I did not think in this controlled environment that the teachers would decide alone to get Jeff drunk.

Another male administrator stood. I cringed. Not again, not another toast directed at Jeff. But I was surprised. With a broad smile this man asked all the assistant female teachers to stand. He called them by name and gave a flowery speech about beauty mixed with intelligence. Then he did a *gan bei* to them. The young female teachers who had been assisting us so well each day looked strained. They accepted the compliment and took a sip of the *baijiu*.

Cassie surprised me and everyone else by giving a brief *gan bei* toast back to the administrator. She looked like the most petite of those who rose for the toast, but she had moxie. I liked Cassie's spirit and wondered at the grit and the energy she showed with her pretty face and charming smile. Then she drained her cup of *baijiu* in a *gan bei* as smooth as any man present.

With his elbows on the table, Jeff held his head in his hands. His face was a much deeper red than a blush. I wondered if he was going to be sick. How embarrassing would that be! I certainly knew how it felt to get sick in front of a whole room of people, but this would be worse for him, a young man who would seem unable to hold his liquor.

Suddenly, I remembered Jessie's instructions, but no Communist Party representative from our host school or from any other organization had been introduced to us. Was such a person at this dinner? Could individuals showing off for a man none of us had met yet have led to the *gan beis* toward Jeff ?

I leaned toward Emily to ask. "Which person here is the Communist Party representative who oversees our host school?"

"He did not come to this dinner. He also will not travel with us tomorrow on our day trip either. He plans to be at breakfast on Sunday."

"Really?"

"Do you need to talk to him before Sunday?"

"No. Sunday will be fine. I just want him to understand that the content I present around our holidays will have some religious information."

"No one can give information to try to convert others here."

"I know that."

"But teachers can answer any question a student asks."

"That's good to know."

She nodded and sat back. I leaned against the elegance of the cushioned glitzy silver chair. Multiple times a day, I thought of Jessie's words. They came like a calming mantra. "Every day will have surprises while you are in China. Embrace them and remember that the Lord is always with you."

Usually, I liked surprises, but my husband didn't. I felt glad for the first time that he had not come to China with me. We talked about working with Amity together. The church he served as pastor would allow him to use his vacation time and mission work weeks or continuing education weeks to give more than his three vacation weeks.

Jerry could have gone with me to work with Amity. I knew that sitting through ceremonial dinners, not knowing the language, not seeing anything in public in English, unfamiliar foods, the board hard bed, strong liquor, a team not committed to the same goals, plus tiptoeing around contro-versial topics would cause him to feel terrible.

I looked around at quiet Tia whose body language revealed her tiredness even though she smiled. I wondered if it really was just the teaching experiences that caused her to feel so fatigued. Maybe it was the heat. I knew that I should find some time to talk alone with her to see if something else was bothering her.

Kathryn was at a different table and looked cheerful. She could enjoy too many *gan beis* unless someone cautioned her. Kathryn cared for people, but gruffly protected herself and her interests. Jaye sat near Kathryn, and frowns flittered across Jaye's face. She did not like dressing up or ceremonies. I thought of asking her why she had signed with Amity, but because I did not want to announce all my own reasons, I would not ask.

Doug had a seat five places away from me. Unflappable Doug, how did he feel about this second SEP experience in China? We had not been here a full week, and I hoped our team would stay well and not succumb to feeling wretched in body, mind, or spirit. Tension came with challenges and the unexpected. Still, I had noticed that the chest-tight feeling of angry dissatisfaction that had traveled with me to China had eased.

Why? Did the distractions of differences drown my anger? Were the prayers of people for all the Amity workers affecting my spirit as much as my growing awareness of having a limit to my own power? I knew so little about this culture that looked self-contained and orderly above what felt like dangerous swirling undercurrents. My ignorance of the language and expectation of more surprises had humbled my spirit.

Had confusion and concerns shown me the futility of my anger over not having the ability to do what I wanted, when I wanted? Could the task of speaking to the Communist Party representative have made me ready to spend more time talking to God?

Chapter 12

Respect, Noise, and Noodles

For breakfast Saturday morning, we reported to the faculty dining room at six o'clock because our hosts had planned a full day trip for us. I told the teachers who arrived as our companions that we called these day trips field trips in the US. Emily said we would have a simple breakfast this morning because we would have a large meal later in the day. Our breakfast in the faculty room was *baozi*, a steamed yeast leavened bread, tea, fresh fruit cups, and porridge made of red beans and dates.

"We've been here a week and haven't seen rice," Jaye said as we ate.

"I know. I thought every meal would have rice," Kathryn agreed.

With his professorial tone, Doug told us, "Inner Mongolia grows wheat and potatoes. In fact, the potatoes for the MacDonalds in China are grown in this province. Noodles are common throughout the north. Rice is common in the south." Doug ate a hearty breakfast every day, digging into whatever was set before us. We knew he always had coffee in his room with a small coffee pot and coffee he had purchased in Nanjing. He didn't like Nescafe instant, the coffee served in China accommodations and hotels.

While I nibbled on the *baozi* and sipped my tea, I thought back to the previous night. I'd finally had a heart-to-heart with God. I doubted the wisdom of planning to do everything on my own power through these weeks in China. I confessed my anger, frustration, fears, and needs. I wanted to feel God's closeness and care. I wanted to trust that no matter what came into our day, God was right there with us and would help us. I knew that my prayers went beyond the ceiling of my dorm room, but I didn't feel different after the prayer.

At 7:20 a.m., we arrived at the main gate. The line of three official large black cars was not a surprise, nor was the sight of Principal Chen, Vice-Principal Zhu, and Emily. The teachers standing near the cars were the surprise: Thomas, Penny, Cassie, Eliza, Marge, Terry, and Jenna.

Thomas, a tall Mongolian, broad-shouldered and slim, would have looked fine in a costume of a Genghis Khan warrior except that he had glasses. His background included a biochemistry degree and five years teaching science. Science had been his passion, but his English was good, and his school needed another English teacher.

His lovely wife Penny, Han Chinese in background, had been invited on this trip too. Cassie, Marge, Jenna, and Eliza attended our host school when they were high school students. That Terry was invited on this field trip was a pleasant surprise. Spending the day in the company of these teachers would add to the treat of whatever excursion the administrators planned.

Everyone divided into cars as guided by Emily and Vice-

Principal Zhu. Doug rode in the front car with Principal Chen, VP Zhu, Thomas, and Penny. The other two cars had a mix of two Americans and the other teachers who had been selected to act as translators and companions. No one talked much in the first hour, but when we reached a toll booth, we had questions and compared tolls in the US to this toll plaza.

Forty yuan toll booth

The toll seemed expensive, about 40 RMB per car. RMB, also known as *yuan*. RMB stands for renminbi, the official currency issued by the People's Bank of China. Renminbi means people's money.

I was told that in 2004 an average family might earn anywhere from 200 to 1200 RMB per month. The toll seemed like it would be too expensive for a family, but we had learned that not many individuals or families owned a car in Wuhai. We rode another hour and came to another set of toll booths. The price was the same, but there was a long row of shops and an advertised rest stop beyond the tolls.

No restrooms at a roadside stop in China had Western style toilets. In some public places, if the rest rooms were just for women, one stall would be labeled, HANDICAPPED. That stall would have a toilet bowl very low to the floor. Opening the door to enter any one of the restrooms always provoked the necessity for an emotional guard against the conditions that would be found around the hole in the ground.

The drivers pulled into this area and spoke to the Chinese teachers in the car with us. Our teacher companions translated, "This will be a short rest stop."

I was in the car with Tia. When we exited, Terry approached us and offered us the small square plastic envelopes that contained thin sheets of paper used as toilet paper. Tia and I said almost at the same time. "Thank you. We have our own. We learned the necessity for taking our own packets as soon as we landed in Guangzhou." Terry nodded as if she appreciated that we had learned this lesson.

At least at this rest stop they were not unisex outhouses. Jaye and Cassie went to that building through the door marked with a stick figure woman. Kathryn practically leapt out of the car but had no interest in the toilet. She dashed toward the little shops looking like someone seeking treasure.

The storekeepers who had been watching the trio of black cars smiled at Kathryn like sharks circling a potential meal. They welcomed her with words she did not understand. Eliza hurried to assist Kathryn in shopping.

When everyone else gathered back at the cars, VP Zhu surprised us by looking around and asking in clear English, "Where is Kathryn?"

A chorus of voices immediately answered in English, "She's shopping." Kathryn appeared at that moment with her hands full of little bags, followed by smiling and attentive shopkeepers and Eliza also carrying bags of Kathryn's purchases.

"*Hao le ma?*" Ready? VP Zhu asked. Emily translated.

"*Wǒmen zǒu ba.*" Principal Chen said as he got back into the lead car.

"Let's go." Terry translated.

We entered Yinchuan, the capital of this province, Ningxia, south of Inner Mongolia. This province had been renamed by Genghis Khan. Now Yinchuan had more than two million people, making it eight times as big as Wuhai.

We were taken to a building known as the Drum Tower. We just walked around the Yinchuan Drum Tower and took pictures.

Emily explained that this had to be a quick stop because there was a more amazing ancient place we would visit. Many cities had Drum Towers because bells and drums were used to announce the time and give other signals. While we walked around the ancient tower and took pictures, Kathryn skittered off to barely visible shops down the main avenue near the Drum Tower square.

After listening to the history of the Drum Tower, we returned to our assigned cars, except for Kathryn.

"Where's Kathryn?" VP Zhu asked again with even more clear English pronunciation.

"She's shopping," Cassie answered and pointed to Eliza who had Kathryn by the elbow with one hand and who carried two large bags of items that Kathryn had purchased. Kathryn looked happy. She did not apologize for leaving the group or for returning late.

Drum Tower of Yinchuan

Principal Chen said something to Emily. The rest of us watched the driver of the second car put Kathryn's new bags in the trunk. When we got back into our cars, the air conditioning let us sigh and settle in with relief. Outside it was one hundred degrees.

Tombs of the Emperors

Marge told us with visible excitement that we were on our way to the most prized site of ancient royalty of the western provinces, the tombs of the emperors. The tombs rose as the ruins of what had been an octagon.

War, weather, and thefts left the tombs outwardly looking only like a pyramid of earth. We could see what had been walls, a platform, and the remains of towers proclaiming the power of the rulers. The parking area was far from the tombs. After walking the wide avenue in the full sun, it felt like we walked through an oven to arrive at the cones of the mausoleums.

The sides looked like they were composed of layers of saddle bag flaps. Marge told us in the eleventh to thirteenth centuries, these UNESCO treasures once had complete stone coverings and carvings.

"What's UNESCO?" Tia asked.

Emily answered, "United Nations Educational, Scientific, and Cultural Organization. It tries to build respect for the history of cultures."

Cassie added, "These tombs are the best remainders of the Western Xia Dynasty, built by a people no longer here."

We had not yet reached the major Tai Tomb when Kathryn announced, "I cannot take this heat. I am going to return to the car." And she did. I found this frustrating as the heat did not bother her when she was shopping. Kathryn never saw the inside of the air-conditioned museum that displayed funeral relics, paintings, and sculptures from times of ancient emperors. Terry walked back to the cars with Kathryn.

Wuhai was surrounded by mountains too and had the fabulous western curve of the Yellow River, but it did not have these cultural heritage tombs. I felt sorry for Terry who had not been able to see the tombs because she had gone back to the car with Kathryn, but I understood that Terry might still feel like an interloper and want to allow the other teachers to have the time in the museum.

After the visit in the museum, my entry into the car woke Kathryn. Terry had rested there with Kathryn. Emily had told us before we left the school that this day was a treat for all the teachers too. None of them had been to these special sites in Ningxia. The school took care of our expenses as well as those of the teachers who came along with us.

In our car, Emily reached into a compartment that held bottles of water and gave one to each of us. I turned it down because the more I drank water, the more I might want a bathroom when none was available. Kathryn said thank you and drank half a bottle without taking a breath.

"So, tell me what I missed," Kathryn smiled and made a smacking sound with her lips upon finishing the last drops of the cold water. I didn't know if she expected an answer from me or from everyone. Our companions looked at me. I thanked God I had read the signs in the museum. I shared some of what I remembered.

Marge knew the most unusual details about the romances and intrigue of some of the twenty emperors buried at this site. She said the real drama came in the thirteenth century when the Mongols first invaded Western Xia. Life became terrifying. Listening to Marge's stories made the ride pass quickly.

We rode through an outer area of Yinchuan and stopped for a meal. It had been a long time since breakfast. The restaurant looked like one half of a long low building constructed many years ago, though it did have a second floor for apartments. The building, made of cement blocks, had a covering of slate gray paint, with windows trimmed in blue.

A pattern of dark and light blue tiles stood out around the door. The signs in front were in Chinese and Mongolian.

"This is a family-owned restaurant, Muslim," Emily told us. "Principal Chen knows the family and often stops here when visiting Yinchuan."

Principal Chen led the way into the restaurant while VP Zhu held the door for all of us. The owner approached our group at once and gave us an enthusiastic greeting. Marge whispered to me that this family was part of the largest ethnic group here, the Hui people. Principal Chen introduced our host as Ahmed.

We were escorted to an area where several rectangular tables had been put together so that our group of fifteen could be seated around the same long table. The drivers of the comfortable cars did not join us. Marge whispered that other shops and small restaurants were in the area. The drivers could do as they pleased.

Principal Chen sat at the head of the table and VP Zhu at the foot. The rest of us lined the sides. Our principal talked with Ahmed about the menu. Then Ahmed introduced his wife, sons, and daughters to us. The family cooked, served, and cleaned in his restaurant.

Platters of watermelon chunks, dates, and raisins arrived at the table along with fried cakes. The tea, which I had never had, was wolfberry, and had a light sweet berry flavor. The dishes at this meal showed the honor Ahmed and his family felt because Principal Chen had brought respected foreigners to their little family establishment.

The main dish for each of us was a bowl of beef broth with chunks of tender beef and wide wheat noodles. Carrots, onions, and small tomatoes made it thick with local favorites. The flavor included cinnamon, cloves, garlic, and pepper.

Principal Chen suddenly raised his hand forward and up to his chin. If we were home, I'd think the person was going to give a blessing over the food, but not here. He spoke to Emily.

"Principal Chen would like to show you how to eat the soup. He has seen Westerners struggle because they do not know the proper way."

Emily paused and looked at the principal. He spoke and she translated. "You should pick up your bowls and drink the broth. This will make it easier to grab the noodles and vegetables with *kuaizi*, chopsticks."

We lifted the bowls and drank some broth. It was too hot to gulp, so we sipped. Then we used chopsticks to carefully eat a vegetable, or a piece of meat, or to lift a dangling noodle to our lips. The administrators and Wuhai teachers watched us.

Suddenly, Principal Chen, who almost always looked serious or blank of expression, laughed, but there was no humor in the sound. It was a bark of disapproval. He said something to Thomas. Without revealing any attitude toward what Principal Chen said, Thomas translated the principal's words.

"You are too quiet. If you appreciate food, especially noodles, and you want the host to know you enjoy the food, you should make noise. Loud noise is approval. Anyone in the restaurant should hear the noise you make as you draw the noodles into your mouth." Then Thomas stopped speaking and looked at Principal Chen. The principal then used his chopsticks to gather some of the thick noodles and made a loud slurping noise that would have horrified every American, Canadian, and English mother I knew.

Obviously, no one here knew that Westerners raised

children to believe eating quietly showed polite behavior. We watched but were hesitant to follow the example. Principal Chen sucked in the last bit of hanging noodles with a final loud slurp. Then he looked expectantly at all of us.

Thomas and VP Zhu saw our reluctance and took a turn to demonstrate making a good amount of noise as they practically inhaled some of the noodles in their bowls. They did not make as much noise as Principal Chen had. I wondered if they could but did not want to outdo Principal Chen.

Then our host spoke. The female assistants picked up their bowls and noisily drew the noodles into their mouths. Principal Chen studied them briefly but turned to look at us. His quiet waiting seemed intimidating.

Doug, who had already nearly emptied his bowl of broth, lifted a light mouthful of noodles with his chopsticks and drew them into his mouth with hardly any noise. His expression and attitude said, *This is how I eat.* Principal Chen looked from Doug to the next two people.

Kathryn and Jaye made a better attempt, but they still had too much broth in their bowls and the noodles slipped out of their chopsticks. Shy Tia came under Principal Chen's stare next. Tia pulled up only one noodle and as she ate it, she hardly made any noise at all. Her blush showed even in the dim lighting of the restaurant.

Memories of a seventh-grade science challenge came to me as I watched Principal Chen and my teammates. In my science class, the teacher passed around a tin of a foreign delicacy, chocolate-covered ants. We might have thought the items chocolate-covered raisins, but our science teacher opened the large tin wide so that we could see the large black lumps of ant bodies covered with chocolate. The teacher passed the tin to the class.

All the boys in our class tried one, making a face or noises and laughing. The girls made faces too, and they passed the tin faster than a hot potato. Every girl refused to eat a chocolate-covered ant until I held the tin. To wipe the smirks off the faces of the boys and the all-knowing grin of our science teacher, I grabbed a clump of chocolate-covered ants, put them in my mouth, and chewed them while smiling.

Principal Chen made me feel the urge to outdo his noisy sucking in of the noodles. Was it wise to try to be as loud as he had been? It certainly would not be ladylike. Was I wrong to want to show him that he could not predict everything about us? Would it tell him that I was not afraid of him and his authority? I was frightened of the authoritative figures who were aligned with the communist government, but I didn't want to show fear.

With my chopsticks, I gathered a thick bunch of golden wheat noodles. I smiled at VP Zhu, Thomas, Emily, and Principal Chen who were seated near one another. I put the edge of the clump of noodles in my mouth. Then I made as much noise as I possibly could by sucking in those noodles with one huge deep vacuum-long suck. My team looked appalled.

Principal Chen's face showed a quick smile. He said, "*Hao.*" My attempt was good. From that moment on, we were not studied or urged to eat any specific way. It seemed we could relax and enjoy the meal without focusing on making more noise.

We were so full when we left the restaurant that most of us thought a nap on our ride to the next spot would work out well. When we got into the cars, we learned that the day's final treat of this trip into Ningxia would extend into the evening. Principal Chen had decided to take us to China's Hollywood of the West, Zhenbeipu West Studio. It was an hour from the restaurant to the vast movie studio, and we had a nap.

Dirt, sand, and two-story fortress walls surrounded the studio grounds. Flags fluttered from spears spread out around the top of battlements that had spaces for firing arrows. VP Zhu went to a small building near the main gate to gain admittance for all of us until closing time.

Walking into the studio grounds transported us to BCE centuries when the Qin, Zhou, Han, and Ming emperors were uniting and protecting their kingdoms. We visited the three main theme areas: a Qing Dynasty town, a Ming Dynasty town, and a twentieth-century town. I liked the Ming dynasty because it had the desolation of ancient times in the desert with detailed recreated scenes of the old towns and daily life.

My teammates wandered through each section, except Kathryn, who'd found the recreation of stalls selling items in the Qing area were real. Sales occurred here: shawls, dishes, wall hangings, and containers of unusual foods and teas. When Cassie introduced Kathryn to the process of bargaining over a price, shopping became a wonderful game.

Our SEP students expressed delight in taking pictures with us and of us. When we saw sights, we wanted to learn about them. With English translations missing, our assistants read any information aloud to us in English. Some of them knew stories about ancient times beyond what the signs showed.

Chinese snacks and Western candy bars could be purchased, carried, and eaten while walking around the sights. I turned down the pickled chicken feet that came in a clear plastic bag. These clawed and lumpy feet came pickled or flavored. Some had a hot spicy flavoring that could disguise any food. The chicken feet were kept in brine until they were soft enough to chew and eat. Thomas said that the chicken feet used for pickling were something China bought from the United States.

"Why does China buy these from the United States? We just throw them away."

"Ms. Virginia, it is because the United States chickens have feet much fatter than any feet of chicken raised in China or in other countries."

Thomas and the other Wuhai teachers wandered like tourists too, but someone was always near us to answer questions and to safeguard our steps. This annoyed Jaye so much that she took out some of her own money to pay for a camel ride through the ancient scenes. If she expected that would take her away from everyone, she was wrong. Principal Chen watched her actions and announced that we should all have a camel ride or a ride in a donkey cart, whichever we chose.

The camels looked thin and tired to me, so I chose a ride in a donkey cart. A pair of donkeys pulled it, and they looked well fed. When I got out of the cart, I stood near a line of warriors who looked out over Ningxia.

This moment and the view made me think of wars, as well as what kind of war happened inside people, inside me. I wanted to be free of the turmoil I'd felt at home. What an incredible day this had been from sites and sights to noodles, noise, and now this feeling of standing in the past. The modern city looked hazy and unreal in the distance.

Warriors of Ningxia

By the time we headed back to Wuhai, we had walked for hours in the desert air throughout the day. Bugs never created a problem. The days were so hot and dry that the only place we might see mosquitos was near a marshy edge of a river or pond.

The highway seemed smooth, but the connecting roads had potholes deep enough to hide a goat. Even in the deluxe comfort of the big black cars, we'd felt every one of those bumps on the way out to Ningxia. On the way back, I fell asleep and felt nothing until we stopped for a traffic light in Wuhai.

I don't always remember my dreams, but when I woke up as our line of cars stopped at the school's tall front gates, meeting the Communist Party representative filled my mind. From my nap time dream, I remembered walking in and out among the line of warriors looking over the desert. No modern city appeared. I knew it was there, but I couldn't see it at all.

The warriors in my dream read my mind. They made comments about the modern city in the distance that I could not see. The Communist Party representative that I had not yet met, followed me in my dream. He spoke to me and the soldiers. The oversized warrior soldiers nodded at his words.

Even though he spoke Chinese, in my dream I understood him, but I could not remember what he said. Dreams often hook into fears, but they also have subconscious insight. I wondered what my intuition would tell me in the morning when I met the man who had authority over everyone and every lesson in our host school.

Chapter 13

Comrade Wang and a Registered Church

Sunday morning dawned clear. The temperature rose quickly from a cool seventy degrees Fahrenheit in the night to eighty by our 7:00 a.m. breakfast time. I arrived in the teachers' dining area a couple of minutes before breakfast. Doug, Tia, Emily, Jenna, and Marge were already there, plus Principal Chen, VP Zhu, and a tall thin gentleman. If he wore robes like those, we saw in the ancient scenes yesterday, he could stand in for a wandering philosopher.

"Ms. Virginia, this is, Tongzhi Wang." Emily said. I had learned that *tongzhi* (同志) meant comrade. Literally it meant common aspiration. Party members used it to refer to members who were leaders. It spoke of one person relating to another as a fellow citizen. To me, it did not sound or feel like a title of equality when Emily said it.

I waited to see if he would offer his hand, Western style. He did not, so I tipped my head in a slight bow. He returned an even more miniscule tip of the head.

Kathryn and Jaye arrived, and Emily introduced

Tongzhi Wang again. More minor bowing was shared. We sat at one round table. Emily and my team were on on my left, Thomas, VP Zhu, Principal Chen, and Tongzhi Wang sat on my right.

I whispered to Emily. "Do we call him Tongzhi Wang or Mr. Wang?"

"Mr. Wang will be fine. I only used the formal title in the introduction."

"Thank you. Jessie told me to explain to the party representative what I am teaching about Western culture and history."

"After the English lessons that we study each morning with the Amity textbook?"

"Yes. In the afternoons we look at educators from around the world, and I am going through all the holidays. If holidays are celebrated in two major ways, like Christmas, one religious and one non-religious, I will describe both."

Emily nodded and looked past me to Comrade Wang.

"I will tell him you want to explain some lesson plans to him. I will translate."

"Thank you." I had no idea what she said as breakfast was served. The party representative had thick black hair combed straight back and the angles of his broad cheekbones reminded me of pictures of a Eurasian lynx, one of the top three predators in Mongolia. Like the lynx, his eyes were a light-brown tawny color, but they looked tired.

Tongzhi Wang stopped talking with Principal Chen and turned his attention fully to me. He looked like he spent lots of time outdoors. Could a person who supervised the teachings at a school be an outdoorsman too?

His direct gaze goaded me to speak even before Emily nodded at me to go ahead., "Mr. Wang, I wanted to let you know that besides working with the English textbooks from Amity each day, our students will also learn about Western culture."

My teammates at the table fell silent. As I continued, I counted on Emily's smooth translating. "Doug has business experience so will give some information and cultural insight into business practices."

Mr. Wang's expression, just like Principal Chen and VP Zhu, did not reveal clues to his emotions, or to his thoughts of approval, or disapproval.

"Kathryn is a medical person and has taught health classes to different ages and groups, so she will share that information on health for students and families. Jaye teaches sports, and we have already seen that young people here, and some of the teachers know about internationally famous athletes and Western sports. Jaye can help them to understand expectations, roles, and strategies.

"Tia works with early elementary children. She will share some of the cultural practices, stories, games, and songs for families and young children.

"I am a literature and humanities teacher, so for my extra lessons, I am teaching about the history and theories of educational leaders and about holiday practices. Over our weeks, I will start with a January holiday and conclude with New Year's Eve, the Western New Year's Eve. I know China's new year is at a different time." I paused after each sentence for Emily to translate.

Everyone in the room stayed still and silent. No noises came from the kitchen either. I especially enunciated the next information.

"I wanted you to know that if you come to visit my class and see names like Jesus, Moses, God, or the Bible, and words like *prayer, church, or faith* I am not teaching religion. I am explaining the holidays and different ways they are celebrated. We have big holidays like Easter and Christmas that are celebrated by people who have a faith and religious practices, and they are also celebrated by people who have no religious beliefs."

The Communist Party representative had enough height to gaze down at me. Without looking at the other administrators, Mr. Wang nodded. He said one sentence which Emily translated.

"Thank you for explaining."

That was it. He returned to his breakfast, eating more of the *baozi*, fruit, porridge, and tea. Everyone else started to eat again. Mr. Wang talked with Principal Chen.

When Tongzhi Wang finished his meal, he stood. The other two administrators also stood. Principal Chen spoke to us, and Emily continued as translator.

"You will all meet at the front gates in thirty minutes to leave for the church. The administrators know that Amity teams expect to attend church services on each Sunday. Wuhai has two churches. We will take you to the nearest one."

The administrators turned and left the dining room. Our team and the teachers with us departed more slowly, identifying some of the combinations for individual translating in the church. I heard Jenna tell Tia, "I am translating for you." Emily gave that message to Kathryn, and Marge told Jaye they would be partnered.

Then, as we left the dining room, Emily spoke to Doug and me. "Ms Virginia, Terry will be at the church and will translate for you. Mr. Doug, Jeff will be at the church and will translate for you."

I walked beside Emily as we went toward the dorm. "Emily, have the administrators been to either of the churches in Wuhai?"

"No. They are curious about why it is important for you to go to a church. Mr. Wang will not go into a church. Maybe Principal Chen or VP Zhu are concerned that in the church you are respected and safe."

"Emily, I think probably no one has explained to you that a church is the people who follow Jesus, not a building."

"You go to the building to talk with others who believe as you do?"

"Yes, because people who follow Jesus are like a family. It is good to meet family members in any part of the world. Even as a child, I learned that if I was lost anywhere, I should find a church and that brothers and sisters there would help me."

"That is why many Christians in China need no building?"

"Christians like to have a special place to gather to worship and learn together, but a building is not necessary. In some countries constructing a meeting place for Christian worship is illegal because Christianity is illegal."

"China protects normal religious activities. Our country has many religious practices. Some are very ancient."

I smiled and nodded. I did not ask who defined 'normal religious activities.'

* * *

The recently washed and polished comfortable black cars whisked us away through the large front gates of the school and onto a main avenue. This time we needed only two cars to transport our team and the SEP participants who had agreed to be individual translators. The principals did not join us. We stayed on the main avenue for a mile, then turned onto a narrow street.

Beside the church

After a short distance, we turned onto an older road. Two blocks farther, we found ourselves on a lane. Once it might have had cement pavement, but time and weather had caused it to crack and crumble.

The wall along the side of the street was made mainly of stones with some old-style mud bricks mixed into the layers. Vegetation, green and flowering, vines, and fully blossomed branches overflowed from the top of the wall. An older couple about to enter through the wooden gate in the wall stopped moving. They stared at the cars, then broke into wide smiles as we exited the vehicles.

What a greeting we received! The older couple had looked at our group and shouted *Huānyíng*, welcome! Some people who must have been inside the gate to the garden and grounds that surrounded the building came out to meet us. Poor Tia, who felt uncomfortable in crowds, endured ten minutes of a group so thick that it could almost carry us into the church.

The whole city knew that five foreigners were in the city for the SEP. Articles in their papers and on one local television broadcast the day we arrived said that all five foreigners were Americans who worked with Amity, and that Amity volunteers were Christians. No one knew if the foreign guests would mix in the community.

Inside the stone wall people gathered in talkative clusters as they edged slowly toward the front doors of the church, a fully clay brick building with only stones like the wall at a foundation level. Their enthusiastic welcome had the power to practically lift us up the few steps to the arched wooden doors, and into the church sanctuary.

I saw a platform, maybe four by six meters at the far end of the room. I'd been in living rooms in the US larger than this entire sanctuary. A cross, dark red, decorated the beige wall behind the pulpit. The wooden pulpit stood front and center on the platform.

Three folding chairs were in a horizontal line behind the pulpit. Pews made of wooden folding chairs filled the center area. Wide aisles on each side also had some folding chairs and the building had some of the same wooden stools that our classrooms had. The space seemed full to standing room only, but our group was led to the second row. The people sitting there smiled at us, got up, and moved to the side aisles.

I felt embarrassed, but we had seen this happen in a church in Nanjing too. Visitors, especially those from far away, were given seats down front. People of all ages who were already seated there quickly moved to clear the space for visitors.

Trees, waist-high, and what we would describe as artificial Christmas trees, stood on the front corners of the pulpit platform. Chinese paper lanterns, white and gold, spread in a half circle cluster connected to one another by red ribbons in each front corner. There was no organ, just a keyboard piano. A young woman sat behind it ready to play.

Everyone wore clothes like people did when going to work, doing errands, or walking their children to school. The front center row and the front row on each of the side sections, were filled with twenty-two people, both men and women, who wore white tops and black or blue trousers. We realized that these people were the choir. They stood, walked onto the platform and sang at two different times during the service.

Few people around us held Bibles, but the ones we could see looked old and worn from use. During the training time in Nanjing, Amity had taken us to a huge printing company, the only one in China that printed Bibles. We had a tour of the facilities and saw each step of the printing process. A few parts included modern digital procedures, but most still followed old time printing and binding methods.

Each of us chose to buy Bibles with all contents in English and Chinese. Our assistants appeared interested in the construction. They took our Bibles and ran hands over the leather texture of the cover, the lining, and lifted the thin pages. The indented places marking different books in the Bible looked like small red indentations.

In China, in this year of 2004, Bibles could be found only in bookstores for foreigners in the most international cities. A few of the largest registered churches had an approved area for selling printed religious materials like Bibles, songbooks, and devotionals. With entrenched restrictions and high costs, Bibles and faith-based reading material were not easily available in any province in China. The fascination our teachers showed in examining our Bibles made me feel like a blindfold had been over my brain and heart. I had taken this book that guided my life and faith for granted too many times.

Jessie had told us that Chinese pastors with seminary degrees are rare in China. Ordination as a requirement is unique to a few regions. Amity administrators had found it common that mature people with years of life experience and a devotion to studying the Bible were appreciated as pastors of churches in China. Young people who proclaimed biblical messages could be pastors, and gender did not matter. In our cultural instruction in Nanjing, we learned that churches often had female pastors.

In this Wuhai church, a woman was the head pastor. I didn't know if she had lived in China before the 1949 revolution, but she looked like she must have. I guessed her age to be at least seventy-five. Petite, full of smiles, the pastor had skin wrinkled by harsh sunshine. Her hair was white and gray and the sparkle in her dark eyes seemed full of spirit. She wore a tunic shirt and trousers like many of the older women we had seen in our time in China. She had fine posture as she stepped forward to pray after her assistant, Pastor Isaiah, welcomed everyone.

In the United States, people I knew emphasized that everything Chairman Mao had done was wrong. They disparaged Mao after he declared equality of the sexes. In 2004, I had not been in many churches in the US that had a female pastor. I knew that some did, but it was uncommon.

Registered churches in China seemed ahead in the equality of women holding roles as leaders in the church.

Outside of the church, I had seen behavior and had heard comments subtly reinforcing that women did not have equality in China. Mao Zedong said that "Chinese women hold up half the sky," but when looking at who held top leadership roles in China, the positions were not even half filled by women.

In this little church, women read scripture and prayed from the pulpit. Now we saw that a woman director led the choir. The choir seemed evenly divided in male and female members. What irony if the Chinese church showed more equality in leadership roles than we saw in the government, the administration of education, or in businesses.

I thought of interactions I'd seen between the women teachers and men. Even someone as respected as Emily changed in attitude and mannerisms when men were present. In one of our team meetings, Doug informed us that femininity in China, especially when assertive, was associated with the evils of individualism and capitalism. He also told us that when Chairman Mao died, the Communist Party emphasized a yin-yang outlook that limited women's political influence.

In this church, the Bibles held by people looked well-worn. The Bibles our team had purchased in Nanjing included Mandarin and English and looked new. Mao had decreed Mandarin the official language of China. This meant that if people could not understand dialects, they could still communicate in writing because literacy stood as a national goal. Unfortunately, we had not heard of any Bibles printed in other dialects or languages of minority groups of China. It was something else I would research at home.

Illiteracy had been high. With great pride, early in our first week of teaching in Wuhai, Emily had told us that in 2004, 90 percent of China's counties had set the goal of spreading nine-year compulsory education to eliminate illiteracy among youths and adults. This led to increasing literacy of 8.03 million illiterate people between 2001 and 2004, more than two million per year. I wondered if anyone in the government, local or national, thought about how literacy opened the world to people, including reading the Bible.

Music, old time hymns, took up the first twenty minutes of the worship service. People sang out with passion and joy. For lively tunes they also clapped their hands. We did not recognize the songs until they sang "What a Friend We Have in Jesus." I didn't know Chinese, but I recognized the melody. I sang along in English.

Doug knew it too and sang in his strong baritone voice. I saw the careful glances that the teachers and the congregation cast his way. Everyone we had met seemed to appreciate music. From the welcome dinners to the music in this church filled with enthusiastic singers, this city's residents showed enjoyment and freedom in singing.

The petite senior citizen female pastor gave a sermon on parables in Luke 15, the lost sheep, the lost coin, and the prodigal son. There were affirmative words shouted out loud toward points the pastor made. I understood the amens and hallelujahs because they sounded like the words in English.

Doug had told us to be prepared for a long sermon. He said all the sermons he had heard in China were twice or even three times as long as the ones we had at home. As I paid attention and tried to recognize any word or phrase, I realized again how listening to a foreign language and trying desperately to understand it took effort. Our students went through this every day for hours and had done well in adjusting to our spoken English.

When it seemed like the service might conclude, an elder announced that baptisms would take place. Pastor Isaiah called the names of all those who would be baptized. The pulpit was moved by two young men to the back of the platform. Pillows were placed in a line across the platform. Adult men and women, ranging from young, middle-aged, and old, went to the platform and facing the congregation, they knelt on the pillows.

A white-haired slightly stooped man stepped to the end of the line of kneeling people and prayed over them. Terry whispered the translation to me. Two elders, one man and one woman, stepped behind each person. The man held a small basin of water. The elder who prayed asked each person a question. The individuals gave a personal testimony of choosing to follow Jesus.

Then Pastor Isaiah moved to stand beside each person. He took water from the basin and sprinkled it on each person's head. A woman elder had a large white cloth to dab away any dripping water and wiped the brows of those baptized. This baptism ceremony occurred four times. In a city surrounded by deserts and mountains of rock, this gentle baptism with drops of water made sense.

Each time Pastor Isaiah baptized a row, the people stood and returned to their seats while the congregation clapped and shouted more amens and hallelujahs. Then another row of individuals moved to kneel on the cushions. I glanced at the teachers to see if any of this was affecting them. Did they think it strange?

I looked at the congregation and longed to know more

about them and Christianity and churches around China. However, from the way we had seen China block sites in our time of using computers, I knew I couldn't do the research I wanted while I was in China. When I returned to the US, I would do searches on many topics.

At home to prepare I did read about the church in China. I learned in 2004, the government approved the Three-Self Church. This simple and full Wuhai church was a Three-Self Church, which meant the leaders had registered their church with the government. They also let the government know about the materials used in the church and the church members.

People who understood the existence of China's house churches and underground faith gatherings knew that the government number of Christians was low. Unregistered churches gathered to worship all over the country. Amity had asked volunteers and staff not to visit unregistered churches. I wondered how these church members and their pastors felt about registering their meetings, members, and materials with the government.

After the service we were invited to stay for a meal. This church had a meal together every Sunday after the morning worship service. We looked toward Emily. She spoke kindly to the people near us. Although we didn't understand her words, we could tell she was refusing for us. Then she and each of our teacher assistants took one of us by the arm. With smiles and waves, we departed. People followed us to the front gate and thanked us for visiting.

"I told them that we had plans for today, but that you might stay next Sunday. You can talk about it and decide. If you stay, you should all stay, along with your teacher assistants. They will remain with you to help translate. I think the church people hope you will join them. Because the Sunday lunches planned for you at the school are very simple, you would probably enjoy their shared dinner. I know some people here, and they are good cooks. Tell me Sunday morning. I can let the cook know your plans."

I thought about the music in the church and how full and happy the voices sounded. Almost three decades of teaching classes, from pre-school through college students, had shown me that people learned quickly with songs. Why couldn't we use music to make the learning in our SEP classes more fun?

The idea of telling the team that we should try to think of more ways to use music in our teaching stayed in my mind with the persistence of the little border terrier we had as a pet at home. Each teacher could choose a song, sing it every day for the weeks ahead, and all the students would easily learn five different songs. If we could think of songs suited to our topics and activities, we could even teach a song a week in our classes.

Would any team member disagree with adding the positive power of music in our classes? One did.

Chapter 14

Not Allowed, Naughty, and Questions

To prepare for our first full week of teaching, we had a team meeting that Sunday evening in Doug's room. We shared ideas for plans and using the Amity textbook. We had many choices to consider, like the timing of the units, warm-up activities, interaction with the main lessons, reading, words and phrases, idioms, discussions, practice, emphasis, review, and summarizing.

It seemed late when Doug asked, "Anything else we should consider?"

"Doug, you have a good voice. I enjoyed hearing you sing the hymns in church. Other people enjoyed your singing too, even though you sang in English. It made me think that we could each come up with a theme song to teach to our classes. We could sing it every day with them as a fun way to practice and hear English."

"It would have to be simple, and I don't have a loud voice," Tia said.

"Oh, they'll laugh and sing along with us even if we don't

sound great. I love singing, but I've never been a choir member." Kathryn added.

"Music lyrics are a very effective way of learning a language," Doug agreed.

"I don't sing, in any of my classes. I won't do it here. We don't all have to do the same thing. I'd feel stupid singing with the classes." Jaye sounded light as a gravestone.

"Jaye, it could be any song." I suggested, "Because you're doing so much about sports for your afternoon enrichment classes, why don't you teach 'Take Me Out to the Ball Game?'"

"It doesn't have to be a Christian song?"

"No. Choose a song you know and like that has clear lyrics. If they learn it fast, we could add in a song each week. There are lots of fun songs."

"Teaching 'Take Me Out to the Ball Game' would be all right. I like that song and sing it at the ball parks."

"But you like baseball and you know the song, so you'd be great at teaching it," Kathryn encouraged her.

"Okay. What are the rest of you going to do?"

"I'm going to teach a song about body parts," Kathryn smiled and sounded happy.

"Ha! What body parts?" Jaye asked.

"It's a children's song, 'Head, Shoulders, Knees and Toes.'"

"Kathryn," Tia said, "if you do that, I know some children's songs I could use too. I could start with the one that kids learn when they come to school, The Wheels on the Bus. There are motions with every song I know from my classes."

"That's a very good idea, Tia," I said. "We have lots of primary school teachers in the SEP, and some of our students are parents. Adding songs will help make our time fun and practical. They will be able to teach the songs to their children."

"Do you have an idea for a motion song, Virginia?" Tia asked.

"I think it is good to get people moving. We have enough room around the edge of all the desks to make a big circle. I think that I'll teach the Hokey Pokey," I added. "What about you Doug?"

"I like the idea of motions with lyrics. I think I'll start this week with, 'If You're Happy and You Know It.' We can do clap your hands, tap your toes, nod your head, stamp your feet. We might all be too tired to do much socializing tomorrow night, but we should let the students know that we will sit outside in the evenings and invite them to drop by so if they want casually use English and maybe sing, we'd be glad to see them. Amity expects us to do the English Corners, free flowing conversational English."

Doug had brought up the need to offer casual time with our students and the community. "Doug, I'll be glad to do that." I responded quickly. Nobody else made a commitment at that team meeting except to agree to announce the casual conversation socializing to their classes.

When I got to my room, I felt thankful for how the day had started. Even though none of the students who had attended the church with us had said anything about the super welcome we received, the music, or the sermon, they had experienced all of it. Perhaps there would be discussions after future visits.

Our team meeting held positives about adding music, but also disappointment since Tia, Jaye, and Kathryn had not shown interest in the English Corner activity. I felt thankful that we all found sleeping improved even though the beds were hard. None of us had anymore eye problems since we used the air conditioners and eye drops.

The first full week of work with our classes had started well. In my years of teaching, I had learned the value of arriving early for extra preparation time and interactions with students. Since my classroom was the first one everyone had to pass to get to the other rooms, I could see every team member tried to arrive early or right on time that first week.

Our students also arrived early or on time. Kathryn and Jaye did not get to their classrooms before all the students arrived, but their homerooms seemed happy. Amity had explained that punctuality in China is a mark of respect.

Mornings zoomed by with the varied lessons. We did conduct enrichment area lessons in the afternoons. Doug and I taught them each afternoon, and our other team members had their desired one afternoon a week off. We had casual conversation on some evenings from eight until nine-thirty with at least a half dozen teachers. The number grew each evening, Tuesday through Thursday. Some of our students asked if they could bring a few of their own junior and senior middle school students in the next week. It was easy to see how the English Corners promoted learning English and about one another.

*   *   *

The highlights of learning in my classes came from positive interactions and from facing any questions students asked or answered. When I started with January holidays, I explained Martin Luther King Jr. Day to them. The classes knew some facts about Reverend King, and showed enthusiasm for

131

learning more, especially about his leading of the justice protests. When I asked if they knew why Rev. King had such a strong belief in equality and justice, I received some interesting answers.

"He knew he lived in a racist country."

"He admired Gandhi."

"He was a hopeful and kind person."

"He could tell what was fair."

"He learned from his father and family."

After these responses, I asked, "Did you know that his father was a pastor too? Rev. King and his father knew that the Bible showed that God loved people and demanded those who had faith to promote justice and to peacefully overcome racism."

We read the "I Have a Dream" speech. We talked about hopes, dreams, and prejudices. I taught the song, "We Shall Overcome." The clear simple message was repetitious but also inspiring. Every class learned "We Shall Overcome" during the week because our schedule allowed each class to have the enrichment materials and activities in the afternoon. When they tried singing together, they sounded wonderful and had harmony. From their enthusiasm it seemed like a message they loved.

Standing by the blackboard where I'd written the lyrics to, "We Shall Overcome," I wondered who would tell Mr. Wang about these discussions about Martin Luther King Jr., justice, and equality. I enjoyed the singing in each class. Combined, they had a power that honored the song, the message, and the leader.

Incongruity swirled through my mind and emotions like an ocean waterspout. Teaching about a civil rights leader in a remote region of China and hearing dozens of teachers singing, "We Shall Overcome," with a sound as good as any civil rights choir gave me chills of the positive kind.

Role-playing in the afternoon classes was a chance for me and the students to experience unexpected hilarity and relaxing laughter. The actions and words they came up with were like a mixture of stand-up comedy and impromptu theater. I paused at one point to emphasize that laughter and music would help their students to relax and learn faster. "It will be great when you start using role playing, music, and lyrics, to add fun to learning in your own classes."

The class became still. Their faces reminded me of the moai stone statues in the Easter Islands representing ancestors, unmoving, and unknowable. In these huge statues people see symbols of religious and political authorities. Made from volcanic stone, the moai stand watch but few have smiles. Those that do have smiles are not happy ones.

"What?" I asked. "What has made you all so still and quiet?"

Students looked from one another, to me, then to Erdeen. Their expressions asked her to give the answer. I saw her take a breath.

In a tone as overwhelming as rock made from molten lava, Erdeen said, "Ms. Virginia, we have no time for teaching songs or having fun with role-playing in our middle school and senior middle school classes. It is not allowed. We must have the students work to earn high marks on the exams."

The lighthearted open spirit of the class drained away. My heart ached to think that these caring young teachers feared introducing songs or activities that brought laughter to their classes. In my years of teaching high school, I had observed some teachers did not care if the students even smiled. Other teachers understood the power of music and fun.

My goal to encourage sparks of courage and curiosity in our time of practiced conversation needed openness without negativity. For this reason, I shared my experiences and asked them to tell me of their classroom experiences or special students. I learned that students with poor behavior, attitudes, or study habits were called naughty.

I told the class that naughty students were discussed in schools where I had taught too. Then I asked them if they had ever seen the naughty student after graduation. Many in my classroom had. This led us to discuss students described as naughty who surprised people by achieving business success or who became leaders in the community through projects that helped improve the community or that solved a problem.

Examples would help and at this moment I was thankful for a get acquainted activity I had done in the second day of classes. I showed pictures of famous individuals, people who had global fame. The class had to call out the names of anyone they recognized. They had recognized Bill Gates but not Brittany Spears. They had recognized Walt Disney but not Robert Reford. They had recognized Queen Elizabeth but not Elizabeth Taylor. I thought of two naughty student examples I could use.

"Bill Gates and Walt Disney struggled in school," I told them. "Many of their teachers thought they did not concentrate or were lazy. With their inconsistent work, you might label them naughty. Teachers who worked with Bill Gates knew he was smart, but he did not show interest or motivation in subjects he did not enjoy. His grades were high in computer science and math, and he did get admitted to Harvard, but he dropped out after two years.

"Walt Disney faced criticism for falling asleep in class. In many subjects he did not earn high grades. Besides going to school, he had a job from a young age, and at home he worked late into the night on his own creative ideas.

"That would not be a combination here, Ms. Virginia." John told me.

"Why not?"

"Students are not allowed to have jobs while they are in school. Going to school is their job."

Kent corrected John. "They are not supposed to hold a job before they are sixteen. After sixteen they may work in a job besides being a student."

"But if they want to go to the university, they will concentrate on school. They must pass Mandarin, math, and English exams with high grades to have any chance of going to a university," Cassie added.

We had more discussion evaluating the pros and cons of working during teen years and of the stresses young people faced. This conversation had revealed honest frustrations. It seemed like these students trusted me with concerns for their teaching and for their students. As I struggled with my trust issues, especially in trusting God, I wanted to find a way to continue building trust with these hard-working SEP students.

Each day of the first week I reminded students that I would allow time for questions every day. I might not have the answers, but I would listen to any question and try to give an answer.

My teammates did not agree. In our early planning meetings, they chose to take the Amity option offered in the training time of keeping to structured activities and avoiding contentious topics. Amity said that if SEP teachers were asked something controversial, they could say, 'I am here to help you with English speaking, comprehension, and teaching, not to talk about politics or topics away from our text.'

Once the classes understood that I would give free time for random questions, the start was tentative. Safe topics arose about schedules for high school students, how Americans chose colleges, salaries for teachers, and why even teenagers in the United States had cars. Issues about families, community life, career options, drugs, and guns followed. Sometimes a simple object lesson led to surprising questions and discussion.

One day I gave out dollar bills and coins for the class to look at and study.

"Why does your paper money say, In God We Trust?"

"I think that started when Lincoln was president, and we had a civil war. I don't know of any war that has been civil, but that is what wars within a country are called. Each side in our civil war wanted reminders that God was on their side. In God We Trust stayed on the money until Theodore Roosevelt was president."

"Why did that president remove it?"

"Isn't it still on your money?'

"I'll answer the second question first. Yes, it is still on the money. President Roosevelt had it removed because he thought it was not respectful to have the word, *God*, on money."

"Who put it back on your money?"

"Another president. President Eisenhower."

"He did not believe it was disrespectful?"

"He believed it important to show that our country did

believe in God. Our Congress agreed that it was respectful, and voted to put it back on the money."

"Does everyone in your country believe in God?"

"No. We have many people who spend no time thinking about religion. Some others who clearly say that they do not believe in God."

"Do you think our paper money is better looking than your paper money?"

"Yes. You have many more colors and variety of pictures on your paper money."

The atmosphere seemed to mellow. My students liked hearing about something admirable or preferred about their country.

Chapter 15

Golden Rule Versions and Choices

B y the middle of week two, the students knew that I meant what I said when I announced they could ask anything. Usually, when someone asked a question, the class members leaned forward expectantly. Some days a question caused everyone to fall silent or to sit straight. No lively discussion followed a discomforting the question.

One young man stood up when I said we could start with questions. His name was Larry, and he had not said much in our class time before this moment.

"Ms. Virginia, are you in favor of the war your president started against Afghanistan?"

If we were the only Americans these teachers would ever meet or converse with, and I had encouraged this open question time, I would respond willingly but carefully. The praying I had started out of concerns for doing the best job possible for Amity had included prayer for wisdom during the open questions time. This time could build trust, respect, and connections.

I nodded in acceptance of the question but paused before answering. I wanted to be honest. "Thank you for your question. I will tell you that my president did not call me to ask if I was in favor of going to war in Afghanistan. I am a mother. I do not know any mothers in favor of war, but the president does not ask for the support of mothers before declaring war. Does your president consult mothers before choosing a military action?"

Larry smiled and did not answer my question. He did not need to because everyone who heard my question to him knew the answer. Most interesting to me was that I never had the same questions repeated from one class to the next. The minutes between classes that we had scheduled as a break time for our students seemed enough time for already asked questions and answers to be shared among all the classes.

The next group, from Doug's Atlanta class, arrived with a cheerfulness that showed they'd had a good session with Doug. This class also had the most male students. Amity usually had more female teacher volunteers for the SEP than males. In a short time, even right from the training time, we knew that the male SEP students appreciated having a male teacher. They spent as much time with Doug as he would give before and after classes, yet only a few arrived for the evening English Corners.

These young male teachers who started their SEP days with Doug chose to sit in the front rows of the classroom. In the US, I rarely saw a young man choose to sit up front. Jeff still showed that he felt out of place by always taking a seat in the last row.

With each class, I assured them that I valued their questions. We all learned with and from one another. They were smart and thoughtful and had already seen how questions and answers helped them to develop knowledge and conversation skills.

In China, students frequently stand beside their desks to ask a question. I had announced that it was question time. Immediately a young man in the front row stood beside his desk. The name card showed his name as Walt.

"Yes, Walt?"

"Ms. Virginia, how do you and Americans feel about the treatment of the prisoners at Abu Ghraib by American soldiers?"

Abu Ghraib, I felt like I'd been punched in the stomach. Just the name brought revolting images to mind. Abu Ghraib stood as one of the ugliest, most disgusting actions of American troops. The images proving torture committed by American troops against incarcerated Iraqi prisoners had appeared in newspapers around the world two months before we arrived in Wuhai. I knew that Chinese papers and news channels had shown the horrible portrayals of American military guards torturing prisoners.

This SEP started in July 2004. Following the attack on the World Trade Tower in New York City on September 11, 2001, George W. Bush had declared war on Afghanistan and promoted a search for as long as it would take to find Osama bin Laden. All our SEP students knew that our military entered Afghanistan, and that in 2003, George W. Bush expanded the war into Iraq. He believed that Saddam Hussein had weapons of mass destruction.

The smiles on faces all disappeared at Walt's question. Some female teachers visibly cringed. Most class members sat like statues on the little wooden benches by each desk.

The students closest to Walt seemed particularly uncomfortable.

All the facts I'd read, news videos I remembered, filled my mind and made me wonder at the stories reported and believed in China. Obviously from the reaction to the question, they knew American soldiers overseeing Abu Gharib had horribly abused Iraqi prisoners. Revolting pictures and countless articles had appeared. In this Wuhai SEP, it had been only three-months since the travesty of inhumane actions by American soldiers toward Abu Gharib prisoners had made global news.

I guessed this was an honest question. Everyone who had walked into my classroom with Walt seemed shocked by his question. It was like an American student asking a guest from China if it was true that Mao had a million people killed in his land reform actions.

Remaining calm outwardly as I tried to think of an appropriate response. I took a slow breath. *Oh God, please help me to give a helpful honest answer.* "Walt, what happened at Abu Gharib shocked me and everyone I know. Across the United States, people felt terrible that American soldiers would torture prisoners. No matter how much training someone has, and no matter how responsible they have been, people can change and make bad choices. They can do something they know is wrong."

The class looked directly at me. Even those who had their heads tipped downward glanced up. I felt like they were waiting for a more elaborate response, something that could help them, help us, understand such inhumane actions. I continued giving an answer slowly choosing my words.

"News traveling so fast around the world showed these

shameful actions by some Americans soldiers. In every country, the comments of newscasters, common people, and leaders have portrayed shock and disgust over what happened at Abu Ghraib. No one knows why people who seemed like regular human beings would treat prisoners sadistically."

"Sadistically, Ms. Virginia?" Walt asked.

"Vicious, brutal, inhuman, heartless, and cruel actions done with pleasure. People who feel pleasure abusing helpless victims are sadists."

Walt continued with clarity and volume, "We saw pictures. One showed the naked prisoners with bags over their heads forced to make a human pyramid, and the American soldiers in the room smiled. One gave a thumbs-up. That is an approval signal."

"Yes. That is a picture of sadism and inhumanity."

How could I move from this miserable subject and have them think about the wider problem with such inhumane actions?

"It makes me sad to say, and this is not to excuse the American soldiers in any way, that I don't think this problem happens in only one country. What causes people to act like this? Power? Fear? Prejudice? Hate? If we look at wars and war crimes, it seems like every military, in every country, even here in China, has some soldiers who treat prisoners in ways that no person should treat another person.

"Do you think that is a fair view of humans? Do you think that in any country there are soldiers who know they should not mistreat other human beings, but do it anyway?"

Walt didn't answer me. I looked around at the concerned faces. No one responded. I thought I should close the class with a familiar and calming activity.

"This topic is painful, but you know that we can learn even from painful discussions. Take your notebooks out. I will put some of the new vocabulary words on the board, along with a saying by Confucius. 'Do not impose on others what you do not wish for yourself.' Under the Confucius statement, I will write the Golden Rule from the words of Jesus. It is similar to the Confucius saying and is well known around the world.

"The Golden Rule says, 'In everything, do to others as you would have them do to you.' People can choose their actions. We can hurt or help people, especially in the career we have chosen as teachers."

Other than taking out their notebooks and writing, the mood felt as heavy as a soaked winter coat. I decided to tell them a story from my high school teaching experience. They must have seen or known of people helping others. They needed to understand that even the primary, or the junior and senior middle students they taught could have a powerful positive effect on others.

"I want to tell you about one of the kindest high school students I ever had the privilege to teach. His name was Billy. He worked hard in school but earning top grades was difficult for him. Billy loved the outdoors and sports. He was a great team member because he did not need to be the star. Billy shared so well that he could help his team members to look like stars. He was popular among students because of his friendly helpfulness, and he did volunteer service work. One of his favorite projects was helping elementary students to enjoy reading.

"Billy discovered a very difficult sport at a rodeo center near us. Do you know what a rodeo is?"

Thomas answered, "A rodeo has some connection with

your west and cowboys They ride dangerous bulls, or horses, called broncos. They ride fast around a big circle and throw ropes around cows and calves."

"That is an excellent description, Thomas. Billy liked all of it, but he especially liked riding bulls and wrestling steers. After he started traveling around the region participating in rodeos, and winning some prizes, he made up a reading program for the primary school. The stories were about cowboys and rodeos. Billy visited the primary schools in his best rodeo clothing and helped launch the reading program.

The children loved it. Cowboy Billy's ideas motivated primary students to read. They loved him and started reading a lot more. Billy still struggled to earn the grades he needed in high school, but he continued to help younger students do better in school. I had Billy in a class for students who had difficulty passing the important senior high school exam that the state required. Billy worked hard on all the assignments.

"One weekend, Billy traveled far away to another state for an event in his rodeo sport. You have provinces, we have states. It was Mother's Day weekend. You celebrate Mother's Day, don't you?"

They nodded but didn't speak.

"Billy called his mother late on Saturday night. He was happy because he had done well at that midwestern rodeo. He told his mother that even though he was driving home he didn't think he would be there in time to celebrate Mother's Day with her the next day, Sunday. But he loved her. He wanted her to know he thought of her and loved her because he knew she would go to bed soon. Billy's mom knew that he loved her, but mothers appreciate knowing they are loved and hearing it when a child says it to them."

I didn't know if every student in the class had a mother who was still living. I didn't know if Chinese or Mongolians said *I love you* often. Perhaps this speaking of love was as rare as compliments.

In all our classes, many of the students had a child of their own. They gave me their total attention as I told them about Billy.

"Billy died in a car accident on his way home. It was not his fault. A large truck hit his small pick-up truck. Reports described the accident as so terrible that Billy must have died quickly, maybe instantly.

"It shocked everyone who knew him in the school, and not just in our community, but also in the surrounding communities. Little children in the elementary school, teachers, administrators, and townspeople who knew him and his family admired and appreciated Billy. Many felt love for him because he had done so much to encourage younger students. Billy had his own struggles trying to earn high grades, but he gave extra time to helping others."

A couple of the women in our SEP class wiped tears from their eyes.

"Billy's mom is a thoughtful, caring, and well-liked teacher. His father owned a popular business. His younger sister and brother looked up to Billy.

"How precious that phone call late Saturday night was to Billy's mom. Billy was eighteen. He died in the year he would have graduated from high school. The church building in his hometown was too small for the funeral. They had to hold it in another town with a larger church building. Even then, so many wanted to be at his funeral service that the seats were full, so people stood inside, and outside."

I paused and wondered how Billy's choices to do good for others connected to the minds and hearts of these adult students. What would Billy's choices mean to them? Did they think about how it connected to their own families or to the students in their own classes? I decided to speak directly to them in their role as teachers.

"Teachers should treat their students with respect and value and show their students how to treat others with respect. We teachers take up hours of our students' lives. No one knows how many years their students have. Just because people are young does not mean they will live to old age."

I moved to the chalkboard to point again to the statements. "Confucius's ideas and the Golden Rule remind us to treat students the way we would like to be treated. We need to do our best to help students see that they have the power to make the world a better place. People of all ages need role models who treat others with respect and kindness.

"We teachers touch the future every day by what we do and say because our students are the future. You are giving me and all the other SEP teachers hours of your lives. I hope you know that Doug, Kathryn, Jaye, Tia, and I feel it is an honor and a privilege to work with you. In all my years of going to school and teaching, the best teachers have been people who keep learning. Teachers have great value in a society, even if they don't pay us well."

That statement at least brought some smiles, but the students left the classroom more quietly this day. Billy had touched so many lives in positive ways. I hoped his story would stay in our SEP students' minds and inspire them in their lives too.

Chapter 16

Needs, Hopes, and Not Just Luck

After the next morning filled with the Amity textbook and activities, the afternoon felt more relaxed. The questions were not tied to political or war topics. One question led me to think about my main personal reason for coming to work for Amity.

"Ms. Virginia, we want more tourists to come to Wuhai. What can we do to bring more tourists here?" The sincere concern in this question reverberated throughout the class. I could see the students' attention and interest reflected in their expressions.

"Travel will have to change. It took me more than thirty hours of travel time to arrive here. Tourists do not want travel to take so long. My trip could have been shorter, if I had not stopped in Guangzhou and Nanjing, but flight costs led me to choose to fly in and out of Guangzhou, and I had Amity classes to take in Nanjing.

"Did you fly here from Nanjing?"

"There are no direct flights from Nanjing to Wuhai. We

traveled from Nanjing to Beijing, from Beijing to your region's capital, Hohhot, and then from Hohhot to Wuhai. This western portion of Inner Mongolia needs to have a direct shorter route. Visitors and tourists must know that they can feel and experience your culture soon after the time they land in China. People want tours that will give unique experiences.

"I have seen some tours organized for Inner Mongolia Autonomous Region, but they are usually towards Hohhot or the northeast. You can have tours that show people your amazing deserts, mountains, rivers, farms, history, food, and art. I am sure you have heard Doug mention that he was in the northeast of this province when he worked with Amity in 2002. He found the climate and the town extremely different from Wuhai. You have unique elements that you should advertise."

They understood that tourists would not arrive until the travel time was made shorter and that the tours offered unique and delightful experiences. Our students showed pride in their portion of the province. They knew that western Inner Mongolia held sights and experiences worth the travel time and the costs for anyone who could afford to explore the world and wanted to learn about Mongolian cultures.

"Ms. Virginia, because your trip is so long why did you choose to come to Inner Mongolia? To Wuhai?"

Would it encourage or discourage them if I talked about my fading sense of energy in teaching, the unexpected changes that I had not faced with flexibility, the insidious discontent that affected relationships? I struggled in a cocoon of layered emotions to analyze my need for renewal.

Disclosing all this to teachers who had so much less than I did at school or at home, did not seem right. I couldn't talk about it now, but when? For now, I would honestly tell them some of my secondary reasons.

"You all know that Amity gives the school requests for SEP teams to your government, so I did not choose the province or the city. When I did see the location, I had a choice. I did not have to agree to come to Wuhai."

"Would you have gone to some other place in China?"

"Only if another team would take me. Amity has teams, and if I turned down this assignment, I would not have had a team."

"Then you could not come to China?"

"Amity would check with all the other teams to see if any of them would take another person who had no team. If another group would take me, I would have gone to their location. If I could not work with an Amity team, I would not have come to China."

"Wouldn't you have come to China as a tourist, by yourself?"

"Maybe, in the future. I don't know. I do not like traveling with tour groups."

"But you chose Amity. You agreed to travel to wherever you were assigned."

"Yes. By living in China and working with people of the country, I think I can learn more about China than by traveling with a tourist group. Plus, as an older teacher, I am always thankful for a chance to help young teachers like you. Amity cares about teachers and it has other wonderful programs, in addition to the SEP.

"Amity has a program for deaf and mentally challenged

children and teens. They help them communicate and prepare them for jobs. They also have programs to help migrants and their families, plus teams of volunteers who are doctors, dentists, and nurses work with Amity around the country. Amity also sends trucks with necessities for areas that have a disaster."

"Did you worry about coming to this small city in the desert?"

"I smile whenever you call this a small city. Wuhai is far bigger than many capital cities of the states in my country."

"You knew it would be hot here, and we heard about the eye problems when you first arrived. We see sweat on your face, but you smile throughout our hot days."

"You have seen some of my pictures of snowstorms in Central Massachusetts."

Heads nodded and many smiles appeared. They had some snow in the winter, and even ice, but the amount of snow that dropped half a meter or more per storm in central Massachusetts amazed them. Seeing pictures of Jerry shoveling snow or using the snow blower to cast snow onto piles that were taller than his six feet fascinated the students.

"I also told you how we need to shovel snow and clear it from our cars many times in an average day, before school, after school, after any errands, before and after any evening meetings. My husband does this at home, but when I am at school, doing errands or going to meetings, I need to clear the car and sometimes shovel snow. When I heard about the wonderful dry desert heat during the days and the comfortable nighttime temperatures, I looked forward to my time here.

"Our house in Massachusetts is very old, though not by

Chinese standards. But in America, an 1896 house is old. It does not have good insulation, and often I feel cold."

"Do you like Wuhai then?"

"I do. You might not know that Christian people do not just believe in chance or luck. We think there is a purpose for life. We believe every experience we encounter has a purpose, even if we cannot guess how it might be important to our lives." The words came out of my mouth before my brain registered how I had ignored this belief while wallowing in my unhappiness in Massachusetts.

"Ms. Virginia, do you mean that you think you are not in Wuhai by chance?"

"Yes." As I said this, I realized that it was truly my belief. "I think part of the reason why I like it here so much is because this is the best place for me this summer. I didn't know about Wuhai or choose it, but I believe life experiences fit into the design God has for our lives. So, I would say, this assignment to Wuhai was the right place for me." My mention of God elicited no comments or questions on that belief, but I wondered if Comrade Wang would hear about it.

"Did you know about our autonomous region before you came here?"

"I knew general information about China provinces and some history."

"Did you learn about China's history in your schools?"

"Not much, just some basic facts. When I knew that I would come to China, Inner Mongolia is what I researched. Unfortunately, the information I found was mainly about the eastern part of your province. I confess that I brought some clothes for that weather, cool days with sudden showers, and chillier nights. I did not see any weather details for Wuhai. In my suitcase, I have a jacket with a warm lining, and it is rainproof. I also have some special trousers for rainy environments, and shoes for walking in mud."

The whole class laughed.

"Ms. Virginia, we have never had that heavy rain weather."

"I realize that now. Your summer weather, which is hot with low humidity, would attract tourists. You can give tips about bringing eye drops."

The topic of bringing more people, more tourists, absorbed the classes. Both in class and out of class we heard the students discussing how to showcase the history, art, geography, family life, and culture of western Inner Mongolia. Some thought their foods would bring tourists. Again, discussion flowed with enthusiasm.

"Hot pot, Ms. Virginia," several voices called out. "Hot pot could cause visitors to love our region," John declared.

"Aren't there many kinds of hot pot meals?" I asked.

"Oh yes, Ms. Virginia."

"Which ones do you know? I have not had any yet."

"Korea and Japan have hot pot."

"But it started in China."

"In the south, spice and broth feature in the hot pot."

"In our region, Northern China, the main ingredient is meat."

"Ms. Virginia, you must have hotpot!"

"We will take you, our foreign teachers, for hot pot. Wuhai has many hot pot restaurants."

"Mongolian hot pot is unique," Erdeen said, and the class gave her their full attention. "Instead of boiling meat and vegetables in spiced broth, we boil milk tea and cook the meat and vegetables in it. Our milk tea broth is tangy."

"Kublai Khan. Tell Ms. Virginia about hot pot for Kublai Khan," one student called out from the back of our room.

Erdeen nodded, "In the Yuan dynasty, Kublai Khan craved stewed mutton. There would soon be a battle, so the cook sliced mutton thin to cook it fast. He put it in boiling water until the meat changed color. Then the cook rolled it in salt. Kublai Khan ate it quickly. That day Kublai Khan won the battle. At the banquet celebrating his victory, the cook was asked to make the instant boiled mutton dish again. Now people add several kinds of meat and vegetables to hot pot. It is a very social dinner time."

"Ms. Virginia, do you have hot pot in your country?"

"I am sure our cities have everything because we have people from around the world, but towns and rural areas do not have much variety, including something like hot pot. And people have to be introduced to new foods. Some people never want to try something new. Maybe that is true here too?"

"No, Ms. Virginia. We like to learn about the world and new foods."

"We will make sure you all go out to one of our hot pot restaurants."

Over the next weeks that happened. For lunch or dinner, we did not have to eat in the dining hall if we informed the school ahead of time that we would be going to a meal with one of the SEP teachers or a group. Although they earned little, the people of Nei Menggu loved sharing a meal and introducing special dishes.

For hot pot, people sit around a table with a simmering pot of soup that stays hot over a flame, usually a gas burner in the middle of the table. With their *kuaizi,* people can choose raw food, meats, and vegetables, on plates all around the pot, and then dip the food into the pot until it is cooked the way they like it. Spices can be added to the broth. Often hot pots have two different broths, and one is extremely spicy. We had hot pot once a week with different groups of teachers at simple local restaurants in our remaining weeks in Wuhai.

Chapter 17

Plans for the Future, Problems of the Present

T he students' concern about tourists did not abate. One afternoon, as soon as the students were seated, Erdeen said, "Ms. Virginia, through the afternoon break, we talked about tourists. May we talk more about what we need to bring tourists to Wuhai?"

The class members had a united expectation for my affirmative answer.

"Sure. What have you been thinking about for ways to bring tourists here?"

"What are the main things we lack?"

"Lack? Let's not focus on what you lack. Think about what you have that would draw tourists. Your autonomous region, Nei Menggu, has everything forests, wetlands, reindeer, desert, rugged mountains, the magnificent Yellow River, precious stones, rare earth minerals, and the amazing double-humped camels. You have unique cultures in ethnic groups with customs, farms, and foods. Inner Mongolia Autonomous Region is the best place to learn pure Mongolian language and culture. You also have calligraphy artists who create poems in their beautiful writing."

The students' expressions showed relief and hope that their area would gain visitors and advance in tourism. Thomas spoke and the class fell silent. They knew that besides teaching, he often translated for Mongolian and Chinese leaders when English emerged as a need for local government leaders speaking with Germans, Australians, and the French. Thomas told us that he found it easier to understand the way Europeans spoke English over the Australians. "I could understand only a few words of the Australians."

Thomas told the whole class, "There are important plans for Wuhai. I think in ten years, we will be an outstanding cultural center with museums, parks, more people, businesses, global connections, and waterpower. This will bring many visitors."

"In ten years?" Jeff asked. Jeff had grown up in the most northeastern part of China, Heilongjiang. In informal conversation of our English corner evenings, we had learned more about Jeff than most of the other students. Jeff's home area bordered Russia. The winter ice sculpture festival in the capital city of Harbin was attended by people from around the world.

Jeff had gone to college in Harbin. When he graduated, he had no job lined up, so, as is the case with other Chinese students who had no definite plans, he was assigned a position by the government based on his degree in English. He was sent to live and work in western Inner Mongolia. There, he met a young Chinese woman born and raised in Wuhai. They married, and now they called Wuhai home.

I didn't know why someone with Jeff's skill had been

assigned to a vocational middle school. China did not have enough places in universities for all the young people who wanted to attend college. Job growth had increased in construction and factory work, but not in areas people thought of as professional careers or expressive artistic options.

The SEP students knew that the country's economy was growing while jobs for their students were not. Even some of the SEP teachers said they would change careers if they had the option for higher pay. They had the intelligence and desire to try other professions, but choices rarely appeared for individuals in the People's Republic.

"Yes, ten years is probable." Thomas continued, "City plans have advanced for connecting businesses to other countries. We have a region that can grow special grapes because of hot days and cool nights. The city leaders are seeking some business interests for wine. They also have plans for building a dam on the Yellow River. Studies for this project have started. When a dam is built, that will change and increase possibilities for farming, water activities, and power in the city."

"Thomas makes good points that should encourage all of you. The Yellow River, right here where the curve touches Wuhai, is a great attraction. You already have some boats that give rides on the river. People around the world have heard about the Yellow River. Tours along the river would definitely interest people, with or without the dam."

"But the Yellow River runs all through China, Ms. Virginia. It starts high in Xizang." This student's comment reminded me that Tibet now had to be called Xizang. Tibet was one of those three Ts we knew not to mention.

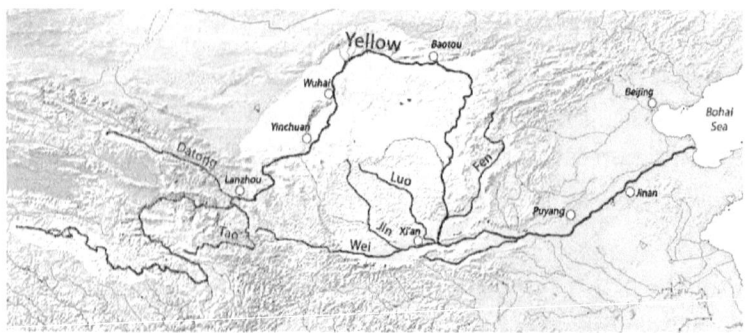

The Yellow River in the People's Republic of China

"Tell me more about what you know about your famous Yellow River. Just call out facts loudly and clearly." Amity wanted us to have the SEP participants speak out loud as often as possible. The spontaneous enthusiastic participation delighted me.

"It is the second longest river in the country."

"It crosses six provinces and two of the autonomous regions."

"My grandmother said it is called China's Sorrow because of floods."

"The Yellow River is longer than fifty-four hundred kilometers."

I had to interrupt them because they needed to know tourists from the US were not good at switching from our measurement system to metrics.

"Think of more facts you can call out, but I need to remind you that while people from the US like to travel, they often do not know a second language well and they are not good at converting their measurements into metrics. If you print or share information for tourists from the US, you will need to let them know that fifty-four hundred kilometers is about 3,355 miles. Also make sure to give temperatures in

Fahrenheit and Celsius because we in the US do not easily convert Celsius to Fahrenheit."

Some of the class looked quite surprised, but they were only quiet for a couple of moments before calling out more facts.

"It is called the Yellow River because of the color of the sediment it carries."

"The Yellow River sediment is carried all the way to the Bohai Sea."

Thomas interrupted, "A dam here will cut the amount of sediment that goes toward the sea, just as the dam at Henan did. A dam will create a huge lake and help this area."

"But the Yellow River will still flow strong."

"The Chinese name is *Huang He*."

"Yes, and it has waterfalls in some provinces."

"There are mountains, plains, temples and caves along the river."

"I have visited islands in the river."

"Some small islands in the river have ancient worship stones. I visited one with my grandparents."

"Some of the islands have rare plants and berries good for health."

A lull fell. The class seemed surprised by how many facts they called out in loud clear English. I also hoped that they felt a bit of awe for the amazing river that curved around their city.

"Thank you all! You did a wonderful job not just speaking English but in educating me about the Yellow River."

Thomas continued, "We have plans for new businesses, new living districts, new buildings for our city government, for two museums, bridges, and roads."

"You sound pretty sure this can all be done in ten years," Cassie remarked still in the loud, clear tone they had used to call out facts. She was smiling, but her words seemed like a challenge. I looked at Cassie and then at the class. *Which of them*, I wondered, *regularly talked to Mr. Wang about our class activities and discussions.*

Could any of our assistants have that role? I glanced at Erdeen. Maybe the young teacher who wanted to get ahead and would participate in everything, like Cassie, would describe the class content? Maybe the quietest member of the class who said little but took notes? Maybe even Thomas?

"Yes. I am sure." Thomas replied. "Our leaders in Wuhai and Hohhot have planned in detail. They have strong plans and will have government support."

Thomas had such fluency in English. I wondered how much longer he would be a teacher. I guessed the local, regional, or even national government would move him away from his teaching to work in an official role. While the class did a closing activity in writing, that I would check later in the evening, I thought about our team visit to Thomas and Penny's home.

Thomas and his wife of one year, Penny, invited us to their home for supper. They lived in an older community not far from the school. Thomas met us at the school and led us to their home, one of many attached homes in a layout of connected buildings that formed a square. The outside of their community square presented few windows, and no doors. Residents had a key to open an iron gate that fit well into an arched brick doorway.

Thomas unlocked the gate, held it open for us and made sure it shut tight. I wondered if security might be a problem. Or perhaps like the old barracks being torn down at our host school, this brick community had been built when groups craved safety from warring factions.

We followed Thomas across a wide grass square in the center of their community. Tables used for playing games like Chinese chess had wooden chairs or benches near them. These were set on the corners of the square. When Thomas noticed us looking around, he said, "The center area is kept clear because many people use it for exercise, like tai chi in the morning."

While we nodded at this information, he turned and pointed to the opposite side of this inner square. We saw a low brick building with no visible windows, but two doors, one on either end. "If you need the toilet, Penny or I will lead you there. They are community toilets, sinks, and showers. One side is for men, and one is for women."

I don't remember that we said anything. We just nodded in acknowledgment. Silently, we walked on behind him. Were the other people on my team thinking about these two young teachers and everyone else in their complex sharing a community bathroom? Thomas and Penny had jobs as professionals after completing university, but they did not have a home with a bathroom of their own. I think the whole team was surprised. Did Thomas and Penny even have running water in their home?

We followed Thomas as he stepped onto a wide gray stone that served as the step into their house. Penny greeted us with her usual beautiful smile. The room we entered had living room furniture in the area closest to the door. Thomas took his outside shoes off and slipped into a simple sandal worn inside a house. Since we did not bring our slippers with us, we kept our shoes on. Thomas and Penny did not ask us to remove them.

A dining area appeared at the back of this room. On the wall to our right was a very large wedding portrait of Penny and Thomas. They both wore traditional outfits.

"That is a wonderful portrait," Doug said.

"You both look good in any outfits," Kathryn added.

"Your dress is beautiful!" Tia exclaimed with a sigh. "I hope to buy that style dress, but not a fancy one for a wedding. Ms. Emily found a woman who makes such dresses. I will go be measured to have one made before we leave."

"I am going do that too," Kathryn announced. None of us knew she had that plan. Her figure was stout, not like Penny's or Tia's slender shapes.

"Oh, you may, I have the dress in our bedroom." Without any hesitation, Penny led us into the bedroom she and Thomas shared. It was as big as the first room we had entered. The bricks in this room, as they had been in the other room, were painted a soft creme color. The floor was cement in both rooms, but carpet was placed near the bed. To our right stood a piece of furniture that reminded me of the wardrobe in the C. S. Lewis, *Chronicles of Narnia*. Penny's wedding dress hung over the head of the bed on a frame like my quilting friends used to display their quilts.

Qipao dress and Male Cheongsam robe

"That looks like it would fit me," Jaye said.

Alarmed, I guessed her next words.

"Penny, may I try it on?" Jaye sounded confident that Penny would say yes.

Tia and Kathryn looked as surprised as I felt. Doug suddenly broke into a coughing fit. I hoped it would distract Penny from even considering Jaye's question.

"Yes. I can lower the frame." Penny started toward the wall.

I found my voice, "No, no, Penny. You must not. It is too precious. Jaye can try on a dress of that style when Tia goes to have one made." I tried to sound casual, but inside I was fuming. Penny was living up to the generous hospitality of an outstanding host. I couldn't believe Jaye would ask that question. I didn't care if I sounded disapproving.

Doug said, "We have gifts. Let us go back into the other room. They are in the bag we left there." Doug turned and managed to swiftly shepherd us out of the bedroom as capably as an Australian shepherd dog.

I felt thankful that we had gotten away from any embarrassment with Jaye trying on Penny's wedding dress. Doug had carried a bag with our gifts when we walked with Thomas from the school to this little enclosed community. In his afternoon browsing through stores in the main downtown area, Doug had found a store that carried some international tins and jars of treats. We had given him some money and he had bought a variety for a gift from us for Thomas and Penny.

We walked to the ochre couch because of the large end table next to it. Doug had put the bag on the table when we went into the bedroom. Now he said, "Please have a look. These gifts are from all of us."

The bag held taffy from Turkey, peaches preserved in whiskey from Scotland, pistachios from Spain, and olives from Italy. Each item elicited questions from Thomas or Penny, so we spent some time standing and talking.

Meanwhile delicious scents came from the kitchen. Penny said, "Please wait a moment before you sit at the table."

She stepped away from us, and Thomas followed. When they came back from the kitchen, he carried a large basin of water, and she held a linen hand towel.

Feeling like we had stepped back in time, we each rinsed our hands in the basin and used the towel Penny offered. Their matter-of-fact graciousness for what they had to offer humbled me. I felt a chastening guilt for what I took for granted and for the aspects of my 1896 house that I focused on in complaints. Silly concerns. With this couple, I saw

God working to awaken a healthier perspective and to increase my gratitude.

"Please have a seat," Penny said as they left the room with the basin and towel.

I took a seat that faced the kitchen. On the far wall, near the window, I could see a water pump and sink set into a wooden cabinet beneath it. The kitchen walls were the same cream color that we had seen in the rest of the home.

As Thomas put a platter with a lamb roast on the table, he said, "We have a coal stove and coal heat, but we did get a refrigerator when the city put electricity into our community." The lamb roast was so tender, it fell apart at the touch of the *kuaizi.*

Penny put down a cool fruit dish with wild berries, currants, and pine nuts. The wonderful roast, along with the fruit and nut dish presented traditional items of this region, and other dishes already on the table showed that this couple adhered to the belief that every excellent dinner should have flavors salty, spicy, sour, sweet, and bitter.

Penny was 100 percent Han Chinese, and Thomas seemed to appreciate the flavor array of Chinese traditional cooking. He had moved up to a top school's English department in Wuhai. Now, with extra work for city officials, he would undoubtedly continue on an upward path. Thomas's skills had high value.

Dessert was watermelon, the most popular fruit in the city and maybe in the country. We had seen watermelon at every meal in Nanjing, and now it was being served here. For some reason our team had a mistaken impression that watermelon was a popular summer fruit for the US, a Fourth of July essential. We had not known that watermelon often appeared as a treat elsewhere, and in China this summer, we had seen it and enjoyed it at almost every meal.

Thomas and Penny had been raised differently. Since Thomas was a Mongolian, he had brothers and sisters. Ethnic minority groups were small compared to the dominant Han ethnic group. Minorities had no limit on the number of children they could have.

Penny, being Chinese, was an only child. Because Thomas was Mongolian, he and Penny had freedom to choose to have more than one child. I wondered if they would.

Conversation flowed with questions and answers. This dinner had all we had hoped for in gaining a view into the daily life of Wuhai and its teachers. We answered many questions from Thomas and Penny too. And then Kathryn brought up what I had hoped we could all avoid for the evening.

As our evening was winding down, Kathryn asked to go to the toilet. It was getting dark, so Penny picked up a battery-powered lantern, and led the way to the communal toilets and showers. When they returned, we said our thanks, sincerely grateful for their hospitality.

Thomas led us back to the school, but we didn't talk much. He and Penny, on their limited income, had created a delicious feast for us. As newlyweds and full-time teachers, they had sixty to seventy students in each class, a tiring responsibility for any conscientious and caring teacher. At their schools, Thomas and Penny shared office space with three to five other teachers. They worked long days, seven until noon, and then three until six. Often teachers worked in their shared office area at their school during the afternoon break or for some time after the school day.

Thomas and Penny lived in a building that formed a community of apartment dwellers within its brick walls. They had three rooms, cement floors, recently added electricity, coal for cooking and heat, few windows, and one small sink where they pumped water like one of my grandmothers had done in her home in rural Maine, and my other grandmother had done in her home in rural Italy.

Millions of people lived simply with daily routines that took us back in time. Humbling. How ungrateful I had been for every modern convenience I had in my home.

When Thomas said goodnight after we entered the host school grounds, he shook hands with each of us and thanked us for visiting his home. We thanked him, said cheerful goodnights. We stood quietly and watched him walk away after he spoke with the guard at the front gate.

"That was a wonderful evening, even seeing the communal bathroom was interesting. I am glad we do not have to cope with that in this dormitory. I am tired, and I'm going right back to the dorm and to bed," Kathryn announced. Tia agreed and walked away with Kathryn.

"You two doing any conversation on the steps of the dorm tonight?" Jaye asked.

Doug said, "No. We announced to the afternoon classes that we would not meet this evening."

"Well then, I guess I'll go back to the dorm now too."

Doug and I followed more slowly. We could see that Jaye was in the dorm before we were halfway across the area that would one day be beautifully landscaped. Right now, it still had remains of the deconstructed old buildings and piles of rubble. Emily told us that all the old buildings and rubble would be gone by September.

"Doug, don't you wish we could see this school when all the new buildings and landscaping is done?"

"I don't really think about that. We'll be home and busy with our new semester."

"But don't you wonder about people like Thomas and Penny and all our other students? Don't you wish you could see how they're doing in five years, or in ten years? Thomas predicts that Wuhai will double in size. He believes there'll be major new business investments here, a dam on the Yellow River, new buildings, communities, and even museums."

"Virginia, you might find it hard to believe, but I don't wonder about any of it. I have done many short-term volunteer projects. I do what I can while I'm there, show respect and concern for my students and responsibilities. But when I leave, that's it. I appreciate the experience, but I go on to other responsibilities, people, and projects. I don't think it is helpful to become emotionally involved with people we will never see again. You should try to develop emotional distance in short-term work."

"Do you think you'll work with Amity again?"

"I will, but it will be in a different location, far from Wuhai. I will give my attention to that location, team, and students."

"But wouldn't you ever want to come back to Wuhai, either before or after the new teaching assignment? I mean if you come all the way to China and can afford it at all in time or money, wouldn't you want to return here?"

"There are many wonderful people and provinces. Even though this is called an Autonomous Region, people regard it as a province. If you come to China again, enjoy the new area. Don't go out of your way to spend money and time returning to a former location. You should not assume that just because our students are attentive and friendly, that we really matter to them. I doubt they will think much about us after we leave. We are just a unique experience for them, foreign teachers in a program their principals told most of them to attend. We can hope our work will help them to feel renewed and more capable in their work as English teachers."

"Doug, that emotional distance escapes me. People who touch my life in special encounters stay with me. No matter the time that passes or the distance between us, they are a part of my life. I wonder about them and pray for them. Since childhood, I have always wanted to know the rest of a story, especially about people who make an imprint on my mind and heart."

"You'll need to get over that if you continue to do short-term work with groups like Amity." Doug said this with a smile as we arrived at the dorm. He did not greet the head housekeeper who sat outside at the far end of the wide porch steps like she did most evenings. He seemed preoccupied and went inside.

I said a simple good evening, *W ǎnshàng h ǎo*. Then I turned to look out over the school grounds toward the modern administration building and beyond that to the track. The air was so much cooler in the evening, often down in the seventies. With no streetlights or business lights to dim the view of the sky, we could look up at the constellations and sequins of stars on midnight blue velvet sky.

Sitting down on a cool marble step near the housekeeper, I was glad I had at least said good evening in Chinese. She said something to me, and I responded with a phrase I had learned from the Pimsleur CD. I thought I was saying 'I'm sorry, I don't understand.'

Her eyes widened. She smiled and said more to me. I just repeated what I thought was, 'I'm sorry, I don't understand.' She smiled even more, then laughed. She got up, came to me, and patted me on the back. It seemed a sympathetic touch.

Then she said goodnight. I understood that and said it back to her. She still giggled when she left me. I hoped I could find out at breakfast, from one of our students, what I had said that caused the head housekeeper to smile, laugh, and pat me sympathetically.

Chapter 18

Misunderstanding and Knowing

W hen I woke up, I remembered right away making the housekeeper laugh by telling her that I did not understand what she said to me. I hoped I could repeat to one of breakfast companions exactly what I had said to the housekeeper. I wanted to know what I had said. With tonal language, like Chinese, a person can easily say something wrong or embarrassing.

By the time I arrived at breakfast, many other ideas filled my mind. I thought of my conversation with Doug and wondered how he could disconnect so easily from his short-term teaching experiences, from the people, and from the place. He saw that as a practical strength. I didn't want that ability.

I would love to see if the plans Thomas had shared with us came true for Wuhai. How would all these SEP participants be doing? How many of them would live in the new Wuhai that Thomas described? Was there any way I could learn about how their careers and the city developed? Would the economy drop or rise with the new plans for a dam and whole new sections of the city? Would people aim to move into the new part of the city? Would they want to share emails with us? Could they email us? The government had control over any internet communications.

If I kept in touch with some of these teachers through letters or email, would I learn about Wuhai's developments? Not even all our SEP students had email. Cell phones were the main method of communication. China's remote areas, like many countries, skipped land lines and offered Voice over Internet Protocols, VOIP. Our students showed surprise that we did not bring cell phones with us from our highly developed first world country. They did not realize that land-line telephones held people back from fully embracing the everywhere possibilities of cell phones.

When I arrived in the faculty dining room for breakfast, Emily, Erdeen, Doug, and Walt were already there. We greeted one another with *Nihao.*

"I have a question for all the Chinese speakers here," I said as I joined them at the table. "Last night I spoke briefly with the housekeeper. She was sitting outside when I decided to rest on the steps. I greeted her, *Wan shang hao.* Then she said something to me, a few sentences.

"I said to her. *Wo bu zhidao,* because I thought that means I don't understand. She smiled, like you are smiling now. She said more to me. I repeated, *wo bu zhidao,* and she laughed and said goodnight. Why did she laugh when I said, I don't understand?"

Erdeen and Walt looked at Emily. She was smiling too. "Ms. Virginia, if you say *wo bu ming bai,* that means I do not understand."

"And I said *wo bu zhidao.*"

"That is more like saying, I don't know anything."

172

We all had a good laugh. The foreign teacher had essentially said, she knew nothing. She had an empty head. Pimsleur's Chinese had shades of meaning to master.

Others arrived to have breakfast, and I realized the day would zoom by again. It was a Friday, a half day. Today June had invited me to go to meet her parents when our morning classes concluded.

* * *

June took me to have lunch with her parents. She frequently had lunch with them, and they asked questions about the foreign teachers. June told me her parents had looked through the Amity textbook and wanted to know what each foreign teacher presented. Today they would see a foreign teacher for themselves.

"My parents are retired. My mother worked for one of the smaller department stores in the center of town, and my father had the responsibility of a janitor at the hospital. Their apartment is very small. They live simply on their retirement."

"I understand. It will be an honor to meet them."

"They have their main meal in the middle of the day. Many people do."

"Some people in my country do that too."

They lived in a complex of seven story apartment buildings. In Nanjing we'd been told that no buildings had elevators unless they had more than nine floors. This arrangement of buildings, one level or multiple stories, created communities. The whole culture had rare instances of anything approaching individualism. This set of buildings seemed modern and plain. I saw no outdoor communal building, but they had a green square as large as the one by Thomas and Penny's home, open for exercise, games, and socializing.

"What floor do your parents live on?"

"The second. When people are older, or if they have some health difficulty, they can usually get an apartment on a lower floor." The cement block building was painted light green. Trim around the windows and the entire metal door was dark green.

Inside, the hallway floor and steps were unpainted cement. A black iron railing, plain, and more like a grip bar ran alongside the stairs. The air smelled of garlic, spices, and summer heat. As we climbed the stairs, I admired how people here adapted to the summer heat. Air-conditioning did not exist in this building.

June knocked once on a painted metal door, dark green like the outside building trim. It opened immediately. This home also had a main room with an area for a couch, chair, lamp, end table, and TV to our right. The left portion of the room had two windows above a counter that went the length of the wall except for the area that had a stove and a sink. A small white electric refrigerator was to our left and the top of it had a stack of red and white patterned bowls on it. The design pattern appeared often in Chinese restaurants I had visited in the US.

Between the back of the couch and the kitchen area was a square wooden table with four wooden chairs. June's mother took both my hands in hers and drew me toward the table. "*Huānyíng, Huānyíng!*"

Her husband appeared from the bedroom that was out of sight. "*Huānyíng, Huānyíng*," he said as he tipped his head in a simple bow toward me.

I said, "*Xiexie*," and bowed in the same way toward him

and his wife. His wife talked very fast, and it was clear that she had told June everyone should sit at the table. June's father sat with his back to the room I could not see. There was another door slightly open, and I saw it was a bathroom. June sat to my right, with her mother to my left, and I sat with my back to the apartment's door and across from June's father.

At each place but mine, I saw chopsticks. There was a tea pot and four of the small handleless porcelain china cups used to drink tea. They matched the pattern of the stack of bowls atop the little refrigerator.

On the table were four shallow, oval, porcelain bowls. They held vegetable dishes that fit the flavors of sour, sweet, spicy, and bitter, some due to herbs, others due to dressings. I guessed this meant the main dish would be salty. A pickle dish with finely chopped narrow cucumbers in a sour sauce, sweet cherry tomatoes, some bitter herbs flavoring a bok choy dish, and something like coleslaw with chilis, ginger, and garlic, looked as delicious as anything in the fancy restaurants we had visited.

June's mother went to the stove. From a medium sized pot, she dished out chicken and rice soup into bowls stacked next to the little two-burner stove. The scent made my mouth water when she put it down in front of me, serving me first as the guest. Then, with my attention on her, June's matronly mother smiled broadly and drew a fork and spoon out of her apron pocket. With a grand flourish and a wide smile, she gave me the utensils. They were stainless steel and new. She spoke, and June translated.

"We bought these especially for you, our guest, to use. We are thankful for your work with our daughter and for honoring us in coming to our home."

Getting-acquainted conversation followed. Somehow amid the translating, June managed to eat her meal. Our lunch time evaporated like steam.

June's mother left the table with my two stainless steel implements as June and I got ready to leave. We could hear her washing them in the kitchen. She returned with them wrapped in an envelope she had made of paper. June translated her mother's words, as she had during the whole lunch time conversation.

"Please take these. We may never have a Westerner visit our home again. When you use them, you can think of us."

"*Xie xie.* You are very kind. It has been an honor to visit you. The lunch was delicious. You are a wonderful cook."

"Now you should leave so that you still have time to rest," June's father said. He had such a deep bass voice. I thought of how our casual conversational evenings at the school had unexpectedly included some music. June had brought her husband. Yuze, who played the guitar and knew many songs in English.

After hugging her mother goodbye, June took my hand, and we walked back to the dorm. We would have time to rest and then another new unexpected experience. A group of teachers, two from each of our homeroom classes, would arrive at three thirty to take us to Wuhai's only bowling alley in their city of 278,000 people. The cost of this entertainment did not fall only on the students escorting us to the bowling alley. Classmates had chipped in so that everyone could bowl at least two games, rent shoes, and have snacks.

The students who could not attend wanted to hear every detail via phone and even more wanted descriptions in class on Monday. None of these students had ever bowled. No one knew who owned the bowling alley or who had an idea to build it, but they exhibited buoyant happiness over treating us to something we had all done in our hometowns.

When I reached my room and sat down on the bed, I glanced out the window and saw another hot and sunny day. I still felt grateful to be warm each day. Our team had grown used to the heat during the days. For our eyes, we still used the air conditioners in our room, but we did not set them on very low temperatures. I guessed the bowling alley might feel chilly to us.

Before I took my nap, I retrieved the fork and spoon from my purse and laid them on the night table. Looking at them made me think of the basic information in the Amity training sessions. People in China ask questions no American would bluntly ask: How old are you? How much do you earn? But there is also a common question, 'Did you eat?' that is asked as a greeting.

Why is this a casual common greeting? As typical as asking in the US, *How are you?* The question, *Did you eat?* connects to hospitality and relationships. If a person has food, they're all right. Food in China plays a main role in life and shows care for another person. At times in China's history, vast famine occurred. Chinese people know that their country still has many people who do not have enough food.

June's parents' home was so small and neat. It exuded homey comfort. The meal had been homemade and scrumptious. I thought of my parents and friends who had declared, "Don't go to China. It's dangerous and dirty. The people won't be friendly."

What could I tell them about my time in Wuhai that might change their opinion?

Chapter 19

Highs and Lows of Looking Down

"I wish someone had told us that people dress up to go bowling here," Tia sounded embarrassed as she looked at her casual clothes. We had arrived at the bowling alley via pedicabs. These three wheeled cabs have one seat that can be shared by two average size people or three skinny people. They have a fabric roof and the pedicab runs on the pedaling power of the driver.

Before we left the pedicab, we could see our students in dressier clothing than they wore to classes. They had not cared that we still wore our classroom outfits from the morning. The bowling alley looked as spacious and clean as the best bowling alleys we had at home.

"You will probably beat us badly," Jeff announced as we prepared to start.

"Why do you think that?" I asked.

"Ms. Jaye is a physical education teacher, Mr. Doug is strong, and you, Ms. Virginia, said you have taken youth groups bowling. Ms. Tia and Ms. Kathryn said they have bowled many times."

"That doesn't mean we are great at it." Jaye laughed. Only Jaye had a high score when we finished playing two games each. Jeff and Cassie had the next highest scores. When we left to return to the school, our student hosts thanked us so much that it felt like we had treated them to bowling.

* * *

"Field trip number two, tomorrow. Are you ready for it?" Jaye asked at our Friday evening team meeting.

"I don't think it'll include many shopping opportunities," Kathryn's expression reminded me of a hound dog.

"You never know, Kathryn. Little shops are tucked away in every section of this city and even in some of the small clusters outside of the city." Doug said.

"I'm nervous about sand surfing." Tia sounded worried. "I know Thomas thinks we can all do it, but I've never done any kind of surfing or skateboarding."

"We'll have a short trip on the river and there's a restaurant on the river where they'll take us for a meal of fresh fish and locally grown wild foods." Doug sounded as if he was looking forward to the next day.

"Wild foods?" Jaye asked as she made a deep frown. "Sounds dangerous."

Doug shook his head as if in disbelief. "Jaye, we have already eaten many local wild foods. Those are called forageable foods. Pine nuts, berries, wild grains, mushrooms, and even fish can count as forgeable."

"Okay, I can eat that stuff."

"At the Nanjing training, I remember Amity told us that host schools usually took teams out to see their cities and the nearby region, but not necessarily each week. It sure seems like our hosts really want us to have a good look at their land and culture." Agreement followed my comment, then the meeting broke up.

I decided to go outside for a little while. Sitting on the wide cool steps and looking at the vast expanse of sky relaxed me, even as I wished I had studied constellations. The housekeeper and one of her assistants were seated on little wooden stools near the entrance to her apartment.

I said good evening, *Wǎnshàng hǎo*, and they returned the greeting to me. Then she said more and smiled. This time I could tell her, "*Wǒ bù míngbái*."

She nodded and did not laugh. I felt glad I could show her that I had learned a little more about her language.

The Saturday of our second field trip had a leisurely start with breakfast not served until 7:30. The breakfast companions were Thomas, Penny, Marge, Kent, John, VP Zhu, and Principal Chen. We hadn't seen him at meals for a while.

"Marge, is Principal Chen going on the field trip with us today?"

"Oh yes. He grew up near the river. He enjoys any chance to take people to see the variety of land around the water."

I noticed that, like me, the female members of our team ate lightly. Not Doug or the locals. They dove into the dishes taking a bit of everything, baozi, red bean porridge, hard boiled eggs, noodle soup, fruit, milk tea, and fried bread.

With the help of our students, we let the principals know that we looked forward to a day of local exploration along the

Yellow River. It took only forty minutes by car to arrive at a hill that sloped down to a dock low in the river. A boat with a small cabin and benches on each side of its deck took us across to a shoreline of reeds.

The reeds reminded me of a tall fringe wall and looked like bullrushes I'd seen along the Nile. The reeds appeared taller than all the women on this field trip. We had to follow a winding path before arriving at the desert. The path through the reeds had some planks that allowed us to avoid walking in water or muddy sediment.

As we walked, the scents changed as much as the sights and textures. Flowing river water morphed to smells of earthy marsh, plant growth at the edge of the marsh, and moist clay. Like a wide border, ochre clay stretched between the edge of the reeds and the slope of the first huge golden sandhill. The scent of the sand dunes, slightly mineral and a bit salty, could have provided an attractive after shave for men. The dunes rose in awesome orange-gold layers.

On the first low rise of sand, Doug and Kathryn stopped and looked up. The dunes were much taller than any of us had expected. Doug and Kathryn declined the sand surfing activity. Principal Chen and VP Zhu would wait with them while the rest of us tried this sand challenge.

Thomas carried a large leather bag, large enough to hold a full set of golf clubs, but Thomas's bag was rectangular. He carried the bag easily up the dunes. Though he appeared as a tall and too thin, he walked up the dunes with the aplomb of a young Genghis Kahn.

We climbed the tallest dune much more slowly than Thomas. That effort seemed like more of a workout than a Stair-Master exercise machine. Climbing the sand dunes made walking on the flat, dry, sandy beaches of the East

Coast in the US seem easy. This sand was different from any I had seen or felt from Miami to Eastport.

At the top of the highest dune, Thomas opened the bag and pulled out seven pieces of cardboard that looked like boards. They reminded me of extra wide skateboards, although they were not as long. They had the thickness of cardboard used in making boxes, and their color almost matched the dunes.

Looking down to Doug and Kathryn, we saw that Principal Chen and VP Zhu had walked away from them to the edge of the sand to smoke. I didn't know if they'd guessed that none of our team smoked, or if they had heard about our negativity toward smoking from students.

Smoking seemed prevalent among men, and Kathryn had thoroughly proclaimed the dangers of smoking in one of her first afternoon health discussions. I took a different tack by telling them that tobacco companies had lost millions of customers in the West because people could see how smoking led to cancer. Those companies would advertise and sell more now to people of Asia. They wanted money.

Thomas placed one piece of carboard on the sand's surface and said, "I've been doing this since I was a primary student. My older brothers taught me how."

"Thomas is good at this. He will be a good teacher." Kent betrayed confident enjoyment. She said, "Thomas taught me and my husband how to sand surf years ago."

Penny and Marge nodded affirmation and had broad smiles.

"My eldest brother told me that in ancient Egypt they used wooden boards to sand surf. You can try it standing or kneeling or sitting." Thomas smiled in a way that showed he believed we would succeed at sand surfing.

"I want to sit," Tia announced.

"I want to try standing," Jaye's preference did not surprise any of us.

"I'll start by standing, but if I fall, I'll try again, sitting, like Tia. Looking down from up here makes it look higher than it felt walking up here." I hoped Thomas would approve of my choice and understand my feelings.

Thomas nodded and continued with his instructions. "Line up beside me and leave the width of both your arms between each person. This is a tall dune, but not steep. Ms. Virginia, if you fall off, just come to the top. You can try it again sitting down. Come here to the edge, stand on the board and..."

Tia's squeal of delight as she began the slide down this tallest dune caused the rest of us to laugh. We watched her ride on her nearly invisible board since its color almost matched the sand. Tia laughed louder than any of us all the way down. It was the first time I could remember hearing her wholehearted laughter.

When Tia reached the bottom of the dune and slid onto the flat area where sand touched clay, Doug and Kathryn applauded her. Tia picked up the board and began to climb to the top again. After just her first step she asked them, "Are you sure you don't want to try? It feels wonderful!"

Doug still resisted the undignified activity. Kathryn gave in to the lure of the experience. In an hour we four women and our assistants had multiple good rides. Only Thomas and Jaye made every slide standing up.

Sand surfing in the desert near the Yellow River

* * *

When the boat took us back to the Wuhai side of the river, the twelve-passenger van that had transported us arrived. The next stop, Marge told us, was a riverside restaurant owned and run by a family Principal Chen knew. The view of the river and the desert to our right and the small farms with mountains to our left reminded us of how unique Wuhai seemed from what we had learned about China. Although we stayed along the river, the shore rose in hills and finally to something that looked like bluffs.

The restaurant stood on thick stilts that allowed half of it to be out over the river. That part, maybe a third of the building, had a roof made of reeds and some tables for customers. The other two thirds rested solidly on a bluff. Surprising to us, the whole building was only slightly larger than one of the classrooms we each worked in. On the land behind the building were outdoor stone grills and clay ovens.

A man who was grilling fish turned and waved. He shouted something, and as Principal Chen led us toward the building, a woman and a young man came to greet us.

They led us up a few steps into the restaurant. To our right, a bar made of wood had a high polish, maybe polyurethane, and decorations behind the bar mixed Chinese and Mongolian symbols. Flowering plants drew the eye to the wide doors to the deck, and then outside.

In our time in China, we did not meet anyone over twenty-five who enjoyed having a meal in a big open room full of strangers like our usual restaurant experience in the US. They preferred a private room for their group, like we had in the faculty dining room at the school. The tables in this restaurant had been aligned so that our whole group could sit together. This arrangement provided a dining room just for us.

The owners of this family restaurant were Chinese, and so they had followed the government rules and had only one child, a son, but they also had employees. One of the employees played the guzheng, a long wooden instrument with more than twenty-one strings. We had their music during the two hours of our lunch. Principal Chen ordered for everyone, and fortunately no noodles had to be noisily inhaled.

We had fish and potato soup in bowls that we lifted to drink the broth. I didn't worry if I made a loud noise. I aimed only to match the noise level of Principal Chen, VP Zhu, Thomas, and John. My teammates, other than lifting the bowls to drink the broth, ate like they would have at home with little to no noise.

Catfish isn't a fish I like, but it is common in the Yellow River. We had spicy roasted catfish. Then a grilled scaleless

185

carp arrived surrounded by roasted barley and wild onions. Large platters with strips of tofu and something called Mandarin fish were placed on the table along with dishes of cabbage and chilis, plus bowls of vegetables blended with soy sauce, ginger, and minced garlic. Individual bowls of rice also arrived.

"Rice," Jaye said loudly.

"Principal Chen heard that you all thought rice was served with every meal in China. He realized that noodles at every meal did not delight you. So today we have rice and in your remaining weeks, the school will serve rice and noodles," John explained. I saw Principal Chen nod and give his infrequent slight smile. With such small indications after translations, I firmly suspected that the principal understood English to at least an intermediate level.

The owner, along with his wife, and son, talked with Principal Chen before we left the restaurant. I saw VP Zhu hand an envelope to the owner.

"Now that we are all full, we should take a walk. It is a healthy custom to walk at least one hundred steps after a big meal," Marge announced. Before we left, we said thank you to the owner and his family.

"Are we going to walk near here?" Tia asked.

"No, not here," Penny said as she took Tia's hand. I noticed that Tia's petite body and gentle voice provoked protective actions from our students. "We are going to the most beautiful park back in the city. We can walk through that beautiful park."

Before I got to the van that would take us back into the city, I walked to the edge of the bluffs to look down at the river. It was the worst choice I could have made after our lunch. At the base of the tall bluffs on this side of the river, trash formed a thick soaked line along the river's edge, both in and out of the water, and car size piles of trash formed small hills at the base of the bluff.

It shocked me. At home, I hated to see even scattered trash along roads and highways. How many years had the people with the restaurant been dumping trash over the side of the bluff? What were the river currents like? And when the river flooded did some trash get washed away? None appeared on the other side of the river.

At the bottom of the bluff, layers of garbage appeared in a tall cone-like pile. And it didn't look like it came just from the restaurant. It seemed to be a local dump that could be hidden in the deep indented curve of the base of the bluff. When I turned away from the awful sight, I realized I was the last foreigner to climb into the van.

Principal Chen stood by the van waiting to see me get into the vehicle. I had no way of knowing whether he had seen my shock and disgust as I turned away from the river. He must know how much trash had piled up there and who had dumped it.

And we had eaten above it and not smelled it. How was that possible? I didn't know whether I would tell my team or not. I kept my head up, and tried to maintain a bland expression, while I worked to forget the sight when I had looked back and down. I did not look back again on that day.

Chapter 20

No Random Choice

"We are going to the most beautiful park in Wuhai," Marge announced as our van moved toward the city. "More of your students will be at the park and some will have their middle school students with them. They are excited to meet you."

Wuhai had small parks around the city, in almost every neighborhood. This special large park had sculptures, exercise equipment, fountains, a small museum of local art, a restaurant, a cafe, and a place Doug had wanted to visit, a museum of rocks and crystals.

John and Kent left for their homes when they got out of the van. Jaye and Tia said they'd like to go back to the school. They had no interest in any kind of petrology or minerology, and they had climbed the dunes more times than anyone to squeeze in as many sand surfing rides as possible. Thomas and Penny volunteered to walk them back to the school. VP Zhu walked back with them.

Principal Chen stayed with us listening and watching as we received descriptions of the park and this part of the city from June, Walt, Peter, Cassie, and Erdeen. A few of their best students had come along to meet the foreign teachers and to hear English conversation. Each one was introduced to Principal Chen who made the decision to let them continue along with all of us.

Not until we stepped into the museum did anyone notice that nothing was in English. The museum information only had the Chinese and Mongolian languages. I realized that I had better mention signage needs to the class when we next discussed the topic of preparing for tourists.

We had seen some attempts of signs in English. They had resulted in what Amity said produced Chinglish, odd wording of messages. A restroom for handicapped women could have a sign, Deformed Women Toilet. A sign over a trash can said it was for Evil Rubbish. In a park we saw a sign that said No Strinding, which we guessed was a misspelling of No Striding, and meant No Running.

The rock and crystal museum did not have one sign in any kind of English. Even the most capable SEP students said that if they had their dictionaries, it would be difficult to put the information together. They didn't even know if they could find all the words for the science of rocks and crystals. The embarrassment they revealed due to taking us to a place where they could not explain any of the information caused many of them to frown or blush.

Then Ye, a student of June's who had listened to our conversation, said, "I can stay and help. I like rocks and crystals. I have visited this museum by myself three times. I have looked up the English words for displays here. I thought the work would help expand my English."

We stopped and stared at Ye. He had said this to us in English. Already Ye had stood out to us. He had come with

June, his middle school teacher, and her husband, Yuze, one evening for casual conversation time. Yuze played the guitar and knew many songs in English.

Ye also knew the English songs. We had heard him sing as smoothly as a native speaker of English. To have this seventeen-year-old declare that he had the ability to talk about rocks and crystals never entered our minds. What kind of motivation backed a random choice to study the vocabulary of rocks and minerals?

We started through the museum. At times Ye had long pauses, but the vocabulary came to him. We learned more in the next ninety minutes about the three major mountains ranges, and about the plains, kinds of coal, quartz, kaolinite, gypsum, pyrite, and of rocks and gems with color and facets that captured geological beauty.

Doug often stopped to study the displays. He smiled as Ye spoke of smoky citrine quartz, fluorite on quartz, chocolate dogtooth calcite. Ye knew the names of the range of colors of crystals, lavender, bright pink, pastel hues, and white. Even though I had never had an interest in quartz, crystals, and rocks, these museum displays had impressive beauty. The colors and crevices looked almost magical.

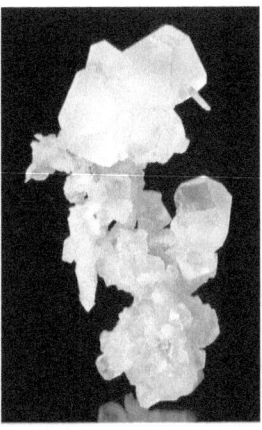

Flourite Crystals Climbing Quartz Octahedron

As Ye explained the information, his teachers listened. I noted Principal Chen's tall figure supervising the cluster around Ye. Did he feel proud that his school had a young man like Ye?

Flourite

Did Ye's facility with English, which was greater than many teachers' proficiency, cause the principal to feel concern about the teachers' skills and motivation to expand their competence with English? I could not discern the answer. Principal Chen excelled in maintaining a bland expression.

I wouldn't say anything to my teammates while we were with the teachers who were our students, but what amazed me most in this whole museum was Ye. Because June had been Ye's middle school teacher, she had seen Ye's advances in English and knew his family. Here we were, just days after Ye and June's husband sang a half-dozen English songs under the gorgeous night sky, and Ye was demonstrating advanced English vocabulary ad fluency. I remembered June told me that Ye struggled taking tests.

In China, the senior high English tests have questions like this: What is the difference between especially and particularly? I told her that I could ask a dozen teachers in my home city, and they would not be able to explain such language details. Ye's English was outstanding. If June had been his English teacher for his middle school years, she should feel proud.

Like Thomas, I saw in Ye an intrinsic motivation to go farther than Wuhai. Ye had a passion to serve his community but also enthusiastic idealism to serve his country. I expected Thomas and Ye would go beyond what they even imagined or hoped for now. How would I ever know what turns their lives would take commensurate with their dreams and abilities? Could I quell my desire to know more of their stories?

Jeff had also brought some of his junior middle school students to the casual conversation evenings. Those thirteen-year-old students' qualities of observation, listening, and trying to use English, had exceeded what some of the teachers of English could do. Jeff said that his best students did well on tests. He concentrated on helping them to know how to take tests. He expected they would have a chance to go to an excellent university.

Which one would go the farthest? Why did I have such a

desire to see how they would advance? Would I have a full chance for a renewed spirit when it seemed unlikely that I would ever see these people again? How did Doug just turn off any desire to see how these students would progress?

Ye's senior year was ahead. Would he be able to score higher on tests than he had in the past? Would he have a chance to go to a university? He worked so hard and had natural people skills. How would I ever know unless I stayed in contact with June who had been his junior middle school teacher and Erdeen who taught Ye now in our host school?

Jeff had told us that his two best students, Koshing and Xiong, came from supportive well-educated families with some economic means, but he assured us that they worked to achieve and learn. In contrast, June had said that her best student, Ye, had loving parents, but he was a late-in-life-child. His mother was a street sweeper, and his father worked in an outdoor market. If China had young heroes from low economic backgrounds, who went on to surprising success, like the Horatio Alger stories, Ye could surely be one.

Doug never talked about other people he had met and worked with in the different countries where he had taught for a year or less. He didn't talk much at all except in his teaching and reviewing of our plans. Even when we sat outside for casual conversation, if anyone asked Doug a personal question, his answer was brief.

I wouldn't ask about his parsimonious personal sharing. Doug probably had a host of reasons he could give me to reject developing deeper connections to the locals. Doug didn't seem cold-hearted as much as guarded.

I wanted to keep caring and building relationships. Even our students' mini stories, that they had shared in discussions reinforced that teachers needed to care about their students. Could I help these students realize the effect they could have on their classes if they could show they cared about more than classwork and test scores? If I really believed there was a purpose, not just chance in life experiences, could I dare trust God would let my plans to revisit Wuhai happen?

My curiosity and appreciation for our students and this whole community had formed a plan to return to China to work with Amity again. If I came back, no matter where I was assigned, I could try to visit Wuhai. I could see the development of lives, careers, and the city.

Teachers had email addresses, and as long as I did not use Gmail, we could exchange communications that way. China did not allow Gmail because Google did not agree to give information on anyone the Chinese government wanted to investigate. Google also remained unwilling to follow China's censorship regulations and desire for digital sovereignty. Only people who purchased a virtual private network, VPN, had global options and VPNs were expensive with temporary effectiveness, to use Gmail.

With ongoing communication, I could provide mentoring for any teachers who wanted more ideas and help with the oddities of English and the tough national exam questions. Wuhai and its people would always be special to me. God could use everything that came into our lives for our good. Sometimes strangers become precious individuals and new friends.

I felt a pang of guilt in my slow recognition that without the move from south Jersey to Central Massachusetts, and the unhappy frustration I felt over my career, I never would have thought of traveling to China. I would not have discovered Amity. I wouldn't have met these teachers and students or been humbled by their work ethic as they lived with simplicity and low pay. I wouldn't have had their stories and future possibilities stir me to find my own team of committed individuals to work in an SEP. I would look for individuals like those I had seen in the Amity training time who worked to prepare together before traveling to China because they were friends.

All of this went through my mind and stayed in my heart as Ye continued in his concentrated effort to describe the value of the largest crystals. Everyone listening learned from him. Standing amidst the incredible beauty of the rocks and crystals and looking at the precious people around me, I said a silent prayer. *"Forgive me for my lack of trust."*

Chapter 21

Desires, Goals, and Hopes

W eek three found most of our team doing well with our schedule and plans. Working with the Amity textbook and presenting our special afternoon topics had built conversation skills. Doug, Tia, Kathryn, and I had found a comfortable pace. Jaye remained a puzzle to all of us as she arrived on time for her classes only once in that week. Kathryn and I had offered to walk to class with her, but she just smiled and said, "Don't worry about me." We did anyway as well as about how the students in her homeroom felt when their teacher was not there until after they all had arrived.

Doug, always prepared, worked conscientiously on every lesson. He gave us no say in his assumption of the role of leader for our team meetings and for interacting with administrators. He held the team meetings, asked questions about lesson plans, and supplies, and helped us gather the extra materials we needed for enrichment activities.

Ye helped all of us gladly. This allowed him more access

to us the foreign native speakers of English, not something any other high school seniors in this city had. Because he knew a wide variety of shop owners and because of his bargaining skills, Ye found any materials we needed and got them for a lower price for us.

His parents had a friend who ran a print shop. That individual knew other small businesses where we could get rolls of newsprint paper and craft materials. Creativity while giving and following directions in a foreign language built crucial communication skills. Ye took the initiative to talk shop owners into lowering their prices to help Wuhai schools. When Ye told us the prices he paid for materials even Emily was surprised.

Like Ye, Thomas and Penny connected to us through unexpected kindnesses and conversations. On Monday evening Thomas and Penny invited us to their house to watch a movie, *Ugly Feet*, about a teacher in a rural town. Only Jaye and I agree to go, and I took a moment before we left to say, "Jaye, please do not ask to try on Penny's wedding gown. That is very inappropriate. Would you do that at home?"

"I have, with some of my friends who got married."

"And did they agree to have you put on their wedding gowns?"

"No, but I thought it was worth a try. I am curious to see if there is any special feeling or if it's just a dress. The red dress Penny has is so dramatic."

"It is gorgeous, but don't ask. All right?"

She just nodded. We bought a basket of fruit as a gift before we took the tricycle style pedicab taxi to Thomas and Penny's community. Thomas waited for us by the gate, and we were welcomed enthusiastically by their neighbors even before we reached Penny and Thomas's front door.

Where they found a movie with English subtitles, I didn't know, but Jaye and I were able to follow the whole story. Ugly Feet is a young teacher who looked very plain. One day a young woman from a city comes to the school for a job as a teacher. Ugly Feet is demoted to be an assistant to this young, smart, stylish, and beautiful city woman.

The beautiful city woman is not suited to provincial life. She has no sense of what her students have in their lives, of their difficulties, or of how to show she cares about having them do well in their lessons. Without Ugly Feet's help, this woman would not have finished one year of teaching in the rural school. She returns to the city, and Ugly Feet gets her old job back. Sadly, the students long for the beautiful city teacher.

Sorry for her poor job as a teacher, the city woman invites Ugly Feet to bring the students to the city as a field trip. Ugly Feet arranges the trip, but when they arrive in the city they're overwhelmed by the differences in sights, sounds, and pace. They're mocked and laughed at by the city people. Ugly Feet and most of her students feel relieved to return to their little country town, although one student looks longingly back at the city.

After the movie, we talked about real and imagined differences between schools in Wuhai, smaller communities, and huge cities like Beijing and Shanghai. Thomas and Penny walked with us to the entrance to their community and thanked us for spending another evening with them.

Thomas called for another tricycle taxi, and he and Penny waited with us until it arrived. Then Thomas gave the taxi driver instructions and money. We were dropped not at the main gate of the school, but at the gate at the end of the alley close to the dorm.

An assistant to the housekeeper sat there all through the evening to be available to open the gate. She did open the gate for us with her usual shy smile. When I got up to my room, I chose several postcards from America and five single dollars to put in an envelope for her. I would give the same to the head housekeeper. They don't tip in China, but these were not tips.

* * *

Classroom time raced onward. Students showed a desire to have more open communication about difficult topics. I thought we were done with such questions but on this Tuesday, I was asked, "Do you think Taiwan should be separate from China?"

Taiwan! Oh dear, another of the T words that we were not supposed to mention or bring into any discussions. The class looked back at me as if to say, *Will you still answer our questions?*

"Separations in countries are sad, but not uncommon." I answered. "Many times, even when there has been a war over differences, separate parts have learned to live beside one another and to build connections with one another. When we had our civil war, Abraham Lincoln said a country divided against itself cannot stand."

"Ms. Virginia, does that mean you think Taiwan will rejoin mainland China?"

"It could happen in part or fully. Many countries that have divided see benefits in cooperating for something like economic advancement. They learn how to trade with each other, like Ireland and England, French Canada and the rest of Canada, Basque Country and Spain, Corsica and France."

"But what do you and your friends think, Ms. Virginia?"

"I have friends who have many different opinions. We do not all agree with one another. But I will tell you, that I would rather see mutual respect, trade, and tourism even if Taiwan stays separate."

Mostly frowning faces looked back at me. What were they thinking? To change the topic, I reminded them that this Wednesday, they would have their last turn to do a role play in English in the large assembly hall. Every class would have groups do presentations. We counted off by five, and they became groups that would create and work on what they would present in their role-play situation.

The distraction worked for several reasons. They were free to create and chat, although they needed to use English. They had always enjoyed role-playing because they could adapt the situations for the shy ones in the group and for the most outgoing. Finally, they liked that the role-play situations could be humorous.

On Wednesday afternoon, we stood together with Emily, Thomas, Marge, Kent, and Ye in the area where all the old buildings had been demolished. Only clearing away the foundation remained. The heat reflected off broken bricks, chunks of wood, and rocks. I wished we had met inside where there was a fan or air-conditioning. How could it be so hot when the sky seemed cloudy?

"Emily, how hot is it now?"

"Forty-one."

"Isn't that a bit over 102 Fahrenheit?"

"Yes."

"Even though it is so hot, the sky is not clear. Is it cloudy today, or is it pollution?"

"Clouds, I think. Wuhai is west of most of the air polluting factories."

"So, it might rain? It hasn't rained since we arrived."

"It rarely rains in July and August. I wish it would rain. Look toward the mountains. Everything will change instantly from just browns and grays to having patches of green if there is rain."

We all looked toward the mountains and at that moment a light rain fell. Only one large dark cloud hung over the school grounds and the mountains, and the rain stopped after ten minutes. I never even thought of getting an umbrella. This rain felt refreshing, and it was magic. That misty rain disappeared, and we saw green patches where there had been none between stones, on the bare dirt patches, and on the sides of the mountains.

"Emily, you're right! Look at the patches of light green in the mountains."

"And here," Doug added. Even on the open areas of the school grounds light-green patches appeared as if the Lucky Charms leprechaun had suddenly visited Wuhai. The magic did not last overnight. In the morning the brown had returned to all the bare earth and the heat rose to one hundred degrees Fahrenheit by noon.

Did such a swift short weather change affect people? I didn't know, but I did know that Tia left her classroom in tears the day after the rain. She made it until the lunch break but left the classroom crying before most of her students recovered from seeing her tears. Delia came to my classroom as my students were leaving and pointed to Tia hurrying over the open ground toward the dorm. I nodded and pushed through the students descending the stairs so I could go after Tia and catch up to her.

* * *

I caught up to Tia when she reached her room. Still wiping tears away, she let me enter behind her and shut the door. She sat on one of the single beds, and I sat on the edge of the other one facing her.

"Tia, what is it?"

"I'm so sorry. We were discussing how important it is for parents to support and encourage children in schoolwork." Her inhalation after this statement was a sob.

I reached out to put a hand on one of her knees and asked gently, "And this really upset you because...?"

"I haven't told anyone what caused me to sign up for Amity. After twenty years, my husband left me. He asked for an uncontested divorce. They go through fast. He said that he wanted to..." She trailed off, then put her face in her hands and cried. I moved to sit beside her and placed my arm around her shoulder. I prayed for Tia to feel some comfort, to have her broken heart heal.

In a minute she finished the statement. "My husband said he wanted to marry the woman who was pregnant with his child. I couldn't have children, even though my husband and I wanted them. His baby with this other woman is due in August. His new love told him she wanted to be married before the baby arrived, so he wanted the quickest divorce. I had no idea he was seeing someone and having an affair. He said he'd been seeing her for almost a year. I never felt so stupid. How did I miss all the signs?"

I did not think Tia expected an answer, so I stayed quietly with her.

"He told me he loves her and wants a family, but he didn't want to adopt a child with me. I suggested that years ago. He said he only wanted a child that he and a woman he loved could conceive. Twenty years of marriage, and it ends. Talking in class about parents helping their children overwhelmed me. I feel so terrible about getting upset in front of my students."

"You had such a hurtful shock, Tia. I'm so sorry. Your students were just concerned about you. You don't have to explain anything to them. Sometimes anyone can recall a memory or experience a feeling that causes tears."

"While they talked about couples parenting, I felt overwhelmed by grief."

"That's understandable."

"I did give him an uncontested divorce. I also found out that many people in our little town knew he was with this woman. It was shameful and embarrassing. Then our church had a presentation on the Amity volunteer program, and I thought, *Yes. I will leave the country to go do some good. I won't have to be home until August.* I wouldn't have to see anyone who knows my husband left me for someone half my age who can give him babies." Tia dissolved into tears again.

We sat quietly for another fifteen minutes. I held her hand and prayed for her to feel strength and that she was not alone. I waited for Tia to say something that would let me know if she needed company for the hours of our break.

"Our team will be having lunch now." She spoke over sniffles.

"Yes, but you don't have to go if you want to stay here

and rest. I can stay with you, or I can go and bring something back for you to eat here."

"Oh, would you do that?"

"Sure. If that's what you want."

"I think it's what I need. I want to do my afternoon work. I can pull myself together. It felt good to tell someone. Thank you for listening and for praying."

Tia made it to her afternoon classes, as she'd planned to. The SEP participants didn't try to find out why Tia had cried. Yes, we had all been asked how old we were, how much money we made, and even the casual social, 'Did you eat?' Now though, weeks into working together, no direct questions were asked of Tia.

Students seemed relieved that Tia returned for the planned afternoon. Our team didn't talk about it at our end of day meeting either. But Doug did shock me when he said near the end of our meeting that we should all hold hands and pray together.

* * *

The day after the revelatory conversation with Tia, Emily asked if we would like to go to the Wuhai city square after dinner. She received an enthusiastic yes from our whole team. We knew the city took pride in having a square that almost matched Tiananmen Square in size. Teachers and students who had come for conversational English joined us at the square. It had cooled down to the mid-eighties by the time we arrived, but families still had children who enjoyed running in and out of the long line of fountains and machines that sprayed mist.

Apartment buildings, restaurants, hotels, a large middle

school, and a museum lined the avenues that framed the city square. The square itself had pop-up shops, refreshments. As it got dark, small white lights and towers of colorful lights came on. Music came on as soon as the lighs did.

The first song featured the haunting music of Wen Li, a singer of Chinese and Mongolian music. Ye translated some of the lyrics that showed a love for the Mongolian values of family and land.

We had arrived at the center of the square. A second song came from the speakers around the square, "My Heart Will Go On," sung by Celine Dion. I stood still in amazement but reached out to take hold of Emily's arm so she stopped beside me.

Wuhai Square, 2004, Inner Mongolia, PRC

"This song is in English!"

"Yes," Emily didn't seem to know why I was surprised.

"I haven't heard any English songs except in our conversational evenings with the guitar players and singers. This is from the famous movie, *Titanic*."

"Yes. The movie did not come here until maybe 2002.

Maybe it is already old in your country. Everyone here likes it very much."

"I love it." Cassie added with enthusiasm as she listened to our conversation. "I have seen it many times, and this song is the best." The other teachers agreed.

"Then I think I will make it a song we learn in the classes. The people in my homeroom will have the most practice, but everyone can learn it."

"You better teach it to all the classes. It is too schmaltzy for me," Doug answered.

"I think it should be something you teach too, Virginia. I am only good at teaching children's songs," Tia added.

"All right. I will probably teach the song with American Sign Language added. I was going to introduce ASL next week in the afternoon enrichment classes because physically forming letters can help students picture spelling and sounds. Even preschool children can learn the alphabet and understand more about making words. This song has sentences, important verbs, contrasts like near and far, and emotions. It will be a good song for signing and thinking in English."

Agreement came from my team and from the students near me. Then we continued walking across the square. Families had come out for the lights, the music, the snacks, and the souvenir sellers with their balloons and toys. Everyone seemed relaxed in the comfortable evening air. Ye approached me when we crossed the widest part of the square and arrived at the avenue.

"I am going home, but Ms. Virginia, may I be a helper in your class for the rest of your time here? I would wash the boards every day. I can make sure there is enough good chalk and water for you and your assistants. I will do any errands to help you or any of the other Amity teachers. Your time is passing fast here."

"It's fine with me, Ye, but I must check with Ms. Emily. She will know if you can be in the classrooms each day. How will I let you know if it is approved?"

"Please ask Ms. Emily to call me."

"Yes. You have wonderful abilities, Ye. Our whole team hopes you will reach the many high goals you have mentioned to us."

"Thank you, Ms. Virginia. It has been my honor to help. I have learned a lot from listening to you, Mr. Doug, Ms. Kathryn, Ms. Tia, and Ms. Jaye. I want to learn more."

"I understand. We appreciate your interest and help. Good night, Ye."

"Good night, Ms. Virginia."

I watched Ye as he left our group. He acted so much more mature than the seventeen-year-olds I knew back in the US. Was it something in his experience of overcoming poor circumstances, having older parents, being an only child, loving a foreign language as much as he seemed to love English or having high ideals and goals?

This trip had broadened my knowledge, experience, and spirit. My hopes for removing anger and feeling renewal had emerged in the time of the SEP. I never would have guessed how strong a connection could develop to people in a few short weeks in this remote area of a Communist country. Even more, I could not have guessed how the people and experiences would teach me about trusting God's timing for my life.

Was this how missionaries experienced a call to work in a specific country, culture, or community? At this point in my life, doing some kind of full-time work in China and living there for years would not fit with my relationships and responsibilities. I could however return and volunteer again with Amity. I could also find a way to have at least a few days to revisit people in Wuhai. To achieve that goal, I would need a lot of guidance to find a special combination in a team of people who could afford the trip in time and money, have a spirit of adventure, strong people skills, and who would have a unified goal of service.

Chapter 22

Museums and Rockets

S unday before week three of our SEP found us welcomed as buoyantly as ever at the Wuhai church. We stayed for the shared meal, and our assistants did too. Terry attended regularly so that didn't surprise us, but Jeff also stayed, as did Kent, Marge, and Cassie. No baptisms occurred on this Sunday, but the choir sang more songs. Doug continued to draw smiles as he sang out fully in English on lyrics we knew.

Mid-afternoons of all our days included rest, reading, going to the computer lab in the administration building for emails, and working on lessons for the coming week. Any emails from family and friends were especially encouraging.

Jerry's email to me appeared every day, though its messages were brief. He usually had some news and questions. I tried to answer his questions but gave him only brief glimpses of my days. I wanted to tell him all about the people and experiences, but I also wanted to do that in person.

Mom disliked computers, so I never had email from her, but father shocked me by emailing several times a week. He gave only a little news but seemed to like the challenge of writing in a code about faith and concerns for me. He sent messages like; I talked to your father today. I told him about your needs. I think he will take care of all of them. With love, Dad.

The Monday of week three, after our evening in Wuhai city square, dawned as hot and sunny as the previous weeks. But a better brightness arrived when Emily showed up at breakfast with the news that Ye could be a helper in my class or in any of the classrooms for the rest of our time in Wuhai.

"I called Ye last night, after Principal Chen approved the plan to have Ye help any of you for the rest of the SEP time. Ye has great skill with English, Ms. Virginia. I know he will appreciate listening to the training and enrichment classes."

During the afternoon break, Emily took me to a department store to buy a CD player and the CD of the music from *Titanic*. I knew that people bargained in small shops and open markets, but that was not true when buying from a department store. The prices posted should be paid without any haggling. Still, Emily managed to examine the CD player with an expression of concern and disappointment.

When she asked the saleswoman about lowering the price, and explained how the CD player would be used to help teachers, the woman went to speak to her manager. We got the large CD player, called a boom box in the US, and the Celine Dion disc, both at half price. I wouldn't take this home with me. The CD player and the CD would be one of the closing day gifts that our students could choose.

Back in my room, I tried the various buttons. Trial and error worked to help me learn how to use it. I enjoyed the music. I also practiced the ASL motions for the chorus. That and the sign language alphabet were all I would teach of

ASL this week. I hoped the teachers would see how spelling words with ASL could help their students picture English spelling and have an opportunity to move while working in a classroom.

China had its own sign language. I didn't know how many of our students knew more Chinese sign language than numbers they had shown me, but learning the English alphabet with signs would make the spelling challenges clearer, memorable, and even fun. English has so many oddities in spelling, and the ASL alphabet could help students remember them more easily.

* * *

Another week zoomed by, and our last field trip had been announced. We would return to Ningxia Autonomous Region. Although it's south of Inner Mongolia, people generally think of Ningxia as North Central China. To the west and south of Ningxia is Gansu Province. To the east is Shaanxi Province.

In the team meeting on Friday, the day before this last Saturday field trip, a heaviness clouded our mood. Why? Was it any specific reason? Doug avoided personal or emotion-based discussions in our meetings, so I addressed this feeling myself.

"Lots of tired faces in here. Will a good night's sleep help us to have more energy for the day tomorrow?"

Jaye said, "I don't mind saying that I did not imagine we would always be with our students and administrators unless we were in our rooms. I've had rare walks alone through Wuhai. I wanted to explore a lot alone. I don't like being supervised, and tomorrow we'll be with people all day too. They call them companions, but I feel like they are guards."

Jaye had an aggrieved tone and spoke loudly. I hoped again no microphones listened in to our conversations. How embarrassing and hurtful this would be.

I could see that Doug had a frown, but he didn't say anything to Jaye.

Tia spoke next. She had shared the reason for her tears with our team in a meeting after the day she cried in class. Now Tia spoke with her usual gentle voice, only sadder.

"Knowing this is our last day trip makes me think of what I will face when I go home. As tiring as some days are here, our students are great, kind and attentive. I feel sad thinking about going home and living alone. I don't mind the company on our walks and activities like Jaye does. I know I have good friends at home, but the people here help me feel cared for and special."

Kathryn nodded in agreement. "Yes, our students pay attention. They make the days special even through the classroom hours. However, I agree with Jaye. I would like to have more free range. We've been supervised consistently." With a laugh, she added, "There are long streets of shops in this city I haven't visited. I could enjoy that alone."

The atmosphere still seemed heavy, so I brought up the shopping trip where Kathryn had left the school grounds without an interpreter. Her shopping trip still made us laugh. "Kathryn, when you tried shopping by yourself here, well, I'm glad I caught up with you to see it with my own eyes. Your acting and charade efforts were spectacular."

* * *

I believed Kathryn had accepted the rule of not going off the school grounds alone, but at the start of the third week, when none of the assistants were around in the afternoon, I saw her walk down the alley next to the dormitory. The gate at the end of the alley wasn't locked until evening. I went after her, but she was through the gate before I caught up.

"Kathryn! Kathryn, where are you going?" I called.

She stopped where the narrow lane met the larger avenue.

"I have to get something at a little general store."

"You can't wait until tomorrow?"

"I need it tonight."

"What is it? Maybe I have it."

"Talcum powder."

"You mean baby powder? I have some. I put a little in each shoe when we leave for the day."

"I can't use that kind of powder. I get a rash from it, but I can use other kinds. Have you noticed how the tiny little stores here have many more products than we might imagine could fit in their space?"

"Yes. I go to the one right outside the gate to get the bottles of jasmine and green tea that I like so much, plus school supplies for daily prizes for our games."

"I used up all my powder because I've found I have to powder my whole body after a shower each day here or I'm just a sweaty mess."

"I'll go with you to the store."

It was just a couple of blocks, but we had to cross a street, which was a wider avenue than the school was on. It even had a streetlight at the corner, but Doug warned us not to trust that vehicles would stop, slow down, or move forward according to the streetlights. He said cities, other than the capital, Hohhot, had few streetlights and only recently added.

In Wuhai, it seemed people stopped for red lights rarely. This was another reason why walking around the city with one of our students seemed wise. If we were out on our own, we tried to stand near some Chinese or Mongolian residents and to cross the street when they did.

Unfortunately, even though other people were out walking, no one else was waiting to cross. Kathryn and I watched for even a thin break in the mix of bicycles, motor bikes, motorcycles, regular rickshaws, electric three wheeled vehicles, donkey carts, and cars. Finally, I saw an opening!

"Go! Go! Go!" I hollered, taking Kathryn's hand, and pulling her across the street. Only as we got to the other side of the avenue did I realize that people on both sides of the street were standing looking around as if searching for something.

Gǒu in Chinese means dog. It sounds like Go. My shouts of Go three emphatic times sounded like *Dog! Dog! Dog!* People on the street looked around for a fearsome canine creature. I explained what was happening to Kathryn who laughed, and we continued walking.

The general store was near the crossing. From a glance in the single large window upon stepping inside, the contents looked like a blend of every mini-mart we could think of crammed into a space the size of my living room, eighteen by sixteen feet. The cash register, resting on a metal box, came to the height of the clerk's belly.

"Do you speak English?" I asked.

"I need body powder," Kathryn said with a smile before the man answered.

"Little." The man replied with a smile of his own. "American teachers, welcome."

"Powder," Kathryn repeated slowly and clearly. "Body powder." She said it loudly like people often do when they speak to someone hard of hearing.

He smiled but shook his head having no idea what 'powder, body powder' was.

Kathryn backed up a step and acted out shaking powder on her chest, under her arms, around her torso. The man smiled broadly. I couldn't help laughing.

"*Qǐng děng yīxià,*" the man said and disappeared into the high stacked shelves.

"What did he say?" Kathryn asked.

"I'm not sure, but I think he meant for us to wait."

He did, because he returned with a woman who might have been his wife. Behind her was an elderly couple, probably the parents of one of them. A child who looked about seven or eight stood with the older couple. With a nod and a hand motion, the man indicated that Kathryn should give her request again.

"Body powder," she repeated. Then she did her act again shaking the powder over her chest area, under her arms, and all around her torso, even over her buttocks this time. I saw surprise on the faces of the man and his family. The child giggled.

I laughed and said, "Kathryn, you're very entertaining, but they don't know what you want."

Kathryn sighed and started to walk down the aisle that had deodorant, toothpaste, and other personal items, but there was no body powder. I looked in other aisles because the organization in any of these shops did not have any Westernized order. The family came out from behind the cash

215

register counter and looked at Kathryn. Did they expect her to do the routine again in one of the aisles?

Kathryn stopped, "I don't think I can find it." She turned to the store owner and said, "Body powder," before starting her act again. Just as she began shaking the invisible powder under her armpits, one of the SEP teachers, Delia, came into the store with her primary school daughter.

"Ms. Kathryn, what is it?" Delia's expression implied that she thought Kathryn exhibited the signs of having some kind of fit. Kathryn stopped her body powder routine the instant Delia asked the question.

"Oh, Delia, thank goodness you're here. I need body powder. I use it every day because of the heat here, but I have run out. I thought if I could show these people how I used the powder, they might understand what I needed."

"Rest, Ms. Kathryn. I will help." Delia talked with the store owner. We saw him nod, and then his wife disappeared down an aisle we had not explored. We waited. In a minute, the woman reappeared with something the size of a shoebox. On the counter in front of all of us, the woman lifted the top covered with pictures of flowers.

Inside we saw an oval plastic container the color of lilacs. She spoke to Kathryn and Delia translated, "She wants you to open the container. She said it has the scent of flowers, but of no single flower."

Kathryn lifted the cover and revealed a rose-colored powder puff. When she lifted that, we saw the large oval container full of fine white powder with a flowery scent.

"Oh, this is great! Thank you. I'll take it. I'll take two!"

We all bowed a bit to one another. Then Kathryn reached out and shook hands enthusiastically. The Chinese family smiled. Kathryn paid for the body powder, and Delia walked us back to the school grounds.

"I guess I made a fool out of myself. Will they think me a crazy Westerner?" Kathryn asked Delia.

"Ms. Kathryn, you showed that you believed they had what you needed, and you had courage to try to communicate. Don't worry, Ms. Kathryn. You made everyone in the store smile. They will never forget your visit." Delia's little girl giggled again when they left us at the alley gate.

When I went to bed after the team meeting, I gave thanks that we had all been able to share a laugh over Kathryn's acting in the little general store. I tried to pray for each team member every day. We all faced some tough moments. Jessie had told us to pray together, but in our meetings, Doug took us through the schedule, plans for the last week, prayed briefly, then ended our meeting.

At the early breakfast, Erdeen joined us and said the other teachers who would go on this trip would meet us at the front gate. Each week, we did not see the administrators often, but Principal Chen and Vice-Principal Zhu stood near the big black cars as our team and Erdeen approached. A feeling of happiness ran through me as I saw Ye standing by Principal Chen, but concern fluttered through my mind too. Would Principal Chen be extra intense in studying Ye? Could this day make or break the possibility of Ye having the aid of a city leader as a patron?

I looked at the teachers who had been chosen to accompany us. I had Erdeen, always a plus to me. Doug had Thomas. Kathryn had Delia. Tia had Penny, and Jaye had one of the most athletic young women in our classes, Kent. When Jaye took her class outside to practice skills related to sports, Kent looked happy and participated with enthusiasm. We used three cars, and I noticed Principal Chen indicated Ye should ride in the front car with the men.

We journeyed back to Ningxia. At this early hour, none of us did much talking. Hardly any cars were on the road. It took two hours to reach a museum devoted to the study of the Silk Road adventures in enterprise and trade. Set in an inconspicuous area and landscaped to fit the desert region and the rocks around it, the museum spread out like a modern art sculpture of rectangles.

Inside, the air-conditioning felt like we had entered a refrigerated locker in contrast to the outdoors. We shivered at first. While VP Zhu got tickets for everyone, we went to the restrooms. Signs appeared in Mandarin, Mongolian, and English. We had so rarely seen anything in English that this was a surprise.

The multiple toilet stalls in the museum were made of marble walls with wooden doors and had a hole in the marble floor. We did see a stall for handicapped individuals, and it had the toilet we westerners preferred. Though we carried our own little packets of toilet paper, still necessary in this rest room, we appreciated the soap dispensers and hot water from the faucets over the trio of marble sinks.

VP Zhu gave us our tickets when we returned to the entry hall. Just a few steps into the museum, we saw large open areas that allowed easy viewing of photos, charts, maps, land, and people. Best of all, the information captions were in Mandarin, Mongolian, and English. The rooms in this modern style museum had sculptures and huge wall hangings, rocks and minerals, photos, paintings, needlework, and maps.

Thomas took the lead in explaining the options. "Here is a map of the museum. Because we have limited time, you should choose what interests you. They have English information here, but a class member will be with you to help if you have any questions."

"How much time do we have here?" Kathryn asked.

"About one hour fifteen minutes."

Doug barely glimpsed at the layout of the museum before he found the room listed for rocks and minerals. He went down the nearest hall. Thomas and Ye hurried after him.

"They have only a tiny museum shop here," Kathryn said. "Did you see it when we came in here?" She sighed as she watched Doug, Thomas, and Ye leave the group.

Jaye looked over all of us with a quick glance and said, "I'm going to use these wide air-conditioned halls for exercise. It will be interesting to see how many laps around the inside of this place I can do in an hour. Then I can look around for the last minutes."

Kent frowned, a rare expression on her face. I knew that she exercised every day and loved sports, so the frown was not for the exercise. She just wouldn't have time to explore the museum. She'd been partnered with Jaye and had to be available to her for the day. Companion or guard? Staying with Jaye was Kent's assigned responsibility.

Principal Chen stood near us. Kathryn turned to him and said, "This trip required such an early morning. I need more sleep. The Silk Road is not more important to me than my sleep. May I return to the cars and sleep while I wait for everyone else?"

Delia translated, and Principal Chen nodded. That nod was all Kathryn needed before she left the group. Disappointment flickered like a fast-moving cloud across Delia's beautiful face. She followed Kathryn out to the cars. We watched them leave.

Tia distracted me when she said, "I could use more rest too. I would like to go back to the car." Penny graciously took Tia's hand and looked at Principal Chen. He nodded before Penny translated. Once again, I suspected that he understood English.

Penny left with Tia. Neither Delia nor Penny had ever been to this museum. Our host school had purchased admission passes for all of us. It seemed Kathryn and Tia didn't think about that. I struggled with anger. I needed to have more generosity toward others' differences. We were tired, but this day was a gift to us.

I felt concern that in this past week, Kathryn, Tia, and Jaye had each expressed feeling that this last week of the SEP would have extra stress. Doug didn't show any extra tension, but he did know and mention how much we needed to do. In our last meeting, Kathryn and Tia spent more time discussing what they would see and do in Beijing before they went home than they did talking about our responsibilities. Jaye didn't say much at all.

The end of teaching in desert heat, adjusting to a different culture, and mentoring young teachers seemed too close for me. I had barely gained the balance I had hoped for in mind and spirit. I wanted to learn more and stay longer. I wondered what my husband would think of living and working in a place like Inner Mongolia. He could teach conversational English, but I doubted he'd be ready to consider such a venture before he retired. He loved his job as much as I had loved mine and our family would be half a world away.

Doug, Jaye, and I spent a little over an hour in the museum but rarely were in the same room together. While admiring one full wall display of Marco Polo's travels on the Silk Road, I read that when Polo made the return trip to Italy, some of his men disappeared into the desert and hills with the beautiful Mongolian women. They never returned to life in Italy. Someone stood beside me while I read this information.

Looking to my right, I saw Principal Chen. He had a remote demeanor most of the time. One smile had brightened his whole expression the previous week when I said, "I notice that you often answer '*maybe*' to a question that could be a yes or a no. Is maybe the way you avoid saying no? I have heard that a direct 'no' answer is considered impolite." He had smiled before Emily's translated my comments and question.

Now, I pointed to the caption below the sign. "You and many of the customs you enjoy remind me of my Italian family. Look at this sign. Maybe one of my ancestors decided to stay in Inner Mongolia. Maybe I am related to people in Wuhai." Erdeen, my helpful shadow, translated. I could tell she did not know if I was joking or serious.

The slight frown that Principal Chen had shown since Kathryn and Tia left the museum disappeared. He surprised me with one word in English. "Maybe." I don't know what shocked me most, that Principal Chen had revealed a sense of humor based on my imaginative view of the past or that he had responded to me in English.

* * *

All the cars had coolers so on the trips we enjoyed cold water. We drank that simple refreshment as the cars pulled out on the way to the next part of our last field trip day. Only we Westerners cared about cold water. People in Wuhai did not think cold drinks helped a person's health. They preferred drinking hot teas.

"Do you know where we are going?" Jaye asked Delia.

"Principal Chen has a good friend who owns one of the largest goat and sheep farms in our region."

"So, we are leaving Ningxia and going back to Nei Menggu?"

"That is the plan."

"Is it farther out, more into the actual desert land or near Wuhai?"

"I do not know. None of us know. It could be on the border of Nei Menggu and Ningxia. The farmer oversees much land. These trips are learning experiences for us too. Principal Chen honors us to be your companions. We enjoy learning with you."

I glanced quickly at Kathryn and Tia to see if they had registered the fact that these trips were treats, honors, for the teachers who went along as translators. Kathryn's eyes were closed. Tia looked out at the hills and mountains.

We were on a road smooth and straight, a new bit of highway. Thomas explained that highways were being built all over the country. Although not many people had cars, the business forecast predicted that this would change in fewer than five years. This newly completed highway showed that the government expected a change in transportation choices and patterns. The road became cement with many cracks.

We turned again, now onto a dirt road. It seemed unusually wide. Clouds of dust or dirt rose as we moved forward. On either side sand dunes rose like blank walls of camel brown. There were no more little houses.

Suddenly, the cars in front of us used an unexpected open area to do a fast 180-degree turn. We realized we must have taken a wrong turn. We did not immediately see why the rushed spin to change directions occurred.

In the turning, we saw what the front car had faced. Ahead stood fences as tall as the remote oil rigs I'd seen in Texas. Beyond the high fences topped with barb wire and reinforced gates guarded by men in military uniforms, low plain military buildings appeared. Although we had only a short glimpse, beyond the barracks I recognized structures like those I saw when I had toured the Kennedy Space Center.

Big cars cannot peal out in rapid turns on dirt roads without stirring up a dust storm. By the time the mustard brown dust settled, nothing of the desert rockets or satellite site could be seen through the car's back window. I wondered if security cameras had taken pictures of the cars, and if Principal Chen, VP Zhu, or any of us would face any difficulties because of a wrong turn.

Chapter 23

Narrow Meandering Paths Are Referred to as Goat Trails

W e arrived at the vast goat and sheep farm later than Principal Chen had planned because of the wrong turn. No one mentioned the wrong turn or sight of the isolated military base as we exited the cars.

Four men as tall as Principal Chen and Doug greeted us with words of welcome and tipped heads as bows. It still surprised me to see such burly men in China. Maybe they were full Mongolian. Their skin might be browned and their eyes tightly creased from ancestry or from spending their lives outdoors.

Their loose-fitting clothing seemed a mix of cotton and typical synthetic material, but the youngest of the four wore baggy jeans. The hot day in this open area had a strong breeze. The men wore long sleeved shirts and trousers that had muddy looking cuffs, and their dirt crusted work boots appeared damp. I could see that the whole yard might have been hosed down. Did they do this because of the guests arriving?

They led us away from the building that looked like a long rough-built semi-ranch dwelling. There were stones low against the ground, the mortar not neatly applied. Bricks and wood formed the walls with no clear pattern. The roof looked like blue metal. Sheds were attached to the building on the back and side nearest us.

"Another blue roof," I remarked. Erdeen immediately translated.

Principal Chen turned to look at the hodge-podge of a building with its blue roof and spoke. Erdeen said, "Principal Chen wants you to know that blue tin is cheap. The old roof here was gray."

"*Xie xie*," I responded and turned to walk to the wooden fence that separated the land around the buildings from the nearest field filled with goats.

"Blue is a color for harmony and protection," Delia added.

The men who had greeted us turned and the tallest man talked to us. We waited for the translation.

"Our goat herd brings money from their meat, but half of our goats bring money because they give the wool for cashmere. It is warm, soft, and lasts many years."

Most of my team paid attention and nodded. We knew what cashmere was, and it had high pricing in any country I had visited.

"You raise sheep too," Doug commented and pointed to the left where the fenced in area was filled with sheep. Thomas was quick to translate Doug's observation and then the answer to Doug.

"Yes. Our sheep are fewer, but we raise both. Now your principal will help us to have a special honor for your visit to our country, farm, and home. He will choose a goat for us to cook for you."

I felt a churning mix of gratitude and fear as I realized we were about to experience an Inner Mongolian special personalized welcome. I looked at the goats and felt a moment of horror that one would be killed to honor us, to feed us, a slaughter on our last field trip. Would they kill the animal in front of us? I felt my heartbeat increase.

Looking at my team, I could see discomfort on their faces, but not on the faces of any of our assistants. To them, this was a special honor, like catching a fish and taking it right into the house to clean and cook. Only these meal choices were mammals, pretty, cute, and curious as they stared back at us.

One is for our welcome meal

Our breakfast had been hours ago, and we'd had no snacks, only water. None of the team was a vegetarian, but I doubted any of us looked at these goats with the immediate thought, '*Oh that one looks like it will taste good!*'

Principal Chen stepped close to the fence. Jaye, Tia, and Kathryn took several steps back. Doug and I stayed, one of us on each side of the principal. We could see him studying the animals. He would point out a goat, and it would be killed for a meal to honor us. My stomach felt like a lump of iron.

Principal Chen studied the goats near us for about two minutes. I watched him lift a hand and point to a goat. I had not personally seen an animal slaughtered, but I had watched a couple of documentaries about slaughterhouses in the US. Their killing process revolted me.

He had chosen a white goat. From the looks of its horns, it was a young male, one that stood not far from the fence. A man from the group that greeted us leaped easily over the fence, pulled a thin rope from his pocket and put it around the goat's neck. He patted it and led it to a gate.

"Good choice," said the man in charge to Principal Chen. Thomas translated. "It will be four hours until the meal is ready. We can go inside and have refreshments and songs. Our wives have been working hard to have many dishes for you. We have musicians inside too."

The young man who brought the goat through the gate went to a space we could not see beyond the house. We looked toward the place where he and the goat disappeared. How would they slaughter it?

I'd seen plenty of information on slaughterhouses for cows, lambs, sheep, pigs, chickens, and turkeys, but I realized I had never seen a goat killed. Would the slaughter be as sad and violent as I imagined?

We stood still until Principal Chen stared at us and asked, "Would you care to see the preparation? Inviting you to witness the process shows high respect for you. To see how the chosen animal is prepared is an honor." Thomas had barely finished translating when Jaye spoke.

"I don't want to see them kill the goat."

"I don't either," Tia said, and tears filled her eyes.

"I will go inside with Jaye and Tia." Kathryn's voice sounded cold as the peal of a death knell.

One of the herdsmen, who had yet to speak, approached the three women and motioned for them to follow him. Penny was the only one to go around to the front of the house with Tia, Jaye, and Kathryn. I followed the head man to the other side of the house along with Kent, Erdeen, Delia, Thomas, Ye, Principal Chen, VP Zhu, and Doug,

The dirt in this courtyard area appeared packed hard as a floor. The youngest man held the goat in the center of the space. I looked at the house. No windows appeared on this side of the house. There was a wooden door at the far end of this part of the building.

Deftly, the young man had shortened the rope. It was up higher under the goat's jaw. Then he tied the rope to a small post in the ground. As I watched him, he put his hands on the goat and guided it to lay down. It did not resist his touch. When it lay down, he pressed on its neck and body so that it lay on its side. The young man stroked the goat's neck from ears to shoulder.

The lead man supervised, but another herdsman squatted down and slid a large low bowl beneath the goat's head and neck. Now the goat's head rested on the edge of the bowl. The young man kept repeatedly stroking the goat's neck.

In the next instant, the man who had brought the bowl pulled out a long piece of metal, as thin as a pencil and pointed on one end. With one quick motion, he pushed the pointed piece of metal straight through the goat's neck. The goat flinched, a quick jerking reaction, but did not bleat or resist.

We heard the metal point of the tool hit the bowl when the man jammed it through the goat's neck. As rapid as a rattler strike, the man pulled the deadly slim pointed weapon out of the goat's neck. The young man continued stroking the animal through the quick stabbing. The goat did not make a move to get up or away.

We could see blood covering the bottom of the bowl. We watched it get deeper. Who had come up with this method of slaughter? I could not imagine any slaughterhouse in the US using such an approach with the large numbers of animals slaughtered each day for their flesh and hides.

The young goat lay quietly bleeding to death from the artery that had been punctured in its neck; the weapon having jabbed in and out in a second. With his hand on the goat, the young man's touch kept the animal calm. The goat lost enough blood that its eyes closed.

This sacrifice, not chosen by the creature killed, would give more than meals. The Mongolians, like the Chinese, and the indigenous people around the globe, did not waste any part of a butchered creature. Indigenous people often gave thanks for the food, a prayer above it or a prayer to it. I saw no discomfort in Principal Chen. Appearing as self-contained as usual, he watched the process that would give us a special feast.

This event, common here and viewed as an honor to guests, could not be rejected without my feeling like the goat died for nothing. It was an odd time to think about Jesus being a sacrifice, a silent lamb, not resisting what the people did to him. He certainly had no one touch him gently in his last moments before death. Still, his bloody death came to mind. I looked at the people watching this death and could not tell what they thought.

Tears filled my eyes, but I widened them to let the tears dry before they fell.

I felt guilty even though this goat had been marked for food before he was chosen to feed us. Principal Chen's choice had just shortened the goat's lifespan.

Dying to give life. Innocent and dying because of the desires and needs of others, I thought of something my father had required me to memorize when I was a teen. From Isaiah, chapter fifty-three, "He was oppressed and afflicted, yet he did not open his mouth; he was led like a lamb to the slaughter, and as a sheep before its shearers is silent, so he did not open his mouth."

My tears were not just for the goat. I felt repentant for all that I had taken for granted in my life and in my faith. I grieved at how difficult trusting God had seemed.

This experience reinforced my need to trust God with my days, even the tough and disappointing ones. We had no idea of the visual and emotional contrasts that would come on this field trip. I realized that I could not predict any of my days, but I could learn more about trusting God to take me through whatever came in any day.

"We can go in now. We have music, drink, and food for the time we wait." The head man spoke. And when Thomas translated, I thought his voice sounded softer than usual. He was a man of the city now, but once he was a young man in a Mongolian family who lived on the outskirts of Wuhai. Surely, he must have seen an animal slaughtered before this. Maybe he had participated in killing one.

I glanced at Doug who stood between Principal Chen and me. Doug nodded at Thomas's words but showed no other expression. Though the whole procedure churned up my emotions, I tried not to show any distress in my expression. We followed the headman back to the entrance yard.

Continuing past the parked black cars, not so shiny now due to the heavy coating of dust from the day's drive, we walked toward the front of the house. There was no porch, just an overhang above the wooden posts that supported its seven-foot height. I could estimate this number by seeing how much space existed between the roof and the height of Principal Chen, Doug, and the tall headman.

We entered through a wide wooden front door. Hostesses in traditional Mongolian garb greeted us. They did not wear toortsogs or pointed genie style shoes. Their hair was pulled back in buns. Only one woman had all gray hair. The other women showed no gray in their dark hair.

The rectangular table of wood, low in height, filled the center of the room. Kathryn, Tia, and Jaye sat on large thick cushions instead of chairs. Four men had greeted us, but only three Mongolian women were in this room. None looked young, so I guessed the young man who had soothed the goat into death did not have a wife in this room. Maybe one of these women was his mother. Perhaps the one with all gray hair was his grandmother. The leather looking skin of the two oldest women reflected years of living in sunshine and harsh winter weather.

One woman gave us the traditional greeting and the offering of the blue silk scarf. We each stood as the scarf and cup were presented to us by the one woman that I thought might be a grandmother. Thankfully, Doug did not ask for tea. As he stood, he picked up a cup from the table. I could see that it contained Mongolian milk tea.

There was also a small handleless porcelain cup at each place that could be used for tea. They brought us wolfberry tea. I felt happy to enjoy it again. I had not tasted it since our visit to Ahmed's restaurant. Before our time in Inner Mongolia, I had never even heard of it or of the red goji berries that give the tea a sweet flavor on their own even if no honey or sugar is added.

Emily had told us that wolfberries strengthened the immune system, eyesight, liver function, and circulation. Why were these little red goji berries called wolfberries? The berry, *lyceum barbarum,* has the written character *"gou"* which connects to the word wolf more than dog. Chinese farmers also observed wolves eating these berries.

Mongolians see wolves as symbols of strength, courage, and honor, and in some of their poetry and ancient stories, Mongols are descendants of wolves. I thought wolves must attack the sheep and goats of Mongolians, and yet wolves are admired. I wondered if anyone could explain that. Maybe I would ask Thomas or Ye.

The Wuhai wolf of legends

Besides his unique knowledge of rocks, crystals, and mining in Wuhai, Ye loved the legends of his province. He had told us many local legends focused on wolves.

When all the welcoming was done, two old men

entered the room. They were wearing something like sturdy moccasins and tunics over heavy trousers that smelled like wool and sweat. They carried instruments. One was the horse head fiddle that we had heard before. It had only two strings yet made a variety of wonderful sounds.

Morin Khuur, the horse-head fiddle

The other was a *tsuur*, a pipe-shaped wooden instrument. One of the younger women brought out an instrument that looked like a zither. Her work-worn hands moved lightly over it. Together the three musicians took us into the Mongolian culture through the sounds of their pipe and string instruments. The youngest Mongolian woman in the room sang a long ballad. Then she taught us all a chorus and sang another solo for us.

We applauded the folk songs and appreciated the information about the Mongolian culture. Our assistants took turns translating. We sipped the drinks, sang along as best we could, and snacked on nuts, fried dough bites, pickled beets, and mini wheels of hard cheese. We were told that all the cheeses came from goats on the ranch. The dishes available showed hospitality with a variety of sour, salty, creamy, spicy, and bitter.

For almost two and a half hours, the music, stories of farming and ranching, snacking, and beverages were shared and enjoyed. Then came an unexpected lull. In those moments of silence, Jaye stood up and asked, "Where is the bathroom?"

Delia translated. Stillness accompanied the silence until one of the women came to stand beside Jaye. She spoke.

Delia said, "Just follow her. She will take you to the place."

"I will come with you," Penny said and stood.

"The place?" Jaye asked as she took the first step after the woman.

Chapter 24

Challenges, Endings, and Flexibility

"We will go with you too," Kathryn announced. We four foreign women and Penny followed one of our hostesses out of the longest side of the L shaped house. We passed sleeping areas, hardly bedrooms as we would describe them, that were empty except for large platform beds with rolled blankets and flat-looking pillows. Then we were escorted through a door at the end of the ell, and outside. The woman offered us the typical individual packets of toilet paper squares.

"We have our own," I said as I showed her my little packet. I looked for an outhouse. Penny spoke to the woman who smiled and pointed toward the short dunes with scrub grass.

Jaye returned to the house as we all did after finding some privacy behind a hillock and some bushes. Tia and I had worn skirts, so our process was much easier and did not necessitate baring our butts to the great outdoors.

As we walked back to the house, Jaye snarled, "Anyone

could have seen us. The men are probably curious to see our white bottoms. I hate this primitive place."

Kathryn responded, "If anyone wandered out somewhere to see my big white bottom, I hope they got a good view." She laughed.

Tia seemed sympathetic toward Jaye but smiled at Kathryn's attitude. I kept quiet and hoped that Jaye would not be sour for the rest of our time on this farm. From the moment we entered the house again, my hope floundered, then failed. I prayed, but again the answer to my prayer did not arrive with the timing Id' hoped for.

Jaye stayed silent and unsmiling through the telling of local myths, more songs, more drinking, and a course of Guriltai Shul, a noodle soup with carrots, tofu, onions, radishes, potatoes, and something like turnip. The soup had a generous amount of pepper, but it did not have the burn to set one's tongue on fire like some of the spicy appetizer dishes we'd had in the restaurants. I didn't try to make a lot of noise while I ate, just tried to match what Erdeen did.

Jaye didn't eat anything. She took small sips of *píjiǔ* from the small glass cup near her place at the table. We each had one. I worried about what she might say if all she did was drink *píjiǔ* instead of eating more, but after that one cup, she had nothing else.

"Will you have something more," Delia asked with gentleness and concern.

"No. If I eat or drink more, I may have to go outdoors again. I don't want to do that." It would have been impossible for our administrators, teachers, and hosts not to see Jaye's lack of participation. Doug and Kathryn noted this too. Together we tried to enter conversation and show enthusiasm for this experience. Tia, a gentle soul, stayed quiet, but

I expected it came from knowing an animal had been killed to honor us.

Everyone else ate and drank, including the three drivers of the big black cars. I did notice that they did not have the hard liquor. People talked and translated until, with a grand flourish, the young herdsman and the two older men who had been out in the yard came in with deep and wide wooden bowls of freshly roasted goat.

Obvious in the delight they felt giving us this great gift, they each put a bowl down on the long table, one at each end and one in the middle. The bowls were full and in easy reach of everyone. I felt relieved they did not bring in a whole roasted goat and cut it up in front of us.

"The roast smells delicious," Doug said as he took one medium sized piece. It was tender and greasy. We could see that Doug's fingers were shiny with the roasted fat that was on the piece he chose. We could also see bits fall off the bone as Doug lifted it. Our hosts, Principal Chen, and VP Zhu looked happy with Doug's praise. We watched him take a good-sized bite. "Delicious," Doug said again.

"*Hao chi*," Principal Chen said as an immediate translation to the head man who owned the farm.

"*Hao chi*," I said to one of the women of the household. Those two short words I could recall and use. I heard them enough to know they meant very delicious. I would remember this additional evidence that Principal Chen knew some English, maybe a lot.

I wished I had instant full recall of everything any member of our team had said in front of the principal. What kind of impression had we made on him? What was he thinking of us now in our actions and reactions?

Jaye sat back an arm's length from the table. Tia reached

for a small piece of the steaming meat. So much of the food this day was eaten without implements. Kathryn chose a piece larger than Tia's. I grabbed a large piece on a bone fearful that the gift of the goat would not appear appreciated enough by us.

Everyone else at the table took whatever piece was nearest from either of the two big bowls, then another and another and another. Nothing in this home would go to waste. Maybe these people hadn't eaten since early morning. Maybe eating a freshly roasted goat was rare for them because they did not want to eat what could be sold. No matter the reason, everyone ate a lot except for Jaye and Tia.

I could tell that the hosts and administrators watched us. We had been given an unusual day, probably one never to be repeated in our lives. How could we best show gratitude for this field trip? I thought we needed to show appreciation for the generosity and work that provided this meal, so I ate more meat than I would have at any other time.

The sun on this summer evening had started down toward the horizon when we finally stood to leave. We said thank you, *Xie xie ni*, many times. Even Jaye said thank you. Our drivers said something to the hosts too, but there was some laughter from the hosts in response to the drivers' comments. We never found out what they said.

Thomas translated the farewells from our hosts, "May you ride comfortably on the road." I thought this sentence went back to the days when people rode horses or even camels. They added, "Please go easy and well."

Darkness on the simple roads seemed deeper with not one streetlight. The dirt roads had the texture of corduroy, and the cement sections with broken areas could have trapped a tire if hit at the wrong angle. Our drivers had experience and skill with such roads. When we reached the newer highway, some streetlights did appear, but the stars and moon provided the most light. I wished they could lighten the mood in the car.

Jaye leaned her head back and closed her eyes. I was thankful that she did not fill the ride with complaints but was frustrated that her discontent had been so obvious. The distance I felt from my present team reinforced my desire to find a group of people who would prioritize being positive individuals and as a team.

Besides openness to adventure. they'd need consideration for the feelings of others, a sense of humor, and faith. How long would it take me to find these people or to see them if God dropped them right in front of me?

Erdeen and Delia stayed quiet too. In the hours back to the school, each of us slept for part of the ride. Only when we entered the dorm and stood as a team at the top of the stairs near our rooms, did Jaye vent. "After a day like today, I can't wait to leave Nei Menggu. Beijing will be civilization." Without waiting for a response from any of us, she went into her room, almost slamming the door shut.

Tia went to her room next. She turned and said a barely whispered goodnight. Tears ran down her face. Kathryn, Doug, and I just stood still and quietly.

Kathryn gave a long loud sigh and said, "I'm sure that my blood pressure is up at this moment, and all that greasy meat did me no good, but it was super tender and tasty. Jaye is in a piss poor mood. I wouldn't want to be one of her gym students when she was in such a mood. I'm glad Principal Chen let me rest in the car this morning. I needed it. I don't know how either of you watched them slaughter that goat."

"It seemed important, respectful because they killed it

for us. They wanted us to experience the Mongolian custom of honoring special guests." Doug responded.

"Kathryn," I said, "I thought it would be worse, the killing of the goat. Compared to the awful and bloody ways that animals are killed in meat plants at home. It went fast and almost seemed gentle."

Kathryn frowned at my response. "Almost gentle, that's hard to believe."

"Killing an animal, even for practical needs, like eating, is difficult for us. Have you ever gotten meat anywhere but in neatly arranged sanitized packaging?" Doug asked.

"My grandparents raised chickens for eggs and meat. I ate the eggs, but those chickens were like pets to me. At their house I did not eat chicken. Goodnight," Kathryn spoke abruptly and left us.

Doug turned to me, "These last teaching days may be more difficult than we imagined. Whether we've loved the time or found it difficult, people find it challenging to face an ending that requires goodbyes and another major transition."

"Remember what Jessie told us about surprises each day?"

Doug said her words of warning almost exactly as I recalled them. "Every day will have surprises while you are in China. Embrace them and remember that the Lord is always with you."

"That's the way I remember her words too. Not all surprises are good surprises. Thanks for your patience with our team. Good night, Doug."

"Good night, Virginia."

*　*　*

Sunday, the mood had not improved for the team. Breakfast held little conversation. I went to my room thinking about my parents. They did not want us to show negative feelings in public. I got used to that and recognized I judged people as inconsiderate when they let out unpleasant emotions, words, and expressions that could affect the happiness of others.

Since we had moved to Massachusetts, I had shown only Jerry my true feelings. Maybe Jaye was admirable in letting her feelings show while I hid mine. There didn't seem to be anything I could do for her. I prayed for all of us to stay steady and upbeat during the last week of classes. Would that prayer be answered for all five of us? Trusting God to do that work was an ongoing battle in my mind and soul.

Chapter 25

Hearts of Christians, Mozart, Donkeys, and Dust Storms

We Amity volunteers and the people who spent the most time with us, started to feel the emotional pressure of the SEP's conclusion. Even at church, they had us stand and offered prayer for our efforts and for our safe return to our homes. All of us, except Jaye, enjoyed the last luncheon with the warm-hearted Wuhai church congregation. Jaye stayed unusually quiet and rarely smiled.

On this Sunday night team meeting, we talked a little about the registered Chinese church. We agreed we had a lot to learn about the struggles of Christians in China. No clear way existed to categorize faith practices in registered churches in comparison to the illegal house churches.

"I was worried about any mention of religion while we were here," Tia said.

"Virginia never got in trouble with any of her teaching about holidays based on religious beliefs. The classes loved the nativity set she used to tell the Christmas story. Comrade

Wang turned out not to be a scary problem, unless that changes in these last days here," Kathryn said.

"I was more concerned about some of the discussion that came out of the questions you answered, Virginia." Doug's tone and expression were stern.

Jaye stayed for this team meeting but said little except, "I'll be glad to get home and to not worry about the Communist Party, where I go to church, the foods we eat, bathrooms, or constant supervision via assigned companions."

Silence followed her words as we each reviewed how it felt to have rare time alone in the city. As if to distract us from Jaye's comments, Doug started one of his semi-lectures reminding us that Christianity has been in China since the 1500s. Chairman Mao expelled all missionaries, but in 1979 the government approved religious practices again. The Three-Self Patriotic Movement (TSPM) and the China Christian Council (CCC) advocate for the government decision that churches must register and apply the three '*self*s:' they must self-govern, self-fund, and self-propagate.

Without using names in case there were microphones in the dorm, we discussed the students we knew who attended unregistered churches, called underground churches. They do not want government monitoring of sermons, worship services, or attendees. Meeting people who followed Jesus in the TSPM and in the unregistered churches, we saw the complications of loving God and others in a country that had comprehensive rules how a person could practice their faith.

Starting Sunday evening, we were awash in invitations from students to activities, homes, and meals. Only Monday through Friday remained with summarizing, preparing for final presentations that would count for successful certification of the course, a closing party on Friday, formal farewell speeches, and photographs. Early on Saturday, we would return to Beijing for two days of debriefing with the Amity organization.

* * *

Mozart. I woke up to Mozart. It was the overture from 'The Marriage of Figaro.' I opened my eyes and sat up. I could hear the music and pinched my arm to make sure I was awake and still in Inner Mongolia at the edge of the huge Gobi. What was going on?

I wasn't the only person who was dressed and out of the dorm early. Our breakfast companions for the day had already arrived. They were talking to the housekeeper near the door into the dining hall. None of them looked surprised to hear vibrant Mozart music this morning.

"Why do I hear Mozart?" I asked Emily.

She smiled with pride. "Students who are in our special musical program come back early. They practice for a couple of hours outdoors beside the administration building, early before the heat of the day. This year they will learn the music of Mozart, Hayden, Borodin, and Xinghai. You will hear them in the mornings now."

"They practice every day? Kathryn asked.

"Yes. Even on Saturday and Sunday. They must practice together every day."

"It's so early," Jaye commented with a wide yawn.

"Our band students practice from six to eight, and you will see some of our athletes too. The teams practice from six thirty to eight thirty each morning. Do you not have some special early morning practices in the US?" The question was directed to me.

"Yes, but not everywhere. It is up to the schools and coaches to decide.

We had an invitation to lunch this last Monday. Separately, each of us had been invited by our homeroom class to have lunch with them at a restaurant. I went with Erdeen during the lunch break to a small restaurant filled by members of my homeroom.

The restaurant specialized in dumplings. I enjoyed dumplings (*jiaozi*) after I got past the first awful day with the spoiled *jiaozi* that caused me to be sick. Now, I felt like I was at a party, and I had a seat for the honored guest at the head table. I was joined there by two students on my left and two on my right. We faced all the other students sitting at round tables.

The servers brought plates of heaping *jiaozi* to each table.

"Each platter has three different kinds of *jiaozi*," Erdeen told me with sparkles of delight in her eyes. I could see that the pottery plates had high edges and three sections.

"Try some from each section," Marge said as the platter for our table arrived.

I did. I used my *kuaizi* to take a selection.

"Guess what they are," someone called out clearly in English. Others repeated the same request.

"This one tastes like shrimp." I took a sip of the tea that had been poured in my cup. I tried one from the next section. "This one is beef."

"You have guessed two out of three," Terry affirmed with a smile.

"This one from the third section, is, what? Lamb or goat? I cannot tell."

"Lamb," someone called out.

When each table had consumed the first platter, servers brought another platter with three sections to each table.

"Guess again," Kent called out.

"Ah, this first one tases like chicken."

"Good guess," I heard from several people.

"The second one, I think is vegetables, maybe some kind of beans and greens?"

"Another good guess. Beans." I heard.

Between each different *jiaozi,* I was careful to sip tea. I took a *jiaozi* from the last section. When I bit into it, it tasted like nothing I had eaten before. In my life I had tasted meat from squirrels, rabbits, bear, duck, venison, moose, and horse meat, but I did not recognize this.

"What's your guess Ms. Virginia?"

I took a second one and chewed it even more slowly. The restaurant wouldn't serve camel. It was illegal to kill wild roving camels for meat, but some camels were raised and domesticated. Maybe they could probably be used for meat.

"This last one, I cannot guess."

"Have more. Have more," the students chanted. They seemed entertained by my inability to guess the contents of this *jiaozi.*

"Have another, Ms. Virginia. Try again."

They were happy with this test for me. I took another and chewed it slowly. Monkey? No. In the south they ate monkeys, dogs, cats, and mice, but the people in this province and most northern provinces did not eat all of those mammals. Mice? Maybe. Doug had told me they served mice at one dinner he attended in the far northeastern part of Inner Mongolia. Neither of us had shared that information with the rest of the team.

Early in our stay, Jaye had asked if people ate dogs in

Wuhai or in other areas of Nei Menggu. The teachers with us were shocked, especially Thomas.

He responded, "Mongolians treat their dogs like a member of the household. Good dogs help raise herds, hunt, and protect the family."

"Oh," Jaye frowned and mumbled, "I thought they ate dogs everywhere in China."

Since Doug had told me that where he had worked in 2002, they did eat mice, could this be the puzzling flavor now?

I could not identify the filling, and did not want to say anything insulting with a guess. This was a special meal these students had chosen and paid for with me as their guest. Platters of *jiaozi* and other dishes in a restaurant would be draining on their budgets even with sharing the cost.

"You have me fooled. I cannot guess what this is. Please tell me."

"Donkey!" they called out happily.

I don't know what I expected, but it never would have been donkey. In my shock, I made a gross error. I laughed, not a laugh of humor but of uncomfortable surprise. I could hardly believe I had eaten dumplings filled with meat from a donkey.

My earliest memories of a donkey were in Bible stories of Mary riding on a donkey on the journey to Bethlehem with Joseph. Our culture had also given me *Brighty of Grand Canyon* and dozens of other books about donkeys: shaggy, funny, stubborn, and magical. My parents had read these stories to me until I could read them myself.

Smiles faded at my burst of laughter. How could I remove this insult to these kind students? I knew my laugh over their choice of donkey had not been a happy sound. *Oh God, give me something to say that will help them to feel that their treat is special to me.*

Into the silence and their serious faces, I said, "I am sorry for my laugh. I am very surprised that this is donkey. Every donkey I have seen here works hard, but the meat in this *jiaozi* is so tender. It is difficult to believe that such delicious meat is donkey."

Smiles returned. I heard sighs of relief. I ate one more *jiaozi* of each kind, including the donkey *jiaozi* lest they think I rejected anything about this meal. "*Hao chi,*" I said when I finished my portion of dumplings. I wondered if anyone else on my team would be served a dish of donkey at the luncheons they attended.

The sky was an odd color when Kent dropped me at the front gate of the school. Like most of the female teachers who rode motor bikes, Kent wore a dress and shoes with medium height heels. After I climbed off the back of her motorbike, I thanked her.

Then I walked slowly around the classroom building thinking of the students at the luncheon. An unusually strong breeze blew in a gust against my back, and dust I could feel and taste swirled around me. I turned to look at the sky. Dark clouds, an odd gray ochre, moved like slow swimmers across the sky. I turned my back to them and continued quickly toward the dorm.

Ye, Jeff, and some of Jeff's students, Marge, and Cassie were on the wide steps at the dorm and cafeteria building. I lifted my hand and waved to them. Suddenly, their smiles disappeared. Marge pointed, but it was not at me.

It was beyond me, behind me. I turned to look back again and saw a rolling, roiling, vast dark cloud rushing across the rocky plain below the mountains. It blocked out all the other clouds I had viewed in the sky. It blocked out a view of everything beneath it. The whirling wind created a wall of opaque dust. If it surrounded me, I doubted I would be able to see or breathe.

"Run! Ms. Virginia! Run!" they shouted from the dorm steps.

I did the best I could with my odd limping gait due to having one leg shorter than the other. Everyone except Cassie and Ye disappeared into the level of the cafeteria. Cassie held the door open, and Ye came down the steps to offer me his hand. He pulled me up the last step and into the cafeteria just as the swirling brown-gray dust storm cloud blotted out any view of the buildings or the school grounds.

Cassie and Ye leaned against the door. Jeff and his students said, "It's a dust storm. A small one, just one big cloud. They come sometimes. Fast. Sometimes they are so big they last longer. They cover everything with dirt and dust."

Fast was right. By the time I caught my breath, the dust cloud storm had passed through the schoolyard and over this dorm and cafeteria building. I thought about all the little shops in the street beyond the alley gate. The people would have had no time to take items inside, and some didn't even have sturdy doors or windows on their shops.

The layer of dust over the cafeteria floor was mainly near the door. I touched my face and hair and could feel a coating of the dust. Ye and Cassie had some on them too.

"Thank you," I said. "It is a good thing you all yelled at me to run," I hoped I sounded appreciative. I went closer to the door and saw the dust outside was thick on the landscape that workers tried so hard to beautify. Jeff and his students

Xiong and Koshing, plus Cassie, Marge, Ye, and I stood looking out through the door Ye had reopened. What did they think about when such a storm blew through their workspaces, homes, and city?

To conclude this incredibly unusual day, Emily invited me to visit with her parents after classes ended for the day. I said goodbye to my rescuers and hurried to my room to clean up and have some rest before the afternoon classes.

I would meet Emily by the front gates of the school. She said that she would come to get me at five-thirty. We could walk to her parents' house from the school.

They lived in one of the oldest communities in Wuhai, within a mile of our host school. First, we walked over the sidewalk along the tree lined main road. All the sidewalks I had seen in China had at least one long row of tactile pavers for people who could not see well or who were blind. The paving ended at the street that ran along the wall around the school's track. Where the sidewalk pavers ended, only a dirt path ran along each side of the street. Dust from the fast-moving storm had been obvious, but human street sweepers with brooms worked daily in the city and were out now.

We crossed the street and walked to a dirt road that went upward toward the mountains. The dust seemed undisturbed on this road until we walked through it and up the slight but steady incline. The ascending road narrowed the more we walked until we came to a place where a brick wall, about thirty feet long, showed that we had come to the end of the road. I could see the tops of trees beyond the wall.

Emily said, "This is my parents' home. They have lived here for forty-five years."

The entrance in the wall appeared as a moon gate, a round doorway that can be shut when wide wooden doors, painted dark red and positioned on each side, are pulled shut. The color of the wooden moon gate doors almost matched the clay-red bricks of the wall. I had learned that red always symbolized joy, good fortune, and feng shui.

"The round doorway is wonderful, Emily. I wish I could have such a door at my home. And why is the dust not so thick here as it was down nearer the school?"

"My parents' home is in an odd space between the mountains. Often the dust storms come at an angle that misses them. The door is very old style. Moon gates in Mandarin are called" (月亮门 *yuèliàngmén*). Emily pointed out how the clay-red bricks had been fitted and shaped right against the round opening.

"My parents can shut and lock the wooden doors over the moon gate each night."

When I followed her inside, her parents put down the brooms they had been using to sweep dust off their stone patio. They hurried to greet us, both more petite than Emily, standing only as high as my shoulders. Because the dust storm sped by without dropping a thick layer of dust here, I could see art in the color and design arrangement of the flowers and heads of vegetables, including different kinds of colorful cabbages that were as beautiful as the vibrant flowers. After welcoming me, Emily's parents showed me around this garden that Emily said formed the true heart of their home.

The mountains started not far beyond the house. Gray-brown, rocky, rugged, the irregular peaks created a dramatic contrast to the balanced beauty of the house and garden. In the enclosed yard, a winding path looped around the different areas, with a pond in the center that had large gold-fish. Rocks and flowers decorated the base of the bamboo trees clustered at each corner of the garden. Delicate weeping willows stood on the side of each group of bamboo trees.

Near the house, an inviting seating arrangement stood ready for us. Well behind the table and chairs, a wide lattice supported grape vines. I looked back toward the moon gate, and saw fruit trees near the wall, cherry, plum, pear, pomegranates, and figs.

"Your garden is like a piece of heaven dropped down by the mountains," I said as I took the seat Emily's father indicated for me at the table. Emily sat to my left, then her mother and her father sat to my right. Just by asking about parts of their garden over the next couple of hours, I learned how many years and how much effort it had taken to create this oasis of rich colors, textures, and scents.

Emily's parents were retired, and besides gardening, they stayed involved with community activities, exercising in the early morning with routines in *qigong* and *tai chi*. Plus, they belonged to a ballroom dance group for couples. Emily's mother was part of a women's group that kept the knowledge and practice of traditional costumes and dances alive by teaching younger women. Their group appeared in celebrations and parades.

Both of Emily's parents moved with an agility that I envied. Although their union had begun as an arranged marriage, they seemed comfortably in love. The visit refreshed many ideas and strengthened my hopes about long years of marriage, I felt sad thinking of the ongoing disappointment with marriage that Tia would have to face at home.

Looking back on the entire day, I thought of how Jessie had done her best to warn us about surprises. I had lacked the imagination to guess at the combination of events in a day: Mozart in the desert, preparing teachers for their final projects, donkey dumplings, riding on the back of a motorbike driven by a teacher in a lovely dress and heels, a dust cloud bigger than the school buildings, a visit to a garden with a moon gate, watching the tenderness between a couple married for over fifty years, and back at the school a subdued dinner with our classroom assistants. We shared reflections on the SEP time.

Emerging from an emotional cloud, I saw how my frustration and anger had caused a gritty storm between me and God. Now I felt like a dry sponge dipped into a spring of fresh water. My selfishly stunted spirit had expanded through the refreshing experiences God provided. Trusting a Creator who loved me and knew everything about all of my days seemed like the wisest path.

Chapter 26

Just Continue Looking Up

"Since we had all our class assistants with us at dinner, I didn't get to ask, how was your time out with Emily?" Tia said as she came out into the hall while I was opening the door to my room.

"It was serene and beautiful. Emily has wonderful parents. They didn't have education beyond middle school, but they made sure she went to college. What did you do after class and before dinner?"

"While you were out, I just rested here. Only four more days. Sometimes that seems so long, and sometimes I feel scared by how soon I'll be back in Massachusetts. You've had some good visits in people's homes. I've only been to Thomas and Penny's. I think my crying in class scared anyone from thinking of having me over. It's okay, though. I've needed lots of quiet time alone and all my students are so kind to me."

"Anyone who knows your situation would understand your stress, Tia."

"What about you? Is there anything else you really wanted to do or see that hasn't happened yet?"

"I need to go to a place that sells weapons."

"Weapons? You want to buy a weapon?"

"My brother collects weapons. I don't want any weapons in my house, but he collects them. He's my only sibling, so I want to get him something special from Nei Menggu, maybe a Mongolian knife. He was against me coming here. I want him to have a souvenir that shows him some of the incredible history of this place."

"How will you find a weapons store?"

"I expect that Ye or Thomas will have some ideas."

"Yes. I'm sure they will. Are you looking forward to leaving? You've seemed content and involved, enough so that you could live here. You haven't seemed to mind having someone with you all the time, no matter if it's for protection or for just keeping an eye on you."

"No. I haven't minded. Emily and others have been such a great help. You know I could have been cheated at the bank the one time I went to change more dollars for yuan. I went up to the teller alone because Emily was talking on her phone. She came up to the counter as the teller was giving me the yuan and boy did she scold that woman! Emily didn't do that loudly, but the woman got red in the face and gave me more money. I do wish I knew the language more than polite phrases."

"Jaye has gotten bitter over the constant companions. Doug doesn't go out much, and Kathryn said she is only disappointed she didn't get to shop more. I'm thankful for the time here, but it has been difficult, harder than I imagined. Have you been surprised?"

"Yes, surprised by what I learned about myself as much as by what I've learned about China. I had no idea what to expect. Being here, working with our students, meeting others, every experience has reminded me that I don't believe anything happens by chance. I'd lost that awareness. Tia, I believe God placed us here. These are the people who we were supposed to meet. This area of China has definitely broken through all the prejudiced comments I've heard from my family and friends."

Tia said, "I hope I can feel safe with God to get me through each day. I never expected to get divorced. Going home to be alone is scary. When are you going home? You're staying longer than the rest of us. I remember you said that was why you walked all around Guangzhou airport getting the layout of it, because you'll be leaving alone from there."

"I'm in China for just a few days after debriefing."

"I wouldn't want to travel around this country by myself. I never did pick up more than a few simple words in Chinese. I'm glad we can all fly to Beijing together for the debriefing, and I'm glad to have company on the way back home. Do you think the debriefing will be just a bunch of questions and forms?"

"I'm not sure, but there will probably be a time for sharing best and worst moments, plus a worship time on Sunday morning."

"Jaye paid extra and got an afternoon flight to Chicago on Sunday, direct from Beijing, so she doesn't have to go back out of Guangzhou like the rest of us will. Kathryn, Doug, and I fly back to the US late Sunday evening. When did they say we will go to the Wuhai airport on Saturday?"

"Not super early, eight, I think. The plane leaves at nine thirty. We'll fly back the way we came, about an hour to Hohhot, then two to Beijing. Amity staff will meet us and take us to the hotel for the debriefing. Your flight home is on Sunday evening?"

"Yes, Sunday evening. I'm glad Doug and Kathryn will be with me. And you're staying until next Sunday, alone? I wouldn't do that." Tia sounded concerned.

"Late afternoon, on Sunday, I'm transferring to another hotel in Beijing. I want to take my time going through the Forbidden City on Monday morning. I'll try to see another museum or more sections of Beijing in the afternoon, as much as I can. I have a ticket go to the Beijing opera on Monday night. On Tuesday, I travel to Xi'an."

"Xi'an? Where's that? And why?"

"I only had the time and money to do one big tourist activity. It was either the Great Wall or the Terra-cotta soldiers. I chose the Terra-cotta soldiers, so Xi'an. Two thousand years ago, Xi'an was the capital of China. People visit Xi'an because so much of its incredible history can be seen in the city wall, one of the few that has lasted almost completely since ancient times. Plus, Xi'an also has famous pagodas that date back to the six hundreds and a mosque that dates back to the middle of the seven hundreds.

"You'll see all that stuff?"

"As much as I can."

"On your own! I admire you but think it's a bit crazy."

"I'd like to count on getting back to China, but I don't know. That's why I am going to try to do all of this even if I am alone."

"The Great Wall is the most famous site. I would go to that or to the summer palace if I had planned to be a tourist. I'm just too tired. If I was doing this over, I'd be a tourist first and then do the Amity program."

"That's sounds like a really good idea. If I come back, I will try that."

"Do you think you'll come back to work with Amity again?"

"I am thinking about it, and I'm praying about it too. I'd like to return."

"Virginia, I really appreciate you praying with me and for me. I pray a lot for strength and wisdom, but I feel better when someone else prays too."

"I wasn't praying much when I signed up for Amity. I was angry with God because of some changes in my life that I didn't expect, and I didn't like."

"Don't I know it! I sure felt hurt and angry this year. I couldn't believe my ears when my husband asked me for a divorce. I wondered why God let it happen. I still do. Is your marriage okay?"

"Yes, but we moved to an area and found unexpected difficulties, for me more than for my husband. He really feels good about his new position. I've been difficult to live with, grouchy, complaining a lot to him a lot before I came here. He kept encouraging me to trust God to renew my career. I've been selfish in my anger and forgot how much mutual encouragement is needed in any relationship."

"That's the truth. I know I have to trust God more. Hey, switching gears. Tell me more about why you chose Xi'an instead of going to the Great Wall."

"I chose Xi'an also because it was the starting point for the Silk Road."

"The Silk Road that comes through Inner Mongolia?"

"Yes. And in Xi'an, farmers digging a well back in 1974 found a huge surprise, one of the biggest of the twentieth century."

"The Terra-cotta soldiers?"

"A vast amount of them, all made of clay. They discovered an army complete with horses, carriages, and chariots. They haven't even uncovered all of what is buried there. When the emperor died, his grand tomb was made like a big treasure chest. It contained everything he had in life in the form of clay statutes for the next life. Wars, robbers, and storms over the decades buried or broke everything built for the emperor."

"Until the farmers accidentally found it when digging?"

"Yes. Pretty amazing find. Early on Thursday evening, I will fly from Xi'an to Guangzhou, then an overnight flight to Los Angeles. From there, I'll head to Seattle, where I'll visit friends that I haven't seen in person for years. I'll spend four days in Seattle, on Bainbridge Island. Then I'll fly to Boston where my husband will meet me."

"I don't know many married women who could be gone for a summer. You and Kathryn have unique marriages compared to most women I know."

I would have said more about how special Jerry's support was in our marriage, but I didn't because I thought about what Tia was facing in her life. Divorce was painful and probably more in her case because of her husband leaving her for a far younger woman who was going to have his baby.

"You and Doug still doing the casual conversation, English Corner, tonight?"

"Yes, today and tomorrow. Then that's it. I should get going because students will arrive by eight."

* * *

A group of nine SEP teachers and three of their students joined us on the steps for this next to the last evening of casual conversations. Yuze brought his guitar. We sang every song the classes had learned. "My Heart Will Go On" came last. Subjects ranged from calligraphy to wolves. Then, near the end of our time, we were quiet. After the crazy dust storm, the night seemed extra clear.

We all looked up because the sky pulled our attention like a magnet. Light years away, the tiny sequins sparkled above us, as bright as diamond chips thrown on midnight blue velvet. God's awesome creation. I glanced at the Chinese and Mongolian students who studied the sky.

These young people around us had grown up in this communist country. No concept of God was taught in their upbringing unless they had family members who talked about faith. I felt sad. Then Thomas changed my feelings, and maybe the thoughts and feelings of everyone.

Thomas, the former physics teacher, a person who had a special love for science said, "Looking at the stars in the heavens on such a clear night as this makes me think an intelligence designed all of it."

No one else spoke. We all just continued looking up.

Tuesday at the lunch break, Ye found me. "Ms. Virginia, Ms. Tia said you need to buy a present for your brother, a Mongolian knife maybe?"

"Yes. That is what I told her. Do you know a place?"

"Yes, Ms. Virginia. We could go there now."

"Thank you, Ye. I would love to do that. Will we walk or take a taxi?"

"I think a taxi. Ms. Marge also knows the man, so she will come with us."

Marge was waiting at the bottom of the stairs. We

walked to the alley by the dorm and took that side gate into the narrow and bustling street. A tricycle pedicab waited there. The driver pedaled fast and in minutes we arrived in a dilapidated side street at a shop that fit the category of hole in the wall.

When my eyes adjusted to the dim light in the shop, I saw floor to ceiling boxes behind a long table. A gray-haired man with skin wrinkled as a raisin, stood in front of the table. He bowed and greeted us.

"*Huānyíng*," he said in a voice roughened by years of smoking.

Marge talked with him, and so did Ye. The man took a few boxes from the shelves behind him, opened them on the table, and pulled a cord that turned on a single bulb ceiling light over the table. I saw three knives that looked as old as Genghis Khan.

The first one, I would never try to buy to take on a flight, not even in a checked bag. It was a sword that looked something like a scimitar, but it did not have as great a curve. It was shorter too, probably better for slashing. I pointed at it and shook my head, no. The man lifted the next box and held it out to me.

This box held a long dagger with etchings and gilding. Its handle was wrapped with leather and the scabbard was made of the same leather and decorated with deep etchings and metal work designs. When I did not move my head in approval or with a negative motion, the man put this box down and picked up the last one.

The man spoke, and Marge translated. "This is a knife of Mongols but shows Chinese influence. The knife is a single edged blade made of black cattle horn with white streaks. The scabbard is wooden, covered with leather and steel. You see it has a brass dragon? This fits on a belt. On the front is the animal revered by the Mongols, a wolf."

"These all look very expensive, Marge. I do not have a lot of money."

"Ye and I will talk for you. You like this last one?"

"I think my brother would like it very much. It is small enough that I can tuck it deep into my checked bag when leaving here. We cannot take any weapons in handbags or carry-on bags."

Marge and Ye gave their best effort at bargaining with this man. I picked up enough words to know they were emphasizing my work for no pay for weeks in the city to help teachers and students, my friendship with the teachers, and my visits to the families. They must have been convincing because the price on the knife box showed 11,000 yuan, which was like $785 in US money. One dollar equaled about fifteen yuan in 2004.

The price offered to me after intense conversation and bargaining was 3,500 yuan, about $250 dollars. My brother had nothing like this in his weapons collection, and I would never have another chance to buy such an item with two expert bargainers, so, I did it. I bought the knife.

The man boxed the knife with care and gave me a broad smile as he handed it to me with a legal bill of sale. I thanked him as did Marge and Ye.

Outside, Marge said, "Ms. Virginia, I am happy we could help you get this gift for your brother."

"It is wonderful, Marge. I thank you and Ye for helping me with this. Ye, you look more serious than you did in the shop. What are you thinking about?"

"I don't know if the security at the airport will let you take the knife home."

"I will have it in checked luggage, not my carry-on. I also have the bill of sale."

"They will open your checked luggage and your carry-on. They may not care about a bill of sale." Ye looked at Marge and neither of them looked as happy as I felt about the purchase. I resolved to wrap the knife in many layers of clothing. An antique weapon, well wrapped, in a checked bag should go through, shouldn't it?

Chapter 27

Mongolian and Chinese Farewells

On the final Wednesday afternoon gathering of all the classes in the big assembly hall, we repeated favorite role-plays that were worthy of any stage. The skits included common scenes like pretending to be sick to get out of going to school to classic and amazing tales of the legendary Monkey King. The presentations entertained everyone.

We laughed until we cried and clapped until our hands hurt. We even had some charades about the movies we had shown over the weeks: *Eight Below, Old Yeller, Black Beauty,* and *How the Grinch Stole Christmas.* Discussion went well past the allotted time. People lingered. Many clasped hands. Some people even gave us hugs.

And we still had one last English Corner. June joined us for our dinner time, and Principal Chen said June should invite Yuze, her husband. Yuze got along well with the teachers who were there in the room with us. He did not say much, but I expect that in listening he could tell his English level was close to some of the teachers.

We went right from dinner to sitting out on the wide steps under that Mongolian evening canopy. I felt refreshed by watching its blue hues from cornflower to cerulean to cobalt to a midnight sapphire. Each transformation captured glitters of stars aglow in the softness of the summer night air.

Cooler temperatures than in the day contributed to relaxation, and there was a sweetness in singing that evening. My heart would indeed go on, but it ached knowing there would be no other night like this one. Could I ever see these wonderful people again? Trusting the future to an unseen God challenged me every day.

We sang until almost eleven. Staff and workers at the school joined us on the steps. The head housekeeper told us, through our assistants, that people gathered out in the street at the end of the alley whenever we started singing. The buoyancy in this last casual evening ebbed away as Yuze stowed his guitar and our students said, "See you tomorrow."

* * *

For our last full Thursday, class time focused on reviewing main points from our text throughout the morning. We discussed not only why their students should learn English but also methods they thought they could use as their new school year started. My class left with noisy chatter in English about the afternoon presentations.

Because our classes had a high number of students, it took all Thursday afternoon for their timed presentations. We went until 6:00 p.m. with the presentations and planned to finish on Friday morning. These counted as their final exams. We called this process a SEP evaluation since the word exam caused such stress.

Thursday evening was quiet. We hadn't met as a team since Monday, and we wouldn't tonight. I wished Doug had called a meeting, but the team members had said they were tired, wanted to pack, and get extra rest. I read, listened to my Pimsleur Chinese, packed a little, but kept out the plain red lined rain jacket that I planned to give to Ye. Though it rarely rained in Wuhai, the jacket was also a wind breaker, and it had a lining that could give warmth in the winter. They rarely had snow, but they did have some below freezing temperatures. And, the jacket was red, a special color anywhere in China. In my heart, I believed Ye would move beyond Wuhai, beyond Inner Mongolia.

Clapping and cheering came from classes as the last students completed their presentations late Friday morning. Delight came in seeing some of the most quiet and tense students present interesting topics and activities. For people who had never worked with native speakers of English, our students had grown in knowledge, designing lessons, listening, and speaking skills. Would they ever really use our activities in teaching their own classes?

Erdeen, Marge, and Emily had assured me that the teachers of early primary grades would teach the songs, poems, and games. Their young people did not play with language sounds and content the way our children's books demonstrated. Dr Seuss. Lloyd Moss, Margaret Wise Brown, Ludwig Bemelman, Jane Yolen, Eric Carle, and Shel Silverstein had been favorites and borrowed often overnight in the lending process we had established in week one.

Teachers of the upper grades would try to incorporate

more opportunities for listening and speaking, but they would find it much more difficult to include fun activities. Learning was a serious process here with the university qualification exam looming ahead of them. Still, they assured us they could find use for the listening comprehension activities. Students would have to listen to recorded English on some exams.

We gave out certificates and walked together to the cafeteria. This Friday, we had lunch with all our SEP students. Even those who usually went home to make lunch for a child or other family members stayed to eat with the whole group in the school cafeteria.

In addition to the dishes the cafeteria served, we had requested and purchased a popular ice cream here, red bean ice cream. No one on my team had ever had ice cream made of beans, not even Doug, but we had tried it from concession stands in the square. It was delicious and our assistants assured us that the SEP students would enjoy the ice cream. Ye found a merchant who, for a good price, sold and delivered individual cups of ice cream to the school cafeteria.

In each class, some students had joined together to purchase gifts that their teacher could fit easily into a suitcase: a scarf, tea, a small book about Inner Mongolia, Nei Menggu postcards, pictures of Genghis Kahn, fans, and calligraphy poems. We had not expected gifts. I felt grateful that they had joined together to buy them so that we knew they did not have to take on extra expenses alone.

Our team had an hour to rest after lunch while the students decorated the classrooms for class parties. Because our classes were so large, even with a set time for every presentation, it had taken hours to listen to the final projects from each SEP participant. We all looked forward to relaxing with a party in the afternoon.

Streamers, posters, banners, flags, and balloons created a festive atmosphere. Our team didn't talk about it, but Jaye was almost a half an hour late getting to her classroom for their party. I had stopped counting the times she was late to class and stopped offering to walk with her as had Kathryn and Tia. Doug never brought up her lateness in team meetings. When would I have done that if I had been the team leader?

I wondered if Jaye apologized to her class or commented on their work decorating the classroom. All their efforts were a gift showing appreciation. Some decorations in each class-room showed artistic talent in painting. Most showed the lovely calligraphy special to this city. Even humor showed up in hand drawn cartoons about the classes or about homework.

Because we'd had a banquet of choices for lunch, far more than students ever had in regular cafeteria lines, refreshments for the parties were simple. The refreshments were watermelon, sunflower seeds, and cake. We supplied the beverages.

Once again, Ye knew little stores nearby that would give us a good deal on hundreds of bottles of water and popular bottled teas, Master Kong, jasmine, peach, green, and black tea. We had trusted Ye with an amount Emily deemed appropriate, and he not only got enough bottled drinks but also arranged to have them delivered to the top-floor classrooms.

Our surprise to the students came when we announced that none of the books, decorations, games (like Boggle, Scrabble, Password, the Pyramid Game), or teaching aids in our classrooms would go home with us. They each could choose something. We suggested that they walk around and look at everything before they made their decisions.

Whatever was left, after all the choices were made, would stay with our host school. Fortunately, we'd brought enough. We had even mailed boxes of books and games from the US to our host school before we left for China. No one had to take only what was left. Everyone could have a choice.

Following the party hour, the school had scheduled a time for taking pictures, class by class, whole group, with teaching assistants, and with administrators. A professional photographer and his assistants arranged us and took the pictures. Then came formal farewells, speeches by the administrators, a speech by Doug translated by John, had projected the speeches clearly. One song played over the loudspeakers..

The melodic strings and rhythm of instrumentation in flutes, piano, and even bagpipes in "My Heart Will Go On" emerged. Without me directing, all the students stood up and did the sign language motions, fluid yet precise, coordinated as only a culture accustomed to group work in everything could achieve. Their voices harmonized and betrayed an emotional connection to the words as a parting statement that this special work together would stay in their minds and hearts. I knew it would stay in mine. I blinked fast and wiped tears away.

The administrators and other city officials present applauded. They knew the song had been taught in ASL. The power of the goodbye in the song, yet the message of an ongoing connection seemed to have touched the spirits of the students, administrators, and visitors involved in Wuhai's closing ceremony for the 2004 SEP.

After the ceremony, some students stayed for individual pictures. By 6 pm everyone had departed. They knew that because this was our last Friday evening in Wuhai, there would be a ceremonial dinner with principals from every school that had sent a participant to the SEP.

Emily suggested that we dress in our best outfits because the local television station would film people entering the grand hotel near the government building. Tia and Kathryn wore the traditional *qipao* dresses that a tailor made for them. Tia's was deep burgundy, and Kathryn's was an emerald green. More surprising was that Jaye had a dress made too. She had kept it a secret from all of us. It was sunset gold and looked gorgeous on her athletic build and with her long blonde hair. I wished she would smile. She looked beautiful, but her expression remained serious, almost frowning.

The three women looked like gems had taken human form, lovely in their tailor-made dresses, make-up, and freshly done hair. I felt like the plain school marm in my midi-length navy blue and white dress. I didn't wear make-up and my unruly naturally curly hair that people often asked to touch formed a brunette cloud around my head. Doug looked more formal in black trousers and a dark patterned shirt. He didn't need a tie. We had rarely seen a man who wore a tie in this summer climate.

Our hosts took us to a hotel that catered to large government events. It had glowing wood furniture, simple chandeliers, walls with a lustrous silk brocade covering, draperies of matching material, sparkling glass goblets, china with a cobalt, white, rust, and red floral design, shining implements, and polished *kuaizi*. Flower arrangements in dark red vases looked like minimalist art. The impression was of quiet assured power.

Only one teacher had been invited from each of our classes. This person would sit beside each of us as an individual translator for the evening. Our team was sprinkled around the tables, none of us near one another. I had Erdeen, Tia had Emily. Jaye had Delia. Kathryn had Kent, and Doug had Thomas. They not only interpreted but also guided us through the moments when we might have made mistakes because we didn't know when to toast or which dishes were spicy, sour, sweet, savory, or bitter.

Toasting commenced early, and the dinner included the traditional Mongolian and Chinese dishes. Representing the Mongolians, we had milk tea, steamed dough made from oats, and lamb banquet dishes that had the roasted mutton. Besides this we had half a dozen cold dishes and another half dozen hot dishes.

I did not get the names of every dish, but Erdeen helped me with some, *qurut*, dried curd cheese, thin sliced strips of beef, *Niislel* salad, which is like a potato salad, cold garlic noodles tossed in a sauce of garlic, ginger, sesame oil, and rice wine, nuts and seed dishes that I recognized. Among the hot dishes we had *huushuur* which tops the center of a pancake with meat flavored with salt and onion. Then the circle of the pancake is folded up to make the *huushuur* like a pouch.

Among the Chinese dishes, we had a cucumber salad made with sesame paste, rice vinegar and garlic, and a radish salad with a green salsa that had a super-hot kick that lasted through other dishes. The clear noodles in chili sauce set mouths on fire. Jaye and Tia refused to taste marinated pig tongue but enjoyed the prawn summer rolls. Hot dishes included stir-fried spinach with garlic, hot and sour soup, spicy mushrooms with bamboo shoots, and eggplant in garlic sauce.

I thought we should have avoided eating for at least two days before this banquet and wondered again if the staff could take the leftovers home. Doug's reputation had preceded him. Everyone present paid attention to his toasts and his responses to toasts. Would Doug come back another time to work with Amity? Would anyone warn his future team or hosts of his vow regarding alcohol? Would any of us keep in touch with one another? My team, except for Jaye, lived within a ninety-minute drive of one another.

Did I want to stay in touch with them? I would probably reach out at least once after we were home, especially to Tia. Would I want to be on a team again with these people? No. But I did believe God put these people into my life for a reason. Working with this group had taught me more about team commitment, goals, and necessary efforts in a different culture.

* * *

Ye came to the school early enough to say goodbye before we went to the airport. I gave him the red-lined rain jacket from LL Bean. He seemed amazed by the rainproof material, many pockets, and the removable gray inner lining that would add warmth in the colder weather.

"I bought this especially for this trip, Ye, because I thought the weather would be like it is in the northeast of Nei Menggu. This jacket is suitable for a man or woman. It is from a famous store in the US. I would like you to have this because you did not choose to take a gift from the party time. You have been a wonderful help, a true gift to us in our time here."

Ye liked the jacket, and it fit him well. He said he had no jacket as comfortable. He put it on in front of our team, and they all complimented him on the fit and how great he looked in the dark red jacket.

As Ye was leaving Principal Chen saw Ye and invited him to go to the airport with us. That was another surprise and treat for us. Although I looked calm when the original group of greeters, minus the superintendent from Hohhot, took us to the airport, my emotions had turbulence of at least a Category 2 hurricane. I wanted to hug people, to say I hoped we can meet again, to promise I would come back to Wuhai if I ever returned to China. I wanted to say they were so special that I would bring my husband to meet them. I didn't say any of this because I didn't want to cry and couldn't know if any of it would happen.

One surprise let some emotion spill out, a mix of anger and sadness. Someone had figured out a way to scam tourists by letting them buy something, but then not letting them have it. When the security people X-rayed all of our checked bags, they said they had to open mine. The knife. I knew it had to be because of the knife, but it had a sales receipt attached to it.

That didn't matter. They unwrapped it, throwing the clothing to one side. Ye and Marge had guessed this might happen. I turned to look at Ye and saw sincere sadness.

In the manner of a scolding that Emily translated while blushing, a security guard said the knife was a precious piece of local culture. It should not have been sold. The security people confiscated it and my sales receipt. No one argued with them, and I certainly would not.

As I stuffed my clothing rapidly back into the suitcase, I told myself it was an expensive lesson about the culture and a possible selling and taking back scam that I had fallen for. Because of the concept of guanxi that the classes had explained to us, I suspected the old man would have the knife returned to him and sell it again, giving the guards money for returning it to him, or maybe the guards just kept such items.

Doug, Kathryn, Jaye, and Tia stood off to the side until I closed my suitcase. A supervising security guard frowned at me throughout the process. He took my case after I closed the latches. The security officer placed it on the conveyor belt. We stood silently and watched it move forward. It passed through now without any more problems.

Principal Chen led us into the waiting room that had a wall of windows facing the runway and a door where we would exit. We shook hands, said many *xie xies*, walked out of the terminal and toward the plane. Even though looking back had caused distress sometimes in my life, I could not resist looking back at this moment. This was my last chance to see some very special people.

The teachers and Ye stood in a row by the big windows and lifted a hand. I thought they would wave goodbye. But no, they lifted a hand to say a sentence in American Sign Language. Principal Chen stood behind the line and smiled.

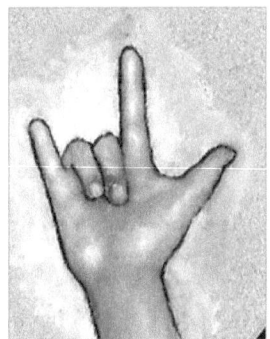

In ASL, I love you.

Chapter 28

Debriefing, Disclosing, and Desires

For the debriefing we stayed in an attractive and clean, but not deluxe Beijing hotel that probably had been in existence for twenty years. Beijing's streets overwhelmed the senses. I felt like a Lilliputian walking on a sleeping giant. Outside the hotel, we could smell food from street venders, vehicle exhaust, animals, heat, and people. Cars did not dominate transportation, so bicycles and motor bikes filled the streets along with buses, pedestrians, pedicabs, rickshaws, and cars made mainly in Germany, China, and Japan.

Whenever we left the Beijing hotel for a walk or sightseeing, we experienced a modern capital with personality and vestiges of more than three thousand years of history.

I didn't know all the leaders of China since Chairman Mao, but I knew some basics about the current president, Hu Jintao. China experienced changes in expectations and hopes in the twenty-first century because of more interaction with the world. Millions more people learned English, and the number of cell phone owners caused changes in the ideas and expectations of the general population. Beijing throbbed with every kind of life.

In 2004 bicycles still far outnumbered cars in every city. This is in Beijing

We saw Jessie again. She greeted teams as they arrived, but her responsibilities and our travel plans did not allow us to have a personal conversation about what she had meant to us. I planned to tell her how important her words and guidance had been to me in an email to her Nanjing address. Jessie met with the teams to ask questions and hear opinions about the SEP. She also gave out the debriefing questionnaires and would compare our comments to her evaluation of the city and host school.

I looked at the debriefing questionnaire. I could answer each question briefly, but I knew they wanted full and descriptive answers. Jessie had explained that to us.

Question 1: Would you return to China as a volunteer with Amity to teach in another remote rural region? *I could answer yes to that, with one condition, only if I brought my own team.*

Question 2: What was the most difficult part of this teaching experience? *My team.*

Question 3: What was the most positive part of the Amity experience? *The teachers who were our students and the hosting community.*

Question 4: Did team members model the highest standards for teaching? *Four out of five did.*

Question 5: Is there any team member you think should not participate with Amity programs in the future. *Yes.*

Question 6: Provide evaluation of team members and describe at least two strengths and two weaknesses of each person. Give examples to support your evaluations. *I could do that but not easily. Writing negative evaluations causes turmoil in me.*

Question 7: Would you recommend this location for Amity placement of a long-term teaching position? *Yes, and I wish I could be that teacher.*

Amity gave us plenty of time to write detailed answers. I wrote paragraphs.

* * *

I wouldn't want to live in China for the rest of my life, but the people in Wuhai had been so open and hospitable that it was like having someone open a door to a hidden treasure room. I would love to spend a year or a few years teaching in Wuhai. Prejudices could be overcome. Precious friendships could be made.

When I was in third grade, I learned a little about the power of China's government and how it changed lives. An older couple, Rev and Mrs. Swift, spent time as guests with my family. The Swifts had been missionaries in China from their newly wed days in 1919. They lived and worked in the same western province of China for decades and were loved by the community.

But in 1953, the Swifts, like any foreigners involved in mission work, had to leave China. The communist government expelled them. If they had chosen to stay, Rev and Mrs. Swift would have been imprisoned or executed. For more than thirty years of their lives, from young newlyweds to late middle age, China had been their home. Chinese and some ethnic dialects were their heart languages. They prayed in it, sang in it, and even dreamed in it.

The Swifts appeared in my memory as frail as Chinese paper art. In the time we had for reflection in the debriefing days, I could see how a seed of interest in China had been planted in the Swift's visits. Now I wanted to return to China to work with Amity, and I wondered if Jerry would ever do the volunteer work with me. I'd seen how the male teachers showed extra enjoyment in talking with a man leading the class.

Jerry liked routines and planning more than surprises and adventures. The Swifts had so many unusual adventures together in their decades in China. Could it work out for Jerry to have so much time away from the church he pastored? How would that affect his ministry? Had Rev and Mrs. Swift both had the same amount of desire to go to China?

My parents had explained that when Chairman Mao kicked out all the foreigners, the Swifts hadn't known what they would do back in the US. They decided to travel around the United States speaking about missions. They told how God had drawn them to China, given them a love for the people there, and provided for them over the years.

That all sounded good, but when I asked my parents how the Swifts earned money, they told me about 'love offerings.' I realized that love offerings were like giving to a charity. So, I asked my parents if the Swifts could buy a house just with money from love offerings. The answer was no. They had found a community built for retired missionaries where the rent was low. I wondered if all the missionaries Chairman Mao had commanded to leave China also went to their home countries as poor people for the rest of their lives. How did they stay happy if they had so little?

Though she looked old to me, Mrs. Swift seemed not only happy, but romantic when she told the story of their first visit to a home in rural China. They were served the best dish for honored guests, rooster head soup. An entire rooster head was cooked coxcomb, beak, eyes, and all. The chicken head was boiled so long that it became totally soft and flavored the broth. The Swifts received the honor of having two roosters killed for their welcome meal. They each could have a rooster head in their bowls. Mrs. Swift took one look and whispered to her husband, "I just can't."

In his masterful Chinese, Mr. Swift thanked the hosts for the special meal but said that his wife had an unsettled stomach. She would enjoy their company but would not eat anything. I must have looked confused because Mr. Swift said to me, "Where we lived, if a person did not eat the special food served in one's honor, it was best to give a good reason and not eat anything else. We did not want them to think we would reject their meal. These poor people had used up two roosters for us."

Mrs. Swift added, "And then they insisted that Allan have both bowls with the rooster heads in them. My husband loved me so much that he ate both bowls of the rooster head soup and praised the family's cooking." She then looked at him with a glance that made me think they were old but still in love.

I thought of Jerry who waited for me back in Massachusetts. When I applied to teach as a volunteer for Amity, memories of the Swifts had rushed into my mind. I remembered telling Jerry the story of the rooster head soup and asking, "Could you eat two bowls of rooster head soup to get us out of an embarrassing predicament?"

"That won't be a challenge I'll face since I don't expect to go to China."

"But could you do it? Eat soft rooster heads in broth flavored from their heads?"

"You're the one going to China. Could you?"

"I asked you first."

"Maybe. I'd have to close my eyes or eat without looking into the bowl very much."

"So. you think you could do it?"

"I would look at you and smile. Only you could have gotten me into such a situation."

On the Sunday afternoon of the debriefing weekend in Beijing, people started leaving for airports or places where they would be tourists instead of teachers. Jaye was one of the earliest people to leave. She went right after the morning worship service. We walked to the front of the hotel with her where she wished us all luck, got into the taxi, waved, shut the door, and was off on her return to Chicago.

My goodbye to Kathryn and Tia had been at the front of the hotel when they got into their taxi. We had talked a lot over lunch, gave hugs to one another, and said we'd be in touch. My goodbye to Doug never happened. He left even earlier than Jaye and didn't let any of us know about his change in plans.

I went to speak to one of the young Amity staff, MeiLi. I had met her in Nanjing during the training days. Her English and understanding of what we Westerners needed was impressive.

"MeiLi, I have to transfer hotels, but instead of a taxi, a friend from Wuhai, a young man in the church we attended there, told me he has a friend with a car service. I can call him, and he will come and take me to the new hotel. Here's the number. Can you help me with the call? I have no idea if the driver has any skill with English."

"It would be my honor." She took the paper and made a call. "The driver will be here in twenty minutes. His English name is Timothy, but you were right to ask for help. He has little English, but he is bringing a friend with him. She is a college student here in Beijing. Her major is English. She has long hair, down to her back, and will wear a tan shirt and blue trousers."

"Thank you. MeiLi, you really have natural ease with people. Your English is excellent. I know you are in college here. Is English your major?"

"I am finishing that major, yes. Amity is a good job for my schedule, but I hope to go to graduate school in an English-speaking country. I am going to apply to schools in Canada, the United States, and England."

"If I can help you, by writing a recommendation for you, please let me do that. Here's my email and phone number. I wrote them on a bunch of labels so that I could give them out easily. After my time here, I can see I need a business card if I return."

"Will you come back again to work for Amity?"

"I hope so. I want to build a team with people who know one another before coming here. If I do return, and if you are still doing training in Nanjing, I will make sure my team attends your sessions. Of all the training sessions I attended in Nanjing, yours were the most helpful." We talked about the sessions she taught until my ride arrived.

After Timothy put my suitcase in the trunk, I said goodbye to Meili.

Beside the clean modern car, the young woman inter-preter spoke to me.

"I'm Naomi. Timothy told me his friend, Joel, from Wuhai, asked for you to be given a ride to your next hotel."

"Joel was one of many helpful and friendly people I met in Wuhai. I met him when I went to church there."

"You went to a church there?" Naomi's eyes widened in sincere surprise.

"Yes, I was a volunteer with the Amity organization. Amity workers always try to go to a church in the town where they teach."

"You know, my name, Naomi, is a Bible name."

"I know that. The book of Ruth in the Bible is one of my favorites."

She leaned closer and said, "I am a Christian."

"That's wonderful. You know I almost guessed that just from your name. It is not an English name that anyone else has said to me since I arrived in China. Do you go to church here in Beijing?"

"I am in a house church."

"Ah, I understand. Amity workers do not go to house churches."

Even more than Timothy's kindness as a favor to his friend Joel, Naomi's help was a God-incidence. She walked into the hotel with me and made sure the registration went smoothly. Naomi appeared surprised when I said, "Look around, Naomi. They must be having some kind of convention for parents of baby girls. Have you ever seen so many young parents with babies wearing pink?" She covered her mouth with her hand, but I heard her laugh.

"Naomi, what did I say that was funny? In Wuhai, I heard that using blue for boys and pink for girls, as is done in English speaking countries, is done here too.

"Ms. Virginia, do you not know what kind of hotel this is?"

"What do you mean, what kind of hotel? I chose it because it is not expensive, I can walk to many special sights from this location, and it has a shuttle to the airport."

"This is an adoption hotel."

"An adoption hotel?"

"Yes. Because it is the son's responsibility to take care of his parents, and because people can have only one child, many couples give a baby girl up for adoption instead of aborting the child. In this hotel, legal paperwork and fees are completed. The couple can then take their baby girl home. Usually, these couples are not from China or even Asia."

I stood in the lobby and saw all these happy young couples in a different light. Only a few of them looked Asian. How much emotion, time, and money had these couples spent before they held a baby girl in their arms? How much courage had it taken couples who could only have one child to give up a baby girl for adoption and hope to have another baby, a boy? How much did it affect them to know they had a daughter growing up far away in another culture?

Naomi stayed with me for the rest of the day. She knew shortcuts to the places I wanted to see and where to get a good meal for an incredibly low price.

When we parted, Naomi said she would return the next day to guide me to the Forbidden City, around Tiananmen Square, and then to the airport. I wouldn't be going to the big international airport but to an older domestic one to get the flight to Xi'an.

"That would be great, Naomi, but only if you let me pay you what the tour guides get. You are in college and need money, I am sure." Even though I was no longer teaching, I heard myself continue in the habit of avoiding contractions and speaking full words instead. I wondered if I should try to stay in practice for returning to China. When that could happen, I didn't know, but what had been a desire, was now a goal.

Chapter 29

The Ongoing Challenge

Xi'an's airport signs included some English. I found the area for taxis and gave the driver a slip of paper with the hotel's name on it that Naomi had written for me. Then I wondered if I was being given an undesired driving tour because it took forty minutes to get to the hotel. We went from wide open countryside to China's versions of suburbs, into the main city, then into the oldest area of the city. I had chosen a hotel within easy walking distance of Xi'an's Drum Tower. China's cities seemed to have a drum tower where time was kept, and proclamations and warnings were given.

Not far from the Xi'an drum tower was the Daming Palace National Heritage Park. The palace had existed since the Tang dynasty in the five and six hundreds. I wanted to see both and to visit the Terracotta soldiers. I also wanted to find time to walk on the wide top of the ancient city walls. That view could be an amazing conclusion to this whole time in China. What a place that would be to look over the city, ancient and new, and to reflect, and pray.

The hotel I'd chosen was a five-star lodging, but it was cheap for me because the dollar was so strong compared to the yuan. This hotel was nicer than any of the chain hotels or bed and breakfasts I had ever stayed in during other travels. A doorman in a handsome uniform of blue, gold, and white opened the glass and brass door for me. An attendant in a similar uniform took my suitcase and led me to the front desk.

Three people were ahead of me, talking to each of the beautifully coiffed and uniformed receptionists. I looked in amazement at the highly polished gloss of every surface, the sparkling chandelier, and the organized reception desk and vases of flowers. Then someone touched my right arm. I turned and looked into the face of Penny, Thomas's wife. Had I fallen into some kind of travel trance and imagined her?

"Ms. Virginia, I am so happy!" She gave me a quick hug. "Thomas had all the correct information about your trip. Do you remember him asking questions? I have been waiting for you to arrive."

"Penny! You're really here?"

She giggled, the first time I had heard such a sound from the shy and gentle young English teacher. "I am here. Ye told us that you would go to Xi'an. Do you remember Thomas asked you about your plans after the SEP? He pried to learn where you would stay after Beijing and why you would go there."

"Yes, I remember being surprised that he kept asking for details about my flights, the hotel, all my plans."

"I have relatives who live here in Xi'an. Thomas thought I could have time to visit with them and to be your guide during your short time here. I took the train."

"You took the train? From Wuhai? How many hours was that for you?"

"Four to Baotou. Fifteen to Xi'an. I read and slept. My aunt met me yesterday morning. I have had a good visit with my family and will have more time before I return to Wuhai for the new school year."

With Penny's help, check-in was super smooth. Then we went to my room on the fifth floor. When I opened the door to the room, I felt embarrassed at the opulence, but Penny made sounds of delight. "May I look around?"

"Sure."

"I have never been in a hotel like this one."

"I haven't either."

"You haven't?"

"No. I could never afford this in my country, Canada, the UK, or France. It is only because the dollar is so strong now against the yuan that I will have two nights here. So, I chose to stay in this hotel to have another new experience."

"We will make sure you have the best time in Xi'an. I like this city very much, but Thomas's family is in Nei Menggu, so we live there. When I was a child, I spent much time here in Xi'an. My mother's parents were married here. My uncle lives here."

"Your uncle? You are Chinese so I thought the government said anyone Chinese who is not an ethnic minority could only have one child."

"That law came in 1979. My uncle was born in 1970 and my mother in 1972."

"Don't the citizens of China who aren't a minority group want to change the law?"

"Yes. I think it will change, but I cannot guess when."

I had placed my suitcase on the posh bench beside the

dark wood desk, still amazed that Thomas and Penny had been so concerned about me that they had planned this surprise. What might have happened, or how would they have felt if I had made last minute changes in my schedule? I could see happiness glowing from Penny, and I gave thanks to God again for unexpected grace and kindness.

"Are you tired? Do you want to rest, Ms. Virginia?"

"No, not at all. I can rest on the long flight home. Let's go out and walk to the Drum Tower. Then some other famous places you think are special."

"Yes, there is much to see in this city, and there is a restaurant famous for dumplings. They make every kind but have special fame for how tiny the dumplings are. Maybe the size of one of your nickels. They have a grand show of Chinese culture on a stage, but even their service in the preparation of the meal near each table is a show. I have never been there, but my aunt told me to introduce it to you."

"It will be a pleasure and an honor to treat you to dinner there. Penny. I will enjoy it more because you are my companion."

Walking in Xi'an throughout the afternoon and evening with Penny was calming. This city had high humidity vastly different from Wuhai, but a companion who knew the city and cared about me made each minute comfortable. The sites in Xi'an were all I'd hoped for, especially walking on the old city walls respected for their age, size, and level of preservation. Walking on the top of the ancient walls of the city with Penny surpassed walking on them alone. We talked about our countries, families, hopes, and goals.

I was glad I could pay for any site that required fees and for our meals. Penny had spent a lot of time and money to be my companion in Xi'an. Again, I felt overwhelmed that she and Thomas had been concerned enough about my last days in China to have her join me. I didn't try to explain to Penny how her kindness hugged my spirit.

God knew more than my plans. He knew the needs and desires of my heart. In my time in China, I'd had more reminders of God's care than I could ever have imagined.

We parted at 9:00 p.m. Penny told me she would return at nine in the morning and take me to the Terracotta Warriors site. It had been thirty years since the first clay soldiers were discovered, and it was only in the late 1990s that China started building an impressive educational site for what many people referred to as the Eighth Wonder of the World. The excavation for parking, roads, sidewalks, workers doing landscaping, and even tour buses created noise and dust as we entered the construction and excavation site.

"This will be one of the most important visitor and archaeology sites in China," Penny assured me as we entered the ticket area.

When we had our tickets that allowed us to go everywhere on the site, I asked, "Penny, do you see the old man at the table outside the gift shop? People are talking with him. Can we see why?"

She nodded, and we walked to the table. On it were photo books about the Terracotta discovery. For a fee, the old man would sign the inside cover of the books that people purchased. Penny talked with the man.

"He is one of the farmers, maybe the only one still living," Penny told me.

"One of the farmers?"

Penny opened the book and showed me a picture of the group of farmers, probably middle-aged or at least looking weary back in the 1970s. "Here he is." She pointed to a man in the photo of the group of farmers. I looked at the picture and then at the man behind the table, probably the same man, just more wrinkled and with gray hair.

He smiled at us. I bought a book and paid the fee to have him sign it. "Do you want a book, Penny? We could get it, and he could sign it for you."

"No, no, Ms. Virginia. This is your day and trip. We should go because there is much to see."

We learned there would be decades more of unearthing discoveries in the huge pits that held everything planned to accompany the emperor into the afterlife. Penny told me the city had plans to make the educational museum one huge site by 2010. I wondered if I could come back to China before or after 2010 and if my husband and some friends would be with me.

Now, Penny assured me, much more had been uncovered and put on display. We saw life size terracotta figures of warriors, horses, battle formations, imperial guards, pottery, wagons, and chariots. Most of the displays appeared in pits tagged in order of the time of their discovery. I knew there were more than a thousand warriors revealed, but the number could hardly be fathomed when Penny and I noticed the difference on every face. The sculptors created each warrior as an individual with a unique face.

It was late afternoon when we returned to the hotel. I had two double beds in my room, so I suggested that we both have a nap and then walk out to enjoy the city evening and another restaurant. Penny agreed. In an hour we were up. Penny said we should visit the Giant Wild Goose Pagoda.

In the evening, we went to another restaurant that Penny's family had recommended. It had long tables and patrons sat wherever there were empty seats. Musicians on a stage at one end of the huge room played traditional Chinese music. The tone and melodic sounds of the music were soft enough that people could have conversations over dinner.

Because this restaurant had a set menu, there were few choices. To start, we select egg drop soup or hot and sour soup. Other dishes were brought to the table on family-style trays or big bowls that everyone would share. The same dishes were delivered to each end of the table and in the center so we could easily reach or pass dishes.

The platters held sweet and sour pork, Cantonese dim sum, and four kinds of dumplings with fillings of pork, ground beef, chicken, and shrimp. Penny explained that Ma Po Tofus, sometimes called Granny's bean curd, came from Sichuan. It was spicy! Chow Mein's stir-fried noodles, with vegetables of onions and celery, cooled the palate after any Sichuan dish. Delivered next were Peking duck, fried rice with a generous variety of vegetables, and *xiaolongbao*, a steamed bun served in a bamboo basket.

Everyone at the table engaged in get-acquainted conversation amid asking someone to pass something. Except for Penny and me, the people around the table were couples. We heard them speak in their own languages to each other, but when speaking to others, we heard English. They spoke with accents from Brazil, Bermuda, Portugal, Germany, Denmark, me from the East Coast of the US, and Penny from Nei Menggu.

"Penny, if you could bring students to a dinner like the one here, they would see how useful English is. Of all the countries represented, it is English that allows us to talk with one another."

"I will tell them, Ms. Virginia. They should know in any

big city they visit that foreigners will probably know English. Then they can talk together."

The meal, sumptuous in appearance, taste, and service, led to overeating. Fortunately, we could walk back to the hotel from this restaurant, which suited the Chinese belief that everyone should walk at least one hundred steps after eating a big meal. The taste of Chinese food, real Chinese food without the sugar and flour added in dishes in the US, woke all my tastebuds.

When we returned to the hotel, my heart clenched. We needed to say goodbye.

"Penny, please tell your family that their recommendations for restaurants were the best. I would not have found anything like them on my own. Your kindness, and the thoughtfulness that you and Thomas displayed is something I will remember my whole life. Let us try to stay in touch. You gave me your email. I really hope one day to return. Wuhai and dear people like you will always be precious to me."

"It is an honor and a privilege Ms. Virginia. Do not forget, Ye told us where you would go after Beijing so Thomas could ask you questions about your plans for Xi'an. Ye knew I had made trips to Xi'an to visit my family."

"You are all generous people, smart and caring. Your students are fortunate to have you and Thomas as teachers because you are excellent role models. As for Ye, I am sure he will have a way to advance to a high position in Wuhai or elsewhere."

"Ms. Virginia, thank you. We have been lucky to know each other."

"Penny, I want to tell you that I do not believe anything happens just by luck. I think there is a God who cares about each of us and who provides in many ways for us. You have given a special gift of friendship to a team of strangers. Out of the places I could have been assigned, it was to the new Amity location of Wuhai. If I ever can return to China, I will make sure to visit Wuhai. I care about you and Thomas, Ye, and all the other dear teachers who worked so hard. Near and far, you are all dear to my heart."

"I will give this message to Thomas and to all your other friends in Wuhai. We will hope to see you again. You are always welcome to come to Wuhai."

It seemed natural to share a hug again and the tears in our eyes blurred a last close-up look of each other. Penny asked, "Will you need help tomorrow going to the airport?"

"No, I have a taxi reserved."

"And you will fly home?"

"I will go to Guangzhou."

"That is such a big city, Ms. Virginia!"

"I won't have to leave the airport. When we first arrived, we had hours to wait in Guangzhou airport before traveling to Nanjing. I looked around because I knew that when I returned, I would not have my team with me. I will be fine. Thank you again for coming here to keep me company. The words, *thank you*, are not enough to express what this visit has meant to me."

I watched Penny leave the hotel room and walk down the hall to the elevator. When I shut the door and looked at the room, I felt thankful the bed had layers of softness. I thought of my hard bed in the Wuhai dorm with the dry air and the mountains in view. People had helped us and made the place and time special.

The flight to Guangzhou reminded me of how much I appreciated the attitude and service on Chinese airlines. I'd traveled on four different Chinese airlines this summer. A person in an economy seat still felt like a valued customer. That was never something I felt in the economy sections of US airlines.

I could not read any Chinese in the airports other than essentials like *entrance, exit, women, men, toilet, tickets, information, and security,* but on the plane the glossy magazines had Chinese and English. Feeling confident that I knew the Guangzhou airport, I relaxed on the flight from Xi'an to Guangzhou.

From my window seat, I watched as we approached the airport. What was this? Where was I? It was an airport I had never seen!

When we arrived at the end of June, we did not know that Guangzhou had almost finished a new International Airport. In the weeks I had been in China, they completed the new airport! Construction went fast in this country, but this surprise left me feeling like Gretel lost in the woods with no Hansel and no breadcrumbs.

This airport had more than quadrupled in size compared to the old one. It was so spacious that real royal palms, not fake palm trees, were growing well in the glass topped central lounges of each section. China's big city airports have beauty, space, cleanliness, and helpful employees. When I asked for assistance, I received it.

Finally, I arrived at the correct wing, I had only my purse to take on board. My suitcase would be checked through to Los Angeles. Service and meals on this Chinese airline were as good as they had been on any flight I'd had into major cities of the People's Republic. I slept for most of my overnight flight back to the US.

In Los Angeles, I would pick up my bag and find my way

to the terminal where I would travel to Seattle. Earlier, I had thought I would return with a nearly empty case because I had taken so much to give away to teachers in China. What my large suitcase held now was my carry-on bag filled with gifts from the teachers, my clothes, and that book of photos signed by the old farmer in Xi'an.

I checked in with American airlines, saw my slightly battered suitcase move away on the conveyor belt, and went to my gate. Each travel arrangement had been on time, and soon I was landing in Seattle. I went to the luggage carousel anxious to pick up my bag and then go to meet my friends.

My suitcase did not appear. When the conveyor belt showed only a few unclaimed boxes and everyone else had departed, I went to find the lost luggage office. They checked and found no sign of my suitcase.

"You mean that from LA to Seattle my suitcase has been lost? It traveled through six provinces in China, major cities and rural towns, and it gets lost between LA and Seattle?"

They seemed sincerely sorry. My Seattle friends shook their heads at what this seemed to reveal about the competence and responsibility of workers in both countries. Fortunately, the wife of this family was my size. We could share clothing. The airport gave me a receipt that I could use for an insurance claim and assured me they would keep searching for the case.

I had five days to enjoy my friend's home on Bainbridge Island. They took me around their island, sightseeing in Seattle, and up the coast almost to Canada. The differences in these environments made China seem like a dream. I read through my diary in the evenings and felt thankful that I had kept it in my large purse, not in the suitcase.

* * *

I called Jerry each day from Seattle. On the last day on Bainbridge Island, I gave him some good news.

"Jerry, we leave for the airport at six a.m., first on the ferry to Seattle, then a drive to the airport, and this afternoon the airport delivered my suitcase. I have no idea where it was found. Nothing seems to be missing. I hope it doesn't get lost again between Seattle and Boston! Everything in it will help me to show you why my location and the work really helped me. I know you prayed for me, and many other people did too."

"That's great, Ginny. It hurt to see you so unhappy here. And listen, I think I have news to top the return of your suitcase."

"What?"

"A letter from Anna Maria College arrived today with information on the day to welcome new faculty and the orientation. It gives your schedule as an adjunct professor."

"That does top my suitcase news! The interview committee made it sound like there would be a job for me, but details weren't confirmed before I left for China."

"I know. You'll be a great adjunct, and I bet you'll be offered a full-time position after a couple of years."

"Jerry, you told me all along to trust that God would provide a career path for me. I could only see the one that had ended."

"You've had life experiences that made trusting people and God difficult."

"I've also had many experiences that showed God cared about me. Sometimes I feel like a turtle, a super slow learner struggling with lessons of trust. You remember my father made me memorize Bible verses. One of the earliest he chose for me to learn was Proverbs 3, verses 5 & 6."

Jerry knew these verses too. He could say them with me. "Proverbs 3:5&6. Trust in the LORD with all your heart, lean not on your own understanding. In all your ways acknowledge Him, and He shall direct your paths."

He said, "We are both learning more about how to do that. I think it's a lifelong lesson. I'm glad we can learn it together."

When I got back to our Massachusetts home, Jerry and I continued our conversations about how my time in China had shown me God's provision. Experiences in that culture, especially in Amity's new location of Wuhai had renewed me.

I had faced each day, from my awful first embarrassment throwing up at the start of class until I left Seattle with my returned suitcase, with a new perspective. Reminders daily reinforced that God knew what the hours ahead of me would include, tough hours or easy hours. Jessie's words rang true for each day, not just in China. "Every day will have surprises. Embrace them. Remember the Lord is always with you."

God had shown help and care beyond what I could have imagined. Having Penny show up in Xi'an felt like a heavenly hug. I told Jerry that I wanted to find a group of people who were ready for an adventure, people with positive outlooks who would gladly help, serve, adapt, and support one another through the SEP weeks.

He said, "I think it is great that Amity encourages people to build a team before they come to China. It seems wise to bring people who know one another, have a goal to serve, and can even prepare ahead of time by collecting materials and ideas. Sounds like you saw that in a number of the groups in those training days in Nanjing."

"Yes, and some of the groups that came were as small as four people or as large as eight. They were friends arriving together and excited about working together."

"I don't know who or when you will find the people who could be a team for you to take to China for another SEP, but I will volunteer to be on your team. I can get my full vacation time from the church and the week they give me for mission work, plus the week for continuing education. I want the adventure of trusting God each day with you in that incredible country. I never would have thought of going to China, but the Amity SEP sounds like it meets many needs for the students, the communities, and the volunteers."

"The financial cost will be higher if we both go, not just for the airfare but for the supplies we each should bring."

"We'll manage."

"I think the costs will limit some people from participating, but for the people who could go, I think they should have a chance to do something special as tourists before starting the Amity work. Like Tia pointed out, people are tired when the SEP finishes."

"I'd like to see the Great Wall."

"I would too, but I am glad I chose Xi'an."

"I wonder who God would have sent along to keep you company if you had told people you were planning to visit the Great Wall after the SEP."

"Very funny. Now I can wonder about that too."

"Ginny, it could require waiting for a while, a year, two, or even more before a team shows up, but you and I have new jobs to learn and grow in, so that will make time fly by. I think God will help us to find the right people for a team and will provide for what we will need."

"If I make it to China again to work with Amity, I want to find a way and the time to visit Wuhai. Maybe the team would go home before I did."

"Before **we** did."

"We. Yes, before **we** did."

"We'll see how we can work it out when you find the people who would go on this adventure. I want to see Wuhai and meet the people. We can pray about it and..."

"And?"

"We can look at the waiting to go to China together as more practice in trusting God's direction and timing."

Appendix 1: Pronunciation

Note: Chinese words have tonal inflections. Use the wrong tone and you can end up saying a totally different word. I didn't attempt to reproduce tone marks in this list.

Jiaozi (djowzih) dumplings with fillings

Gan Bei (gan bay) bottoms up in drinking

Baijiu (Buyjo) a clear strong liquor

Nǐ chī le ma (knee chir le ma?) Have you eaten/ Did you eat yet/ Did you eat?

Guanxi (gwanshee) sharing based on mutual respect and exchanging favors

Buzz (booot'z) Mongolian meat dumpling

Baozi (boughzih_a steamed sweet yeast roll bread usually with a filling

Suutei tsai (sootee ai t'sigh) Mongolian milk tea

Hao (how) good   Hen hao (hen how) very good

Tongzhi (taung jir) Comrade

Toortsog (tortsaug) hats for people of Mongolia

Kuazi (Kwaizih) Chopsticks

Morin Khuur (morin kur) horse-head fiddle with just two strings

Nihao (Kneehow) Hello/you good

Wǎnshàng hǎo (Wan shang how) Good evening

wǒ bù zhīdào (Whoa boo jeedow) I don't know (could also imply not knowing anything)

wǒ bù míngbái (Whoa boo ming by) I don't understand

Huānyíng (Hwan ying) Welcome

Xie Xie (sieh sieh) thank you

Hao Chi (how Chir) Delicious

Hao le ma? (How luh ma?) Ready?

Huang He (Hwang Huh) Yellow River

Wǒmen zǒu ba (Women zoabah) Let's go.

Wǎnshàng hǎo (Wan shang how) Good evening.

Wo bu zhidao (Whoa boo djeetao) I know nothing.

Wo bu ming—bai (Whoa boo mingby) I do not understand.

Deel (del) a long tunic with long sleeves and a high collar. Some have buttons on the right shoulder or knots of fabric to hold the material in place.

Feng shui (fung shway) an ancient Chinese system of arranging spaces or objects to create balance and harmony, rooted in Taoism's belief that the life force flow can be affected by the environment.

Yuèliàngmén (yu liahng men) moon gates are circular openings in a garden wall that serves as a pedestrian passageway. The round opening symbolizes the moon.

Guzheng (goo jun) is a Chinese narrow wooden instrument with 21 or more strings

Guriltai Shul (Gooriltie sool) a noodle soup with carrots,

potatoes, tofu, radishes, onions, something like turnip, generously peppered

Qurut (Q rut) dried curd cheese

Niislel Salad (Nigh I lel) like a potato salad

Khuushuur (horshur) in the center of a pancake place meat flavored with salt, scallions, and onion and the circle of the pancake is folded up to make the huushuur look like a pouch.

Appendix 2: Why should I learn English?

Ideas from teachers of English in Wuhai.

1.English is spoken in the most countries around the world.
2. English offers insight into other cultures.
3. English increases communication opportunities.
4. English strengthens thinking skills. (Knowledge, Comprehension, Application, Analysis, Synthesis, and Evaluation)
5. English increases friendship opportunities.
6. English has many interesting elements.
7. Learning English is a national goal in China.
8. Knowing English supports China's international goals and efforts.
9. Knowing English well can lead to good college years.
10. Knowing English can increase job possibilities and options.
11. Knowing English well will help Chinese students to pass the required tests.
12. English skills help in travel.
13. English skills open more entertainment possibilities.

14. Knowing English can lead to some unexpected and unusual opportunities.
15. English skills help one to inform others well.
16. English skills increase bargaining power.
17. Knowing English opens doors to information in the news.
18. English is used in international conferences and contests.
19. English skills help one to understand athletics in English-speaking countries.
20. Maritime captains of huge vessels must know English.
21. Airline pilots and crews must know English.
22. Air traffic controllers must know English.
23. People who work in any industry or business that has international customers or clients need to know English.
24. Advances in government jobs can occur more quickly for those who know English.
25. In case of international emergencies, English is very helpful.
26. Knowing a worldwide language can increase understanding and respect among people from other countries.
27. Scientists have found that learning something difficult, along with continuous growth in that subject can delay brain disorders in old age.
28. Scientists have found that learning with songs, varied pitches, motion, and playful activities increases the ability to learn and retain information.

Appendix 3: Recipes

Hot Pot (Simplified)

Asian grocery stores will have thinly sliced lamb and other sliced meats for hot pot.

Boil chicken (leg, thigh pieces) in water with sliced ginger, minced garlic (some people just choose to cook stock) Skim off any froth appearing on the surface. Lower the heat and leave to simmer for 1½ to – 2 hours until the water becomes opaque. Pour the liquid into the pot you plan to use for the hot pot meal. Top up with hot water if necessary. Add rehydrated shiitake mushroom, scallions, Chinese dates and goji berries. Season with white pepper and salt. For spicy hot pot broth, add chilis. For a hearty flavor add fermented black beans, Sichuan peppers and rice wine.

(The soup base can be kept in the freezer for a long time.)

When the broth starts boiling, use chopsticks or other long implements to dip ingredients into the broth. Usually, a variety of meats and vegetables surround the hot pot, and the flavor of the hotpot broth and high temperature will cook everything quickly. As the meal progresses, the broth will reduce its volume. Simply add more hot water.

Frequent ingredients for hot pot: thinly sliced lamb, thinly sliced beef, thinly sliced pork, bean curd, leafy greens like bok choy and cabbages, mushrooms, root vegetables, tofu, noodles, shrimp.

Hot pot and additional elements

Jiaozi

The classic Chinese dumpling is filled with a pork and garlic chive and scallion base. Mushrooms can be added. Chinese dumplings can be boiled, steamed (zhengjiao), and pan-fried. When they are pan-fried, they are called pot stickers.

Dumpling filling

• 8 ounces cabbage (about 1/4 head), plus extra leaves for lining if steaming
• 8 ounces ground pork
• 1/2 bunch scallions (green and white parts), finely chopped

- 1/2 cup finely chopped garlic chives
- 1 clove garlic, finely chopped
- 2 teaspoons grated peeled ginger
- 2 tablespoons soy sauce
- 1/2 teaspoon toasted (Asian) sesame oil
- 1 pound round wheat dumpling or potsticker wrappers

The dipping sauce
- 1/4 cup soy sauce
- 2 tablespoons rice vinegar
- 1 teaspoon thinly sliced scallions, white part only
- 1/4 teaspoon toasted sesame seeds

***Filling the dumplings*:** Have a small bowl of water ready. Place a dumpling wrapper in the flat of your hand. Place a tablespoon of the filling in the center of the wrapper. Dip a finger in the water and use it to wet the edges of the wrapper. Fold the dumpling in half to form a half-moon shape, press out the air, and seal the dumpling. Press firmly to seal the dumpling closed. Place on a baking sheet. Repeat until all the filling is used. You might have extra wrappers.

***Freezing the dumplings*:** Dumplings can be frozen for up to three months. Freeze them as a single layer. Separate layers with parchment paper. Freeze until solid, then you can transfer them to a sealed freezer bag.

Dumpling wrappers must be uniform in size.
If you want to make dumpling wrappers from scratch, there are many good recipes online. Vegetarian dumplings will have loose fillings. Wrappers should be larger.

Acknowledgments

This memoir, the first in a series, shares glimpses into a culture and people who do not have open global interaction, but have hopes, dreams, and goals for their lives, their families, friends, and young people. I thank all the people represented in this book for their care and generosity.

Thank you to my husband, Jerry, for his Alpha reading, questions, and encouragement. He was part of my team in my second, third, and fifth summers in China. Thank you to Dr. Paul Erickson who shared his passion for Asia with me and encouraged me to step out on faith that this would be a life-changing experience. Thank you to Carolyn Allard who encourages my writing and who has been an excellent copy line editor. Thank you to the many family members and friends who provide positive boosts for my writing efforts.

Thank you to Rachael Herron who started my journey of writing memoirs and to Alison Wearing who helped me mature in the effort. Thanks to Ashland's 'Must Love Words' writing group for reading chapter drafts and giving feedback. Thanks to MaryAnne Slack, Lisa LeBlanc, Val Kerin, Caitlin Reidy, and Victoria Rector, of Advancing Writing Endeavors (AWE) for their ongoing encouragement. Thank you to my beta readers Adele Ciriacy, Jerry Heslinga, Rebecca Jones, Lucinda Bradley, and Lieutenant Fred Lussier (Massachusetts State Police, ret.).

An extra special *xie xie,* thank you, to my dear friend Ruby Huang who has so patiently helped me with Chinese over the years and to Sandra Kurtz who most consistently pushes me to write.

To Dr. Gordon Saunders, thank you for using your artistic, analytic, and writing tips to guide through revisions, create a cover, complete the developmental edit, and the interior design edits for the published work.

About the Author

Virginia Heslinga, Ed. D. is Associate Professor of Humanities at Anna Maria College in Paxton, Massachusetts. She is a recipient of the Living the Mission Award, which is presented to a member of the faculty who understands and appreciates the importance of educating the whole student and who seizes every opportunity to do so. In April 2024, Virginia presented her memoir, *Grace Interlaced*, in the Anna Maria College LaVigne Lecture Series.

For more than forty-nine years, Virginia has taught in a variety of schools, public, private, alternative, homeschools, religious, juvenile detention, and online. She has worked in this country and others with every age group. Virginia has published articles in education journals, written curriculum, released a memoir about a fire that devastated her family and changed her life, *Grace Interlaced* (2023). The Spanish translation of Virginia's memoir, *Gracia entrelazada* was completed by Carlos Miranda, Ph.D., MITI, and published in December 2024. The revised second edition of Dr. Heslinga's historical novel, *Wounded Dove* (2024), based on real events in the life of Danish immigrants in Worcester County, Massachusetts, tells of a time with little support for a girl stricken with polio in the New England polio epidemic in the early 1900s.

Virginia describes herself as a child of God, a wife, a mother, a grandmother, an educator, an author, a traveler, and a lifelong learner. She gives thanks for the blessings of a loving and supportive family and friends near and far.

If you enjoyed *China Sweet and Sour: 2004*, please tell others what you appreciated by writing a review. Most widely read reviews appear on Amazon which automatically posts to Goodreads. Some other review sites include Book Page, Reddit, Story Graph, Barnes and Noble, and Kobo.

www.ingramcontent.com/pod-product-compliance
Lightning Source LLC
Chambersburg PA
CBHW030358130626
46549CB00004B/1544